History of the Opera
by Henry Sutherland Edwards

MICROFILMED

HISTORY

OF

THE OPERA,

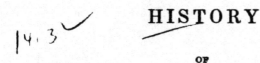

From its Origin in Italy to the present Time.

WITH ANECDOTES

OF THE MOST CELEBRATED COMPOSERS AND VOCALISTS OF EUROPE.

BY

SUTHERLAND EDWARDS,

AUTHOR OF "RUSSIANS AT HOME," ETC.

"QUIS TAM DULCIS SONUS QUI MEAS COMPLET AURES?"
"WHAT IS ALL THIS NOISE ABOUT?"

VOL II.

LONDON:

WM. H. ALLEN & CO., 13, WATERLOO PLACE.

1862.

1823

LONDON:
LEWIS AND SON, PRINTERS, SWAN BUILDINGS, (49) MOORGATE STREET.

CONTENTS.

————◆————

CHAPTER XI.

CONTENTS.

CHAPTER XVI.

CHAPTER XVII.

CHAPTER XVIII.

CHAPTER XIX.

HISTORY OF THE OPERA.

CHAPTER XI.

THE OPERA IN ENGLAND AT THE END OF THE EIGHTEENTH AND BEGINNING OF THE NINETEENTH CENTURY.

HITHERTO I have been obliged to trace the origin and progress of the Opera in various parts of Europe. At present there is one Opera for all the world, that is to say, the same operatic works are performed every where, if not,

> " De Paris à Pékin, de Japon jusqu'à Rome,"

at least, in a great many other equally distant cities, and which Boileau never heard of ; as, for instance, from St. Petersburgh to Philadelphia, and from New Orleans to Melbourne. But for the French Revolution, and the Napoleonic wars, the universality of Opera would have been attained long since. The directors of the French Opera, after producing the works of Gluck and Piccinni, found it impossible, as we shall see in the next chapter, to attract the public by means of the ancient *répertoire,* and were obliged to call in the modern Italian composers to their aid. An Italian troop was engaged to perform at the Académie Royale, alternately with the French company, and the best opera buffas of Piccinni, Traetta, Paisiello, and Anfossi were represented, first in Italian, and afterwards in French.   Sacchini and Salieri were engaged to compose operas on French texts specially for the Académie.   In 1787, Salieri's *Tarare* (libretto by Beaumarchais),* was brought out with immense success ; the same year, the same theatre saw the production of Paisiello's *Il re Teodoro,* translated into French ; and, also the same year, Paisiello's *Marchese di Tulipano* was played at Versailles, by a detachment from the Italian company engaged at our own King's Theatre.

This is said to have been the first instance of an Italian troop performing alternately in London and in Paris.   A proposition had been made under the Regency of Philip of Orleans, for the engagement of Handel's celebrated company ;† but, although the agreement was drawn up and signed, from various causes, and principally through the jealousy of the

---

* For an interesting account of the production of this work, see " Beaumarchais's Life and Times," by Louis de Loménie.   See also the Preface to *Tarare,* in Beaumarchais's " Dramatic Works."

† See vol. I.

"Academicians," it was never carried out. The London-Italian company of 1787 performed at Versailles, before the Court and a large number of aristocratic subscribers, many of whom had been solicited to support the enterprise by the queen herself. Storace, the *prima donna assoluta* of the King's Theatre, would not accompany the other singers to Paris. Madame Benini, however, the *altra prima donna* went, and delighted the French amateurs. Lord Mount Edgcumbe, in his interesting volume of "Musical Reminiscences," tells us that she "had a voice of exquisite sweetness, and a finished taste and neatness in her manner of singing; but that she had so little power, that she could not be heard to advantage in so large a theatre : her performance in a small one was perfect." Among the other vocalists who made the journey from London to Paris, were Mengozzi the tenor, who was Madame Benini's husband, and Morelli the bass. " The latter had a voice of great power, and good quality, and he was a very good actor. Having been running footman to Lord Cowper at Florence," continues Lord Mount Edgcumbe, "he could not be a great musician." Benini, Mengozzi, and Morelli, again visited Paris in 1788, but did not make their appearance there in 1789, the year of the taking of the Bastille. The *répertoire* of these singers included operas by Paisiello, Cimarosa, Sarti, and Anfossi, and they were particularly successful in Paisiello's *Gli Schiavi per Amore*. When this opera was produced in London in 1787 (with Storace, not Benini, in the principal female part), it was so much admired that it ran to the end of the season without any change. Another Italian company gave several series of performances in Paris between 1789 and 1792, and then for nine years France was without any Italian Opera at all.

Storace was by birth and parentage, on her mother's side, English; but she went early to Italy, "and," says the author from whom I have just quoted, "was never heard in this country till her reputation as the first buffa of her time was fully established." Her husband was Fisher, a violinist (whose portrait has been painted by Reynolds); but she never bore his name, and the marriage was rapidly followed by a separation. Mrs. Storace settled entirely in England, and after quitting the King's Theatre accepted an engagement at Drury Lane. Here English Opera was raised to a pitch of excellence previously unknown, thanks to her singing, together with that of Mrs. Crouch, Mrs. Bland, Kelly, and Bannister. The musical director was Mrs. Storace's brother, Stephen Storace, the arranger of the pasticcios entitled the *Haunted Tower*, and the *Siege of Belgrade*.

Madame Mara made her first appearance at the King's Theatre the year before Storace's *début*. She had previously sung in London at the Pantheon Concerts, and at the second Handel Festival (1785), in Westminster Abbey. I have already spoken of this vocalist's performances and adventures at the court of Frederick the Great, at Vienna, and at Paris, where her worshippers at the Concerts Spirituels formed themselves into the sect of " Maratistes," as opposed to that of the " Todistes," or believers in Madame Todi.*

Lord Mount Edgcumbe, during a visit to Paris, heard Madame Mara at one of the Concerts Spirituels, in the old theatre of the Tuileries. She had just returned from the Handel Commemoration, and sang, among other things, " I know that my Redeemer liveth," which was announced in the bills as being "Musique de Handel, paroles de *Milton*." " The French," says Lord Mount Edgcumbe, " had not the taste to like it."

The first opera in which Madame Mara appeared at the King's Theatre was *Didone*, a pasticcio, in which four songs of different characters, by Sacchini, Piccinni, and two other composers, were introduced. She afterwards sang with Miss Cecilia Davies (*L'Inglesina*) in Sacchini's *Perseo*.

At this period Handel's operas were already so much out of fashion, though esteemed as highly as ever by musicians and by the more venerable of connoisseurs, that when *Giulio Cesare* was revived, with Mara and Rubinelli (both of whom sang the music incomparably well), in the principal parts, it

* *Question*. Quelle est la meilleure? *Answer*. C'est Mara. *Rejoinder*. C'est bientôt dit (*bien Todi*).—(From a joke-book of th·· period).

had no success with the general public; nor were any of Handel's operas afterwards performed at the King's Theatre. *Giulio Cesare,* in which many of the most favourite songs from Handel's other operas (" Verdi prati," " Dove sei," " Rendi sereno il ciglio," and others) were interpolated, answered the purpose for which it was produced, and attracted George III. two or three times to the theatre. Moreover (to quote Lord Mount Edgcumbe's words), " it filled the house, by attracting the exclusive lovers of the old style, who held cheap all other operatic performances."

In 1789 (the year in which the supposed sexagenarian, Madeleine Guimard, " still full of grace and gentility," made her appearance) the King's Theatre was burnt to the ground—not without a suspicion of its having been maliciously set on fire, which was increased by the suspected person soon after committing suicide. Arrangements were made for carrying on the Opera at the little theatre in the Haymarket, where Mara was engaged as the first woman in serious operas, and Storace in comic. The company afterwards moved to the Pantheon, " which," says Lord Mount Edgcumbe, " in its original state was the largest and most beautiful room in London, and a very model of fine architecture. It was the chef-d'œuvre of Wyatt, who himself contrived and executed its transformation, taking care not to injure any part of the building, and so concealing the columns and closing its dome, that it might be easily restored after its temporary purpose was answered, it being then in contemplation to erect an entirely new and magnificent opera-house elsewhere, a project which could never be realised. Mr. Wyatt, by this conversion, produced one of the prettiest, and by far the most genteel and comfortable theatres I ever saw, of a moderate size and excellent shape, and admirably adapted both for seeing and hearing. There the regular Opera was successfully carried on, with two very good companies and ballets. Pacchierotti, Mara, and Lazzarini, a very pleasing singer with a sweet tenor voice, being at the head of the serious; and Casentini, a pretty woman and genteel actress, with Lazzarini, for tenor, Morelli and Ciprani principal buffos, composing the comic. This was the first time that Pacchierotti * had met with a good *prima donna* since Madame Lebrun, and his duettos with Mara were the most perfect pieces of execution I ever heard. The operas in which they performed together were Sacchini's *Rinaldo* and Bertoni's *Quinto Fabio* revived, and a charming new one by Sarti, called *Idalide*, or *La Vergine del Sole*. The best comic were La Molinara, and La bella Pescatrice, by Guglielmi. On the whole I never enjoyed the opera so much as at this theatre."

The Pantheon enterprise, however, like most operatic speculations in England, did not pay, and at the end of the first season (1791) the manager had incurred debts to the amount of thirty thousand

* A celebrated male soprano, and one of the last of the tribe.

pounds.   In the meanwhile the King's Theatre had been rebuilt, but the proprietor, now that the Opera was established at the Pantheon, found himself unable to obtain a license for dramatic performances, and had to content himself with giving concerts at which the principal singer was the celebrated David. It was proposed that the new Opera house should take the debts of the Pantheon, and with them its operatic license, but the offer was not accepted, and in 1792 the Pantheon was destroyed by fire—in this case the result, clearly, of accident.

At last the schism which had divided the musical world was put an end to, and an arrangement was made for opening the King's Theatre in the winter of 1793.   There was not time to bring over a new company, but one was formed out of the singers already in London, with Mara at their head and with Kelly for the tenor.

Mara was now beginning to decline in voice and in popularity.   When she was no longer engaged at the Italian Opera, she sang at concerts and for a short time at Covent Garden, where she appeared as " Polly " in *The Beggars' Opera*.   She afterwards sang with the Drury Lane company while they performed at the King's Theatre during the rebuilding of their own house, which had been pulled down to be succeeded by a much larger one.   She appeared in an English serious opera, called *Dido*, " in which," says Lord Mount Edgcumbe, " she retained one song of her *Didone*, the brilliant *bravura, Son Re-*

gina. It did not greatly succeed, though the music was good and well sung. This is not surprising," he adds, "the serious opera being ill suited to our stage, and our language to recitative. None ever succeeded but Dr. Arne's *Artaxerxes*, which was, at first, supported by some Italian singers, Tenducci being the original Arbaces." It is noticeable that in the aforesaid English *Dido* Kelly was the tenor, while Mrs. Crouch took the part of first man, which at this time in Italy was always given to a sopranist.

Madame Mara's husband, the ex-violinist of the Berlin orchestra, appears never to have been a good musician, and always an idle drunkard. His wife at last got disgusted with his habits, and probably, also, with his performance on the violin,* for she went off with a flute-player named Florio to Russia, where she lived for many years. When she was about seventy she re-appeared in England and gave a concert at the King's Theatre, but without any sort of success. Her wonderful powers were said to have returned, but when she sang her voice was generally compared to a penny trumpet. Madame Mara then returned to Moscow, where she suffered greatly by the fire of 1812. She afterwards resided at some town in the Baltic provinces, and died there at a very advanced age.

The next great vocalist who visited England after

* Some writers speak of Mara as a violinist, others as a violon-cellist.

Mara's *début*, was Banti.   She had commenced life as
a street singer; but her fine voice having attracted the
attention of De Vismes, the director of the Académie,
he told her to come to him at the Opera, where the
future *prima donna*, after hearing an air of Sacchini's
three times, sang it perfectly from beginning to end.
De Vismes at once engaged her; and soon afterwards
she made her first appearance with the most brilliant
success.   Although Banti was now put under the best
masters, she was of such an indolent, careless disposition, that she never could be got to learn even the first
elements of music.   Nevertheless, she was so happily
endowed by nature, that it gave her no trouble to perfect herself in the most difficult parts; and whatever
she sang, she rendered with the most charming expression imaginable.   Lord Mount Edgcumbe, who does
not mention the fact of her having sung at the French
Opera, says that Banti was the most delightful singer
he ever heard (though, when she appeared at the
King's Theatre in 1799, she must have been forty-two
years of age*); and tells us that, "in her, genius
supplied the place of science; and the most correct
ear, with the most exquisite taste, enabled her to sing
with more effect, more expression, and more apparent
knowledge of her art, than many much better professors."

It is said of Banti, that when she was singing
in Paris, though she never made the slightest mis-

* Banti was born at Crema, in 1757.

take in concerted pieces, she sometimes executed her airs after a very strange fashion. For instance : in the *allegro* of a cavatina, after singing the principal motive, and the intermediary phrase or "second part," she would, in a fit of absence, re-commence the air from the very beginning; go on with it until the turning point at the end of the second part; again re-commence and continue this proceeding, until at last the conductor warned her that next time she had better think of terminating the piece. In the meanwhile the public, delighted with Banti's voice, is said to have been quite satisfied with this novel mode of performance.

Banti made her *début* in England in Bianchi's *Semiramide*, in which she introduced an air from one of Guglielmi's oratorios, with a violin *obbligato* accompaniment, played first by Cramer, afterward by Viotti, Salomon, and Weichsell, the brother of Mrs. Billington. This song was of great length, and very fatiguing ; but Banti was always encored in it, and never omitted to repeat it.

At her benefit in the following year (1800) Banti performed in an opera, founded on the *Zenobia* of Metastasio, by Lord Mount Edgcumbe, the author of the interesting "Reminiscences," to which, in the course of the present chapter I shall frequently have to refer. The "first man's" part was allotted to Roselli, a sopranist, who, however, had to transfer it to Viganoni, a tenor. Roselli, whose voice was failing him, soon afterwards left the country; and no other male soprano made his appearance at the King's Theatre until the arrival of Velluti, who sang twenty-five years afterwards in Meyerbeer's *Crociato.*

Banti's favourite operas were Gluck's *Alceste*, in which she was called upon to repeat three of her airs every night; the *Iphigénie en Tauride*, by the same author; Paisiello's *Elfrida*, and *Nina* or *La Pazza per Amore*; Nasolini's * *Mitridate*; and several operas by Bianchi, composed expressly for her.

Before Banti's departure from England, she prevailed on Mrs. Billington to perform with her on the night of her benefit, leaving to the latter the privilege of assuming the principal character in any opera she might select. *Merope* was chosen. Mrs. Billington took the part of the heroine, and Banti that of "Polifonte," though written for a tenor voice. The curiosity to hear these two celebrated singers in the same piece was so great, that the theatre was filled with what we so often read of in the newspapers, but so seldom see in actual life,—" an overflowing audience;" many ladies being obliged, for want of better places, to find seats on the stage.

Banti died at Bologna, in 1806, bequeathing her larynx (of extraordinary size) to the town, the municipality of which caused it to be duly preserved in a glass bottle. Poor woman! she had by time dissipated the whole of her fortune, and had nothing else to leave.

* Nasolini, a composer of great promise, died at a very early age.

Mrs. Billington, Banti's contemporary, after singing not only in England, but at all the best theatres of Italy, left the stage in 1809. In 1794, while she was engaged at Naples, at the San Carlo, a violent eruption of Mount Vesuvius took place, which the Neapolitans attributed to the presence of an English heretic on their stage. Mrs. Billington's friends were even alarmed for her personal safety, when, fortunately, the eruption ceased, and the audience, relieved of their superstitious fears, applauded the admirable vocalist in all liberty and confidence. Mrs. Billington was an excellent musician, and before coming out as a singer had distinguished herself in early life (when Miss Weichsell) as a pianoforte player. She appears to have been but an indifferent actress, and, in her singing, to have owed her success less to her expression than to her "agility," which is said to have been marvellous. Her execution was distinguished by the utmost neatness and precision. Her voice was sweet and flexible, but not remarkable for fulness of tone, which formed the great beauty of Banti's singing. Mrs. Billington appeared with particular success in Bach's *Clemenza di Scipione*, in which the part of the heroine had been originally played in England by Miss Davies (*L'Inglesina*); Paisiello's *Elfrida*; Winter's *Armida*, and *Castore e Polluce*; and Mozart's *Clemenza di Tito*—the first of that master's works ever performed in England. At this time, neither the *Nozze di Figaro*, nor Mozart's other masterpiece, *Don Giovanni* (produced at Prague in 1787), seem to have been at all known either in England or in France.

After Banti's departure from England, and while Mrs. Billington was still at the King's Theatre, Grassini was engaged to sing alternately with the latter vocalist. She made her first appearance in *La Vergine del Sole* an opera by Mayer (the future preceptor of Donizetti), but in this work she succeeded more through her acting and her beauty than by her singing. Indeed, so equivocal was her reception, that on the occasion of her benefit, she felt it desirable to ask Mrs. Billington to appear with her. Mrs. Billington consented; and Winter composed an opera called *Il Ratto di Proserpina*, specially for the rival singers, Mrs. Billington taking the part of "Ceres," and Grassini that of "Proserpine." Now the tide of favour suddenly turned, and we are told that Grassini's performance gained all the applause; and that "her graceful figure, her fine expression of face, together with the sweet manner in which she sang several simple airs, stamped her at once the reigning favourite." Indeed, not only was Grassini rapturously applauded in public, but she was "taken up by the first society, *fêted*, caressed, and introduced as a regular guest in most of the fashionable assemblies." "Of her *private* claims to that distinction," adds Lord Mount Edgcumbe, "it is best to be silent; but her manners and exterior behaviour were proper and genteel."

At this period 1804-5, the tenors at the King's

Theatre were Viganoni and Braham. Respecting the latter, who, in England, France and Italy, in English and in Italian operas, on the stage and in concert rooms, must have sung altogether for something like half a century, I must again quote the author of "Musical Reminiscences," who heard him in his prime. "All must acknowledge," he says, "that his voice is of the finest quality, of great power and occasional sweetness. It is equally certain that he has great knowledge of music, and *can* sing extremely well. It is therefore the more to be regretted that he should ever do otherwise; that he should ever quit the natural register of his voice by raising it to an unpleasant falsetto, or force it by too violent exertion; that he should depart from a good style, and correct taste, which he knows and can follow as well as any man, to adopt at times the overflorid and frittered Italian manner; at others, to fall into the coarseness and vulgarity of the English. The fact is, that he can be two distinct singers, according to the audience before whom he performs, and that to gain applause he condescends to sing as ill at the playhouse as he has done well at the Opera. His compositions have the same variety, and he can equally write a popular noisy song for the one, or its very opposite, for the other. A duetto of his, introduced into the opera of *Gli Orazj*, sung by himself and Grassini, had great beauty, and was in excellent taste. * * * * Braham has done material injury to English singing, by producing a host of imitators.

What is in itself not good, but may be endured from a fine performer, becomes insufferable in bad imitation. Catalani has done less mischief, only because her powers are *unique*, and her astonishing execution unattainable. Many men endeavour to rival Braham, no woman can aspire to being a Catalani."

When both Grassini and Mrs. Billington retired, (1806), the place of both was supplied by the celebrated Catalani, the vocal queen of her time. She made her first appearance in Portogallo's *Semiramide*, (which is said to have been a very inferior opera to Bianchi's, on the same subject), and, among other works, had to perform in the *Clemenzo di Tito*, of Mozart, whose music she is said to have disliked on the ground that it kept the singer too much under the control of the orchestra. Nevertheless, she introduced the *Nozze di Figaro* into England, and herself played the part of " Susanna " with admirable success.

" Her voice," says Ferrari (Jacques Godefroi, a pupil of Paisiello), " was sonorous, powerful, and full of charm and suavity. This organ, of so rare a beauty, might be compared for splendour to the voice of Banti ; for expression, to that of Grassini ; for sweet energy, to that of Pasta ; uniting the delicious flexibility of Sontag to the three registers of Malibran. Madame Catalani had formed her style on that of Pacchierotti, Marchesi, Crescentini ;* her groups, roulades, triplets, and *mordenti*, were of admi-

* All three sopranists.

rable perfection; her well articulated execution lost
nothing of its purity in the most rapid and most
difficult passages. She animated the singers, the
chorus, the orchestra, even in the finales and concerted pieces. Her beautiful notes rose above and
dominated the *ensemble* of the voices and instruments;
nor could Beethoven, Rossini or any other musical
Lucifer, have covered this divine voice with the
tumult of the orchestra. Our *virtuosa* was not a
profound musician; but, guided by what she did
know, and by her practised ear, she could learn in a
moment the most complicated pieces."

" Her firm, strong, brilliant, voluminous voice, was
of a most agreeable *timbre*," says Castil Blaze; "it
was an admirable soprano of prodigious compass, from
la to the upper *sol*, marvellous in point of agility, and
producing a sensation difficult to describe. Madame
Catalani's manner of singing left something to desire
in the noble, broad, sustained style. Mesdames Grassini and Barilli surpassed her on this point, but with
regard to difficulties of execution and *brio*, Madame
Catalani could ring out one of her favourite airs and
exclaim, *Son Regina !* She was then without a rival.
I never heard anything like it. She excelled in chro-
matic passages, ascending and descending, of extreme
rapidity. Her execution, marvellous in audacity,
made talents of the first order pale before it, and
instrumentalists no longer dared figure by her side.
When Tulou, however, presented himself, his flute

was applauded with enthusiasm after Madame Catalani's voice.   The experiment was a dangerous one,
and the victory was only the more brilliant for the
adventurous young artist.   There was no end to the
compliments addressed to him on his success."

On her way to London, in the summer of 1806,
Catalani, whose reputation was then at its height,
passed through Paris, and sang before the Emperor
at St. Cloud.   Napoleon gave her 5,000 francs for
this performance, besides a pension of 1,200 francs,
and the use of the Opera, with all expences paid, for
two concerts, of which the receipts amounted to
49,000 francs.   The French emperor, during his victorious career, had acquired the habit of carrying off
singers as captives, and enrolling them, in spite of
themselves, in his musical service.   The same dictato-
rial system, however, failed when applied to Catalani.

" Where are you going, that you wish to leave
Paris?" said Napoleon.

" To London, Sire," answered the singer.

" You must remain in Paris," replied Napoleon,
" you will be well paid and your talents will be better
appreciated here.   You will have a hundred thousand
francs a year, and two months' leave of absence.
That is settled.   Adieu, Madame."

Catalani went away without daring to say that she
did not mean to break her engagement with the
manager of the King's Theatre.   In order to keep it
she was obliged to embark secretly at Morlaix.

I have spoken of this celebrated vocalist's first appearance in London, and, having given an Italian and a French account of her singing, I may as well complete the description by quoting the remarks made by an Englishman, Lord Mount Edgcumbe, on her voice and style of execution.

"It is well known," he says, "that her voice is of a most uncommon quality, and capable of exertions almost supernatural. Her throat seems endued (as has been remarked by medical men) with a power of expansion and muscular motion by no means usual, and when she throws out all her voice to the utmost, it has a volume and strength that are quite surprising, while its agility in divisions, running up and down the scale in semi-tones, and its compass in jumping over two octaves at once, are equally astonishing. It were to be wished she was less lavish in the display of these wonderful powers, and sought to please more than to surprise; but her taste is vicious, her excessive love of ornament spoiling every simple air, and her greatest delight (indeed her chief merit) being in songs of a bold and spirited character, where much is left to her discretion (or indiscretion) without being confined by accompaniment, but in which she can indulge in *ad libitum* passages with a luxuriance and redundancy no other singer ever possessed, or if possessing, ever practised, and which she carries to a fantastical excess. She is fond of singing variations on some known simple air, and latterly has pushed this taste to the very height of absurdity, by singing, even without words, variations composed for the fiddle."

Allusion is here doubtless made to the *air varié* by Pierre Rode, the violinist, which, from Catalani to Alboni and our own Louisa Pyne, has been such a favourite show-piece with all vocalists of brilliant executive powers, more especially in England. The vocal variations on Rode's air, however, were written in London, specially for Catalani, by Drouet the flute-player.

Catalani returned to Paris in October, 1815, when there was no longer any chance of Napoleon reproaching her for her abrupt departure nine years before. She solicited and obtained the "privilege" of the Italian theatre; but here the celebrated system of her husband, M. Valabrèque (in which the best possible operatic company consisted only of *ma femme et trois ou quatre poupées*) quite broke down. Madame Catalani gave up the theatre, with the subvention of 160,000 francs allowed her by the government, in 1818, M. Valabrèque having previously enunciated in a pamphlet the reasons which led to this abandonment. Great expenses had been incurred in fitting up the theatre, and, moreover, the management had been forced to pay its rent. The pamphlet concluded with a paragraph which was scarcely civil on the part of a foreigner who had been most hospitably received, towards a nation situated as France was just then. It is sufficiently curious to be quoted.

"Consider, moreover," said the discomforted director, or rather the discomforted husband of the directress, "that in the time when several provinces beyond the mountains belonged to France, twenty thousand Italians were constantly attracted to the capital and supplied numerous audiences for the Italian theatre; that, moreover, the artists who were chiefly remarked at the theatres of Milan, Florence, Venice and Genoa, could be engaged for Paris by order of the government, and that in such a case the administration was reimbursed for a portion of the extra engagements."

Catalani had left the King's Theatre in 1813, two years before she assumed the management of the Italian Theatre of Paris. With some brief intervals she had been singing in London since 1806, and after quitting England, she was for many years without appearing on any stage, if we except the short period during which she directed the Théâtre Feydau. Her terms were so inordinate that managers were naturally afraid of them, and Catalani found it more to her advantage to travel about Europe, giving concerts at which she was the sole performer of importance, than to accept such an engagement as could be offered to her at a theatre. She gave several concerts of this kind in England, whither she returned twice after she had ceased to appear at the Opera. She is said to have obtained more success in England than in any other country, and least of all in Italy.

When she appeared at the King's Theatre in 1824, and sang in Mayer's *Fanatico per la Musica*, the frequenters of the Opera, who remembered her performance in the same work eighteen years before, were surprised that so long an interval had produced so little change in the singer. The success of the first night was prodigious; but Mr. Ebers (in his "Seven Years of the King's Theatre"), tells us that "repetitions of this opera, again and again, diminished the audiences most perceptibly, though some new air was on each performance introduced, to display the power of the Catalani. * * * In this opera the sweet and soothing voice of Caradori was an agreeable relief to the bewildering force of the great wonder."

In one season of four months in London, Madame Catalani, by her system of concerts, gained upwards of ten thousand pounds, and doubled that sum during a subsequent tour in the provinces, in Ireland and Scotland. She sang for the last time in public at Dublin, in 1828.

As to the sort of engagement she approved of, some notion may be formed from the following draft of a contract submitted by her to Mr. Ebers in 1826:—

" Conditions between Mr. Ebers and M. P. de Valabrèque.

" 1. Every box and every admission shall be considered as belonging to the management. The free admissions shall be given with paper orders, and differently shaped from the paid tickets. Their number shall be limited. The manager, as well as Madame Catalani, shall each have a good box.

" 2. Madame Catalani shall choose and direct the operas in which she is to sing; she shall likewise have the choice of the performers in them; she will have no orders to receive from any one; she will find all her own dresses.

" 3. Madame Catalani shall have two benefits, to be divided with the manager; Madame Catalani's share shall be free : she will fix her own days.

" 4. Madame Catalani and her husband shall have a right to superintend the receipts.

" 5. Every six weeks Madame Catalani shall receive the payment of her share of the receipts, and of the subscription.

" 6. Madame Catalani shall sing at no other place but the King's Theatre, during the season ; in the concerts or oratorios, where she may sing, she will be entitled to no other share but that specified as under.

" 7. During the season, Madame Catalani shall be at liberty to go to Bath, Oxford, or Cambridge.

" 8. Madame Catalani shall not sing oftener than her health will allow her. She promises to contribute to the utmost of her power to the good of the theatre. On his side, Mr. Ebers engages to treat Madame Catalani with every possible care.

" 9. This engagement, and these conditions, will be binding for this season, which will begin
                    and end
and continue during all the seasons that the theatre shall be under the management of Mr. Ebers, unless Madame Catalani's health, or state of her voice, should not allow her to continue.

" 10. Madame Catalani, in return for the conditions above mentioned, shall receive the half part of the amount of all the receipts which shall be made in the course of the season, including the subscription to the boxes, the amount of those sold separately, the monies received at the doors of the theatre, and of the concert-room ; in short, the said half part of the general receipts of the theatre for the season.

" 11. It is well understood that Madame Catalani's share shall be free from every kind of deduction, it being granted her in lieu of salary. It is likewise well understood, that every expense of the theatre during the season shall be Mr. Ebers'; such as the rent of the theatre, the performers' salaries, the tradespeople's bills ; in short, every possible expense ; and Madame Catalani shall be entirely exonerated from any one charge.

" This engagement shall be translated into English, taking care that the conditions shall remain precisely as in the original, and shall be so worded as to stipulate that Madame Catalani, on receiving her share of the receipts of the theatre, shall in no ways whatever be considered as partner of the manager of the establishment.

" 12. The present engagement being made with the full approbation of both parties, Mr. Ebers and M. Valabrèque pledge their word of honour to fulfil it in every one of its parts."

I must now add that Madame Catalani, by all accounts, possessed an excellent disposition, that her private life was irreproachable, and that while gaining immense sums, she also gave immense sums away in charity. Indeed, the proceeds of her concerts, for the benefit of the poor and sick have been estimated at eighty thousand pounds, besides which she performed numerous acts of generosity towards individuals. Nor does she appear to have possessed that excessive and exclusive admiration for Madame Catalani's talent which was certainly entertained by her husband, M. Valabrèque. Otherwise there can be no truth in the well known story of her giving, by way of homage, the shawl which had just been presented to her by the Empress of Russia, to a Moscow gipsey—one of those singing *tsigankie* who execute with such originality and true expression their own characteristic melodies.

After having delighted the world for thirty-five years, Madame Catalani retired to a charming villa near Florence. The invasion of the cholera made her leave this retreat and go to Paris; where, in 1849, in her seventieth year, she fell a victim to the very scourge she had hoped to avoid.

As for the husband, Valabrèque, he appears to have been mean, officious, conceited (of his wife's talent!) and generally stupid. M. Castil Blaze solemnly affirms, that when Madame Catalani was rehearsing at the Italian Opera of Paris an air which she was to sing in the evening to a pianoforte accompaniment, she found the instrument too high, and told Valabrèque to see that it was lowered; upon which (declares M. Blaze) Valabrèque called for a carpenter and caused the unfortunate piano's feet to be amputated!

"Still too high?" cried Madame Catalani's husband, when he was accused in the evening of having neglected her orders. "Why, how much did you lower it, Charles?" addressing the carpenter.

"Two inches, Sir," was the reply.

The historian of the above anecdote calls Tamburini, Lablache, and Tadolini, as well as Rossini and Berryer, the celebrated advocate, to witness that the mutilated instrument had afterward four knobs of wood glued to its legs by the same Charles who executed in so faithful a manner M. Valabrèque's absurd behest. It continued to wear these pattens until its existence was terminated in the fire of 1838—in which by the way, the composer of *William Tell,* who at that time nominally directed the theatre, and who had apartments on the third floor, would inevitably have perished had he not left Paris for Italy the day before!

Before concluding this chapter, I will refer once more to the "Musical Reminiscences" of Lord

Mount Edgcumbe, whose opinions on singers seem to me more valuable than those he has expressed about contemporary composers, and who had frequent and constant opportunities of hearing the five great female vocalists engaged at the King's Theatre, between the years 1786 and 1814.

" They may be divided," he says, " into two classes, of which Madame Mara and Mrs. Billington form the first ; and they were in most respects so similar, that the same observations will apply equally to both.   Both were excellent musicians, thoroughly skilled in their profession ; both had voices of uncommon sweetness and agility, particularly suited to the bravura style, and executed to perfection and with good taste, every thing they sung.   But neither was an Italian, and consequently both were deficient in recitative : neither had much feeling or theatrical talent, and they were absolutely null as actresses ; therefore they were more calculated to give pleasure in the concert-room than on the stage.

The other three, on the contrary, had great and distinguished dramatic talents, and seemed born for the theatrical profession.   They were all likewise but indifferently skilled in music, supplying by genius what they wanted in science, and thereby producing the greatest and most striking effects on the stage : these are their points of resemblance.   Their distinctive differences, I should say, were these : Grassini was all grace, Catalani all fire, Banti all feeling."

The composers, in whose music the above singers chiefly excelled, were Gluck, Piccinni, Guglielmi, Cimarosa, and Paisiello. We have seen that " Susanna " in the *Nozze di Figaro*, was one of Catalani's favourite parts ; but as yet Mozart's music was very little known in England, and it was not until 1817 that his *Don Giovanni* was produced at the King's Theatre.

After Gluck and Piccinni, the most admired composers, and the natural successors of the two great rivals in point of time, were Cimarosa and Paisiello. Guglielmi was considerably their senior, and on returning to Naples in 1777, after having spent fifteen years away from his country, in Vienna, and in London, he found that his two younger competitors had quite supplanted him in public favour. His works, composed between the years 1755 and 1762, had become antiquated, and were no longer performed. All this, instead of discouraging the experienced musician (Guglielmi was then fifty years of age) only inspired him with fresh energy. He found, however, a determined and unscrupulous adversary in Paisiello, who filled the theatre with his partisans the night on which Guglielmi was to produce his *Serva innamorata,* and occasioned such a disturbance, that for some time it was impossible to attend to the music.

The noise was especially great at the commencement of a certain quintett, on which, it was said, the success of the work depended.   Guglielmi was celebrated for the ingenuity and beauty of his concerted pieces, but there did not seem to be much chance, as affairs stood on this particular evening, of his quintett being heard at all.   Fortunately, while it was being executed, the door of the royal box opened, and the king appeared.   Instantly the most profound silence reigned throughout the theatre, the piece was re-commenced, and Guglielmi was saved.   More than that, the enthusiasm of the audience was raised, and went on increasing to such a point, that at the end of the performance the composer was taken from his box, and carried home in triumph to his hotel.

From this moment Paisiello, with all his jealousy, was obliged to discontinue his intrigues against a musician, whom Naples had once more adopted. Cimarosa had taken no part in the plot against Guglielmi; but he was by no means delighted with Guglielmi's success.   Prince San Severo, who admired the works of all three, invited them to a magnificent banquet where he made them embrace one another, and swear eternal friendship.*   Let us hope that he was not the cause of either of them committing perjury.

* It will be remembered that Berton, the director of the French Academy, entertained Gluck and Piccinni in a similar manner. (See vol. I.)

Paisiello seems to have been an intriguer all his life, and to have been constantly in dread of rivals; though he probably had less reason to fear them than any other composer of the period. However, at the age of seventy-five, when he had given up writing altogether, we find him, a few months before his death, getting up a cabal against the youthful Rossini, who was indeed destined to eclipse him, and to efface even the memory of his *Barbiere di Siviglia*, by his own admirable opera on the same subject. It is as if, painting on the same canvas, he had simply painted out the work of his predecessor.

Cimarosa, though he may have possessed a more dignified sense than Paisiello of what was due to himself, had less vanity. A story is told of a painter wishing to flatter the composer of *Il Matrimonio Segretto*, and saying that he looked upon him as superior to Mozart.

" Superior to Mozart ! " exclaimed Cimarosa. " What should you think, Sir, of a musician, who told you that you were a greater painter than Raphael?"

Among the other composers who adorned the end of the eighteenth and the beginning of the nine-teenth century, may be mentioned Sacchini, the

successor of Piccinni in Paris; Salieri, the envious
rival of Mozart, and (in Paris) the successor of Gluck;
Paer, in whose *Camilla* Rossini played the child's part
at the age of seven (1799); Mayer, the future master
of Donizetti; and Zingarelli, the future master of
Bellini, one of whose operas was founded on the same
libretto which afterwards served the pupil for his
Capuletti i Montecchi.

Piccinni is not connected in any direct manner
with the present day; but it is nevertheless to Piccinni that we owe the first idea of those magnificent
finales which, more than half a century afterwards,
contributed so much to the success of Rossini's operas,
and of which the first complete specimens, including
several movements with changes of key and of rhythm,
occur in *La Cecchina ossia la Buona Figliuola*, produced at Rome in 1760.

Logroscino, who sometimes passes as the inventor
of these finales, and who lived a quarter of a century
earlier, wrote them only on one theme.

The composer who introduced dramatic finales into
serious opera, was Paisiello.

It may interest the reader to know, that the finale
of *Don Giovanni* lasts fifteen minutes.

That of the *Barber of Seville* lasts twenty-one minutes and a-half.

That of *Otello* lasts twenty-four minutes.

The quintett of *Gazza Ladra* lasts twenty-seven minutes.

The finale of *Semiramide* lasts half an hour—or perhaps a minute or two less, if we allow for the increased velocity at which quick movements are "taken" by the conductors of the present day.

CHAPTER XII.

OPERA IN FRANCE, AFTER THE DEPARTURE OF GLUCK.

A FEW months before Gluck left Paris for the last time, an insurrection broke out at the Opera. The revolutionary spirit was abroad in Paris. The success of the American War of Independence, the tumultuous meetings of the French Parliament, the increasing resistance to authority which now manifested itself everywhere in France; all these stimulants to revolt seem to have taken effect on the singers and dancers of the Académie. The company resolved to carry on the theatre itself, for its own benefit, and the director, Devismes, was called upon to abdicate. The principal insurgents held what they called " Congress," at the house of Madeleine Guimard, and the God of Dancing, Auguste Vestris, declared loudly that he was the Washington of the affair.

Every day some fresh act of insubordination was committed, and the chiefs of the plot had to be

forced to appear on the stage by the direct interference of the police.

"The minister desires me to dance," said Mademoiselle Guimard on one of these occasions; *"eh
bien qu'il y prenne garde, je pourrais bien le faire
sauter."*

The influential leader just named conducted the
intrigue with great skill and discretion.

"One thing, above all!" she said to her fellow
conspirators; "no combined resignations,—that is
what ruined the Parliament."

To the minister, Amelot, the destroyer and recon-
structor of the Parliament of Dijon, Sophie Arnould
observed, in reference to his interference with the
affairs of the Académie—

"You should remember, that it is easier to compose a parliament than to compose an opera."

Auguste Vestris having spoken very insolently to
Devismes, the latter said to him—

"Do you know, sir, to whom you are speaking?"

"To whom? to the farmer of my talent," replied
the dancer.

Things were brought to a crisis by the *fêtes* given
to celebrate the birth of Marie Antoinette's first
child, December, 1778. The city of Paris proposed
to spend enormous sums in festivities and illumina-
tions; but the king and queen benevolently suggested
that, instead of being wasted in useless display, the
money should be given away in marriage portions to
a hundred deserving young girls; and their majesties

gave fifty thousand francs themselves for the same object. Losing sight of the Opera for the moment, I must relate, in as few words as possible, a charming little anecdote that is told of one of the applicants for a dowry. Lise was the name of this innocent and *naïve* young person, who, on being asked some question respecting her lover, replied, that she had none; and that she thought the municipality provided everything ! The municipality found the necessary admirer, and could have had no difficulty in doing so, if we may judge from the graceful bust of Lise, executed in marble by the celebrated sculptor, Houdon.

The Académie, which at this time belonged to the city, determined to follow its example, and to give away at least one marriage portion. Twelve hundred francs were subscribed and placed in the hands of Mademoiselle Guimard, the treasurer elect. The nuptial banquet was to take place at the winter Vauxhall (*Gallicè* " Wauxhall "); and all Paris was in a state of eager excitement to be present at what promised to be a most brilliant and original entertainment. It was not allowed, however, to take place, the authorities choosing to look upon it as a parody of the *fête* given by the city.

The doors of the " Wauxhall " being closed to the subscribers, Mademoiselle Guimard invited them to meet at her palace, in the Chaussée d'Antin. The municipality again interfered ; and in the middle of the banquet Vestris and Dauberval were arrested by *lettres de cachet* and taken to For-l'Evêque, on the ground that they had refused to dance the Tuesday previous in the *divertissement* of *Armide*.

Gaetan Vestris was present at the arrest of his son, and excited the mirth of the assembly by the pompous, though affectionate, manner in which he bade him farewell. After embracing him tenderly, he said—

" Go, Augustus ; go to prison. This is the grandest day of your life ! Take my carriage, and ask for the room of my friend, the King of Poland; and live magnificently—charge everything to me."

On another occasion, when Gaetan was not so well pleased with his Augustus, he said to him :

" What! the Queen of France does her duty, by requesting you to dance before the King of Sweden, and you do not do yours ? You shall no longer bear my name. I will have no misunderstanding between the house of Vestris and the house of Bourbon ; they have hitherto always lived on good terms."

For his refusal to dance, Augustus was this time sentenced to six months' imprisonment ; but the opera goers were so eager for his re-appearance that he was set free long before the expiration of the appointed term.

He made his *rentrée* amid the groans and hisses of the audience, who seemed determined to give him a lesson for his impertinence.

Then Gaetan, magnificently attired, appeared on the stage, and addressed the public as follows :—

" You wish my son to go down on his knees. I do not say that he does not deserve your displeasure; but remember, that the dancer whom you have so often applauded has not studied the *pose* you now require of him."

" Let him speak; let him endeavour to justify himself," cried a voice from the pit.

" He *shall* speak; he *shall* justify himself," replied the father. And, turning to his son, he added: " Dance, Auguste!"

Auguste danced; and every one in the theatre applauded.

The orchestra took no part in the operatic insurrection; and we have seen that the musicians were not invited to contribute anything to the dowry, offered by the Académie to virtue in love and in distress. De Vismes proposed to reward his instrumentalists by giving up to them a third of the receipts from some special representation of Gluck's *Iphigénie en Tauride*. The band rejected the offer, as not sufficiently liberal, and by refusing to play on the evening in question, made the performance a failure.

The Academic revolt was at last put an end to, by the city of Paris cancelling de Vismes's lease, and taking upon itself the management of the theatre, de Vismes receiving a large sum in compensation, and the appointment of director at a fixed salary.

Beaumarchais, while assisting the national revolution with the *Marriage of Figaro*, is known to have aided in a more direct manner the revolution which was now imminent at the opera. It is said, that he was anxious to establish an operatic republic in the hope of being made president of it himself. He is known to have been a good musician. I have spoken of his having held the honourable, if not lucrative, post of music-master to the daughters of Louis XV. (by whom he was as well paid as was Piccinni by that monarch's successor);* and a better proof of his talent is afforded, by his having composed all the music of his *Barber of Seville* and *Marriage of Figaro*, except the air of *Malbrook* in the latter comedy.

Beaumarchais had been much impressed by the genius of Gluck. He met him one evening in the *foyer* of the Opera, and spoke to him so clearly and so well about music that the great composer said to him : " You must surely be M. de Beaumarchais." They agreed to write an opera together, and some years afterwards, when Gluck had left Paris for Vienna, the poet sent the composer the *libretto* of *Tarare*. Gluck wrote to say that he was delighted with the work, but that he was now too old to undertake the task of setting it to music, and would entrust it to his favourite pupil, Salieri.

---

* We sometimes hear complaints of the want of munificence shown by modern constitutional sovereigns, in their dealings with artists and musicians. At least, however, they pay them. Louis XV. and Louis XVI. not only did not pay their daughters' music-masters, but allowed the royal young ladies to sponge upon them for what music they required.

Gluck benefitted French opera in two ways.   He endowed the Académie with several master-pieces, and moreover, destroyed, or was the main instrument in destroying, its old *répertoire*, which after the works of Gluck and Piccinni was found intolerable.   It was now no longer the fashion to exclude foreign composers from the first musical theatre in France, and Gluck and Piccinni were followed by Sacchini and Salieri.   Strange to say, Sacchini, when he first made his appearance at the Académie with his *Olympiade*, was deprived of a hearing through the jealousy of Gluck, who, on being informed, at Vienna, that the work in question was in rehearsal, hurried to Paris and had influence enough to get it withdrawn.   Worse than this, when the *Olympiade* was produced at the Comédie Italienne, with great success, Gluck and his partisans put a stop to the representation by enforcing one of the privileges of the Académie, which rendered it illegal for any other theatre to perform operas with choruses or with more than seven singers on the stage.

No work by Sacchini or Salieri was produced at the Académie until after the theatre in the Palais Royal was burnt down, in 1781.   In this fire, which took place about eighteen months after Gluck had retired from Paris, and five months after the production of Piccinni's *Iphigenia in Tauris*, the old *répertoire* would seem to have been consumed, for no opera by Lulli was afterwards played in France, and only one by Rameau, — *Castor and Pollux*, which, revived in 1791, was not favourably received.

It was in June, 1781, after a representation of Gluck's *Orphée*, that the Académie Royale was burnt to the ground. *Coronis* (music by Rey, the conductor of the orchestra) was the last piece of the evening, and before it was finished, during the *divertissement*, one of the scenes caught fire. Dauberval, the principal dancer, had enough presence of mind to order the curtain down at once. The public wanted no more of *Coronis*, and went quietly away without calling for the conclusion of Rey's opera, and without having the least idea of what was taking place behind the curtain. In the meanwhile the fire had spread on the stage beyond the possibility of extinction. Singers, dancers, musicians, and scene-shifters, rushed in terror from the theatre, and about a dozen persons, who were unable to escape, perished in the conflagration. Madeleine Guimard was nearly burnt to death in her dressing-room, which was surrounded by flames. One of the carpenters, however, penetrated into her *loge*, wrapped her up in a counterpane (she was entirely undressed), and bore her triumphantly through the fire to a place of safety.

" Save my child! save my child!" cried Rey, in despair; and as soon as he saw the score of *Coronis* out of danger he went away, giving the flames full permission to burn everything else. All the manuscripts were saved, thanks to the courageous exertions of Lefebvre, the librarian, who remained below in the music room even while the stage was burning, until the last sheet had been removed.

"The Opera is burnt down," said a Parisian to a Parisian the next morning.

"So much the better," was the reply. "It had been there such a time!"

This remark was ingenious but not true, for the Académie Royale de Musique had only been standing eighteen years. It was burnt down before, in 1763, on which occasion Voltaire, in a letter to M. d'Argental, wrote as follows: "*on dit que ce spectacle était si mauvais qu'il fallait tôt ou tard que la vengeance divine éclatât.*" The theatre destroyed by fire in 1763* was in the Palais Royal, and it was reconstructed on the same spot. After the fire of 1781, the Porte St. Martin theatre was built, and the Opera was carried on there ten years, after which it was removed to the opera-house in the Rue Richelieu, which was pulled down after the assassination of the Duc de Berri. But we are advancing beyond the limits of the present chapter.

The new Opera House was built in eighty-six days. The members of the company received orders not to

* In chronicling the material changes that have taken place at the French Opera, I must not forget the story of the new curtain, displayed for the first time, in 1753, or rather the admirable inscription suggested for it by Diderot—*Hic Marsias Apollinem.* Pergolese's *Servante Maitresse* (*La Serva padrona*) had just been "*écorchée*" by the orchestra of the Académie.

leave Paris, and during the interval were paid their
salaries regularly as if for performing. The work
began on the 2nd of August, and was finished on the
27th of October. Lenoir, the architect, had told
Marie Antoinette that the theatre could be completed in time for the first performance to take place
on the 30th of October.

"Say the 31st," replied the queen; "and if on
that day I receive the key of my box, I promise you
the Order of St. Michael in exchange."

The key was sent to her majesty on the 26th, who
not only decorated Lenoir with the *cordon* of St.
Michael, but also conferred on him a pension of six
thousand francs; and on the 27th the theatre was
opened to the public.

In 1784, Sacchini's *Chimène*, adapted from *Il
Gran Cid*, an opera he had written for the King's
Theatre in 1773, was produced at the Académie with
great success. The principal part in this work was
sustained by Huberti, a singer much admired by Piccinni, who wrote some airs in the *cantabile* style
specially for her, and said that, without her, his
opera of *Dido*, in which she played the principal
part, was "without Dido." M. Castil Blaze tells us
that she was the first true singer who appeared at
the Académie. Grimm declares, that she sang like
Todi and acted like Clairon. Finally, when Madame
de Saint Huberti was performing at Strasburgh, in

1787, a young officer of artillery, named Napoleon Bonaparte, addressed the following witty and complimentary verses to her :—

> " Romains qui vous vantez d'une illustre origine
>   Voyez d'où dépendait votre empire naissant :
>   Didon n'eut pas de charme assez puissant
>   Pour arrêter la fuite où son amant s'obstine ;
>   Mais si l'autre Didon, ornement de ces lieux,
>   Eût été reine de Carthage,
>   Il eût, pour la servir, abandonné ses dieux,
>   Et votre beau pays serait encore sauvage."

Sacchini's first opera, *Œdipe à Colosse*, was not produced at the Académie until 1787, a few months after his death. It was now no question, of whether he was a worthy successor of Gluck or a formidable opponent to Piccinni. His opera was admired for itself, and the public applauded it with genuine enthusiasm.

In the meanwhile, Salieri, the direct inheritor of Gluck's mantle (as far as that poetic garment could be transferred by the mere will of the original possessor) had brought out his *Danaïdes*—announced at first as the work of Gluck himself and composed under his auspices. Salieri had also set *Tarare* to music. "This is the first *libretto* of modern times," says M. Castil Blaze, "in which the author has ventured to join buffoonery to tragedy—a happy alliance, which permits the musician to vary his colours and display all the resources of genius and art." The routine-lovers of the French Académie, the pedants, the blunderers, were indignant with the new work; and its author entrusted Figaro with the task of defending it.

"Either you must write nothing interesting," said Figaro, " or fools will run you down."

The same author then notices, as a remarkable coincidence, that " Beaumarchais and Da Ponte, at four hundred leagues distance from one another, invented, at the same time, the class of opera since known as " romantic." Beaumarchais's *Tarare* had been intended for Gluck ; Da Ponte's *Don Giovanni*, as every one knows, found its true composer in Mozart.

CHAPTER XIII.

THE FRENCH OPERA BEFORE AND AFTER THE REVOLUTION.

A COMPLETE history of the French Opera would include something like a history of French society, if not of France generally. It would, at least, show the effect of the great political changes which the country has undergone, and would remind us here and there of her celebrated victories, and occasionally even of her reverses. Under the despotism, we have seen how a simple *lettre de cachet* sufficed to condemn an *abbé* with a good voice, or a young girl with a pretty face, to the Opera, just as a person obnoxious to the state or to any very influential personage was sent to the Bastille. During the Regency, half the audience at the Opera went there drunk; and almost until the period of the Revolution the *abbés*, the *mousquetaires*, and the *grands seigneurs*, quarrelled, fought, and behaved in many respects as if the theatre were, not their own private house, but their own particular tap-room. Music profited by the Revolution, in so far that the privileges of the Académie were abolished, and, as a natural consequence, a number of new musical works produced at a variety of theatres which would otherwise never have seen the light ; but the position of singers and dancers was by no means a pleasant one under the Convention, and the tyranny of the republican chiefs was far more oppressive, and of a more brutal kind, than any that had been exercised at the Académie in the days of the monarchy. The disobedient daughters, whose admirers got them " inscribed " on the books of the Opera so as to free them from parental control, would, under another system, have run away from home. No one, in practice, was injured very much by the regulation, scandalous and immoral as it undoubtedly was; for, before the name was put down, all the harm, in most cases, was already done. Sophie Arnould, it is true, is said to have been registered at the Opera without the consent of her mother, and, what seems very extraordinary—not at the suggestion of a lover ; but Madame Arnould was quite reconciled to her daughter's being upon the stage before she eloped with the Count de Lauragais. To put the case briefly : the *académiciens* (and above all, the *académiciennes*) in the immoral atmosphere of the court, were fêted, flattered, and grew rich, though, owing to their boundless extravagance, they often died poor : whereas, during the republic, they met with neither sympathy nor respect, and in the worst days of the Convention lived, in a more literal sense than would be readily imagined, almost beneath the shadow of the guillotine.

In favour of the old French society, when it was at its very worst, that is to say, during the reign of Louis XV., it may be mentioned that the king's mistresses did not venture to brave general opinion, so far as to present themselves publicly at the Opera.   Madame Dubarry announced more than once that she intended to visit the Académie, and went so far as to take boxes for herself and suite, but at the last moment her courage (if courage and not shamelessness be the proper word) failed her, and she stayed away. On the other hand, towards the end of this reign, the licentiousness of the court had become so great, that brevets, conferring the rights and privileges of married ladies on ladies unmarried, were introduced.   Any young girl who held a *" brevet de dame "* could present herself at the Opera, which etiquette would otherwise have rendered impossible.   " The number of these brevets," says *Bachaumont*, " increased prodigiously under Louis XVI., and very young persons have been known to obtain them.   Freed thus from the modesty, simplicity, and retirement of the virginal state, they give themselves up with impunity to all sorts of scandals.   *   *   *   Such disorder has opened the eyes of the government ; and this prince, the friend of decency and morality, has at last shown himself very particular on the subject. It is now only by the greatest favour that one of these brevets can be obtained."*

Mémoires Secrètes, vol. xxi., page 121.

No *brevets* were required of the fishwomen and charcoal men of Paris, who, on certain fêtes, such as the Sovereign's birth day, were always present at the gratuitous performances given at the Opera. On these occasions the balcony was always reserved for them, the *charbonniers* being placed on the king's side, the *poissardes* on the queen's. At the close of the representation the performers invited their favoured guests on to the stage, the orchestra played the airs from some popular ballet, and a grand ball took place, in which the *charbonniers* chose their partners from among the operatic *danseuses*, while the *poissardes* gave their hands to Vestris, Dauberval, &c.

During Passion week and Easter, the Opera was shut, but the great operatic vocalists could be heard elsewhere, either at the Jesuits' church or at the Abbaye of Longchamp, to which latter establishment it is generally imagined that the Parisian public used to be attracted by the singing of the nuns. What is far more extraordinary is, that the Parisians always laboured under that delusion themselves. " The Parisians," says M. Castil Blaze, in his " History of the Grand Opera," " always such fine connoisseurs in music, never penetrated the mystery of this incognito. The railing and the green curtain, behind which the voices were concealed, sufficed to render the singers unrecognisable to the *dilettanti* who heard them constantly at the opera."

Adjoining the Jesuits' church was a theatre, also belonging to the Jesuits, for which, between the years 1659 and 1761, eighty pieces of various kinds, including tragedies, operas and ballets, were written. Some of these productions were in Latin, some in French, some in Latin and French together. The *virtuosi* of the Académie used to perform in them and afterwards proceed to the church to sing motets. " This church is so much the church of the Opera," says Freneuse, " that those who do not go to one console themselves by attending vespers at the other, where they find the same thing at less cost." He adds, that " an actor newly engaged, would not think himself fully recognised unless asked to sing for the Jesuits." As for the actresses, " in their honor the price which would be given at the door of the opera is given for a chair in the church. People look out for Urgande, Arcabonne, Armide, and applaud them. (I have seen them applaud la Moreau and la Chérat, at the midnight mass.) These performances replace those which are suspended at the opera."

There would be no end to this chapter (and many persons would think it better not written) if I were to enter into details on the subject of the relations between the singers and dancers of the Académie, and the Grands Seigneurs of the period. I may observe, however, that the latter appear to have been far more generous, without being more vicious, and that they seem to have lived in better taste than their modern imitators, who usually ruin themselves by means of race-horses, or, in France, on the Stock Exchange. The Count de Lauragais paid an immense sum to the directors of the Académie, to compensate them for abolishing the seats on the stage (probably impertinent visitors used to annoy him by staring at Sophie Arnould) ; the Duke de Bouillon spent nine hundred thousand livres on Mademoiselle la Guerre (Gluck's *Iphigénie*) ; the Prince de Soubise nearly as much on Mademoiselle Guimard—who at least gave a portion of it away in charity, and who, as we have seen, was an intelligent patroness of David, the painter.

When the Prince de Guéméné became insolvent, the Prince de Soubise, his father-in-law, ceased to attend the Opera. There were three thousand creditors, and the debts amounted to forty million livres. The heads of the family felt called upon to make a sacrifice, and the Prince de Soubise was no longer in a position to give *petits soupers* to his *protégées* at the Académie. Under these circumstances, the " ladies of the *ballet* " assembled in the dressing-room of Mademoiselle Guimard, their chief, and prepared the following touching, and really very becoming letter, to their embarrassed patron :—

" Monseigneur,
" Accustomed to see you amongst us at the representations at the Lyrical Theatre, we have observed with the most bitter regret that you not only tear

yourself away from the pleasures of the performance, but also that none of us are now invited to
the little suppers you used so frequently to give, in
which we had turn by turn the happiness of interesting you.   Report has only too well informed us of
the cause of your seclusion, and of your just grief.
Hitherto we have feared to importune you, allowing
sensibility to give way to respect.   We should not
dare, even now, to break silence, without the pressing
motive to which our delicacy is unable any longer to
resist.

" We had flattered ourselves, Monseigneur, that
the Prince de Guéméné's bankruptcy, to employ an
expression which is re-echoed in the *foyers*, the clubs,
the newspapers of France, and all Europe, would not
be so considerable, so enormous, as was announced ;
and, above all, that the wise precautions taken by
the King to assure the claimants the amount of their
debts, and to avoid expenses and depredations more
fatal even than the insolvency itself, would not dis-
appoint the general expectation.   But affairs are
doubtless in such disorder, that there is now no hope.
We judge of it by the generous sacrifices to which
the heads of your illustrious house, following your
example, have resigned themselves.   We should
think ourselves guilty of ingratitude, Monseigneur,
if we were not to imitate you in seconding your
humanity, and if we were not to return you the pen-
sions which your munificence has lavished upon us.
Apply these revenues, Monseigneur, to the consola-

tion of so many retired officers, so many poor men of letters, so many unfortunate servants whom M. le Prince de Guéméné drags into ruin with him.

" As for us, we have other resources : and we shall have lost nothing, Monseigneur, if we preserve your esteem. We shall even have gained, if, by refusing your gifts now, we force our detractors to agree that we were not unworthy of them.

" We are, with profound respect,
" Monseigneur,
" Your most Serene Highness's very humble and " devoted Servants,
" GUIMARD, HEINEL," &c.

With twenty other names.

Auguste Vestris spent and owed a great deal of money ; the father honoured the engagements of the young dancer, but threatened him with imprisonment if he did not alter his conduct, and concluded by saying :—" Understand, Sir, that I will have no Guéméné in *my* family."

Although ballet dancers were important persons in those days, they were as nothing compared to the institution to which they belonged. Figaro, in his celebrated soliloquy, observes, with reference to the great liberty of the press accorded by the government, that provided he does not speak of a great many very different things, among which the Opera is included, he is at liberty to publish whatever he likes " under the inspection of three or four censors."

Beaumarchais was more serious than would be generally supposed, in including the Opera among the subjects which a writer dared not touch upon, or, if so, only with the greatest respect.　Rousseau tells us in more than one place, that it was considered dangerous to say anything against the Opera ; and Mademoiselle Théodore (the interesting *danseuse* beforementioned, who consulted the fantastic moralist on the conduct she ought to pursue as a member of the ballet), was actually imprisoned, and exiled from Paris for eighteen days, because she had ventured to ridicule the management of the Académie, in some letters addressed to a private friend.　The author of the *Nouvelle Héloise* should have warned her to be more careful.

On the 12th July, 1789, the bills were torn down from the doors of the Opera.　The Parisians were about to take the Bastille.　Having taken it, they allowed the Académie to continue its performance, and it re-opened on the 21st of the same month. In Warsaw, during the " demonstrations " of last March, the Opera was closed.　It remains closed now * (end of November), and will re-open——neither Russians nor Poles can say when !　No one tears the bills down, because no one thinks of putting them up ; it being perfectly understood by the administration, which is a department of the Govern-

* This prevented me, when I was in Warsaw, from hearing M. Moniuszko's Polish opera of *Halka*.

ment), that the Warsaw public are not disposed at present for amusement of any kind.

In 1789, the revolutionary spirit manifested itself among the company engaged at the French Opera. An anonymous letter—or rather a letter in the name of all the company, printed, but not signed—was addressed to the administration of the theatre. It pointed out a number of abuses, and bore this epigraph, strongly redolent of the period: *" Tu dors Brutus, et Rome est dans les fers !"*

In 1790 the city of Paris assumed once more the management of the Académie, the artistic direction being entrusted to a committee composed of the chiefs of the various departments, and of the principal singers and dancers. One of the novelties produced was a "melodrama founded on passages from the Scriptures," called "The Taking of the Bastille," written specially for Notre Dame, where it was performed for the first time, and where it was followed by a grand *Te Deum*. In this *Te Deum* few of the lovers of the Opera could have joined, for one of the first effects of the revolution was naturally to drive the best singers and dancers away from Paris. Lord Mount Edgcumbe tells us that Mademoiselle Guimard was dancing in London in 1789. Madame Huberti, who was, by all accounts, the best singer the French had ever heard at the Académie, left Paris early in 1790,

We know how injurious a distant war, a dissolution

of parliament, a death in the royal family are to the fortunes of an operatic season in London. Fancy what must have been the effect of the French revolution on the Académie after 1789 ! The subscription list for boxes showed, in a few years, a diminution of from 475,000 *livres* to 000,000! Some, of the subscribers had gone into exile, more or less voluntary, some had been banished, others had been guillotined. M. Castil Blaze, from whose interesting works I have obtained a great number of particulars concerning the French Opera at the time of the revolution, tells us that the Queen used to pay 7,000 livres for her box. The Duke d'Orléans paid 7,000 for his own private box, and joined the Duke de Choiseul and Necker in a subscription of 8,200 francs for another. The Princess de Lamballe and Madame de Genlis gave 3,600 francs for a "post chaise;" (there were other boxes, called "spittoons"—the *baignoires* of the present day—"cymbals," &c.; names which they evidently owed to their position and form). On the other hand, there were 288 free admissions, of which, thirty-two were given to authors, and eight to newspapers—*La Gazette de France, Le Journal de Paris,* and *Le Mercure.* The remaining 248 were reserved for the Hôtel de Ville, the King's Household, the actors of the Comédie Française, and the singers and dancers of the Opera itself.

The howling of the *ça ira* put an end for ever to the Concert Spirituel, where the Parisians for nearly eighty years had been in the habit of hearing excellent instrumental soloists, and some of the best of the Italian singers, when there was as yet no Italian Opera in Paris. The last *concert spirituel* took place at the theatre of the Tuileries in 1791.

Louis XVI. and his family fled from Paris on the 28th June, 1791. The next day, and before the king was brought back to the Tuileries, the title of the chief lyric theatre was changed, and from the "Académie *Royale*" became simply the "Opera." At the same time the custom was introduced of announcing the performers' names, which was evidently an advantage for the public, and which was also not without its benefit, for the inferior singers and dancers who, when they unexpectedly made their appearance to replace their betters, used often to get hissed in a manner which their own simple want of merit scarcely justified. "*Est ce que je savais qu'on lâcherait le Ponthieu?*" exclaimed an unhappy ticket-seller one evening, when an indignant amateur rushed out of the theatre and began to cane the recipient of his ill-spent money. We may fancy how Ponthieu himself must have been received inside the house.

By an order of the Committee of Public Safety, dated the 16th of the September following, the title of the Opera was again changed to *Académie Royale de Musique*. This was intended as a compliment to the king, who had signed the Constitution on the 14th, and who was to go to the Opera six days

afterwards.   On the 20th the royal visit took place.
" *Castor and Pollux* was played," says M. Castil
Blaze, " and not *Iphigénie en Aulide*, as is asserted
by some ill-informed historians, who even go so far
as to pretend that the chorus *Chantons, célébrons
notre reine* was, as on another occasion, hailed with
transports of enthusiasm, and that the public called
for it a second time.   The house was well filled, but
not crammed * (*comble*), as is proved by the amount
of the receipts—6,636 livres, 15 sous.   The same
opera of Rameau's, vamped by Candeille, had produced 6,857 livres on the 14th of the preceding June.
The representation of *Castor and Pollux* in presence
of the royal family took place on Tuesday the 20th
September, and not on the 21st, the Wednesday, at
that time, not being an opera night.   On the 19th,
Monday, the people had assisted at a *special performance* of the same work given, gratuitously, in
honour of the Constitution.   The Royalists were
present in great numbers at the representation of the
20th September, and some lines which could be applied to the Queen were loudly applauded.   Marie-
Antoinette was delighted, and said to the ladies who
accompanied her, " You see that the people is really
good, and wishes only to love us."   Encouraged by so
flattering a reception, she determined to go the next

* To say that a theatre is "full" in the present day, means very
little.   The play-bills and even the newspapers speak of " a full
house " when it is half empty.   If a theatre is tolerably full, it is
said to be " crowded " or " crammed ; " if quite full, " crammed to
suffocation."   And that even in the coldest weather !

night to the Opéra Comique, but the king refused to accompany her. The piece performed was *Les Evéne-ments imprévus*. In the duet of the second act, before singing the words *"Ah comme j'aime ma maitresse"* Madame Dugazon looked towards the Queen, when a number of voices cried out from the pit, *Plus de maitresse! Plus de maitre! Vive la liberté!* This cry was answered from the boxes with *Vive la reine! Vive le roi!* Sabres and sword-sticks were drawn, and a battle began.

The Queen escaped from the theatre in the midst of the tumult. Cries of *à bas la reine!* followed her to her carriage, which went off at a gallop, with mud and stones thrown after it. Marie Antoinette returned to the Tuileries in despair. On the first of October, fourteen days afterwards, the title of *Opéra National* was substituted for that of *Académie Royale de Musique*. The Constitution being signed, there was no longer any reason for being civil to Louis XVI. This was the third change of title in less than four months. The majority of the buffoons, (M. Castil Blaze still speaks)," who now write histories more or less Girondist, or romantic of the French Re-volution, do not take the trouble to verify their facts and dates. I have told you simply that the dauphin-ess Marie Antoinette made her first appearance at the Opera on the 16th June, 1773, in company with her husband. Others, more ingenious no doubt, substi-tute the 21st January for the 16th June, in order to establish a sort of fatality by connecting days, months and years. To prophecy after the event is only too easy, above all, if you take the liberty of advancing by five months, the day which it is desired to render fatal. These same buffoons, (says M. Castil Blaze), who now go to the Opera on Monday, Wednesday and Friday, sometimes on Sunday, think people have done the same for the last two centuries. As they have not the slightest suspicion that the evenings of performance at the Académie Royale were changed in 1817, we find them maundering, paddling, splashing about, and finally altering figures and days, in order to make the events of the last century accord with the dates of our own epoch. That is why we are told that the Royal Family went for the last time to this theatre on Wednesday, the 21st September, 1791, instead of Tuesday, the 20th. Indeed how is it possible to go to the Opera on a Tuesday? That is why it is stated with the most laughable aplomb, that on the 21st October, 1793, *Roland* was performed, and on the 16th of October following, the *Siege of Thionville*, the *Offering to Liberty*, and the ballet of *Telemachus*. Each of these history-writing novelists fills or empties the house according to his political opinions; applauds the French people or deplores its blindness; but all the liberalism or sentiment manufactured by them is thrown away. Monday, the 21st of January, Wednesday the 16th of October, 1793, not being opera nights at that time, the Opera did not on those evenings throw open its doors to the public. On

Tuesday, the 22nd of January, the day after the death of Louis XVI., *Roland* was represented; the amount of the receipts, 492 livres, 8 sous, proves that the house was empty. No free admissions were given then. On Tuesday, October the 15th, 1793, the eve of the execution of Marie Antoinette, the *Siege of Thionville*, the *Offering to Liberty*, *Telemachus*, in which "*la Citoyenne Perignon*" was to appear— a forced performance—only produced 3,251 livres. On Friday, the 18th of October, the next day but one after this horrible catastrophe, *Armide* and the *Offering to Liberty*—a forced performance and some-thing more—produced 2,641 livres, which would have filled about a third of the house."*

The 10th August, 1792, was the last day of the French monarchy. On the Sunday previous, during the Vespers said at the Chapel of the Tuileries in presence of the king, the singers with one accord tripled the sound of their voices when they came to the following verse in the *Magnificat: Deposuit po-tentes de sede, et exaltavit humiles*. Indignant at their

---

* M. de Lamartine before writing the *History of the Restoration*, did not even take the trouble to find out whether or not the Duke of Wellington led a cavalry charge at the Battle of Waterloo. The same author, in his *History of the Girondist*, gives an interesting picture of Charlotte Corday's house at Caen, considered as a ruin. Being at Caen some years ago, I had no trouble in finding Charlotte Corday's house, but looked in vain for the moss, the trickling water, &c., introduced by M. de Lamartine in his poetical, but somewhat too fanciful description. The house was "in good repair," as the auctioneers say, and persons who had lived a great many years in the same street assured me that they had never known it as a ruin.—S.E.

audacity, the royalists thundered forth the *Domine salvum fac regem*, adding these words with increased energy and enthusiasm, *et reginam!* The greatest excitement and agitation prevailed in the Chapel during the rest of the service.

To conclude the list of musical performances which have derived a gloomy celebrity from their connexion with the last days of Louis XVI., I may reproduce the programme issued by the directors of the Opéra National, on the first anniversary of his execution, 21st January, 1794.

IN BEHALF OF AND FOR THE PEOPLE,
GRATIS,
In joyful commemoration of the Death of the Tyrant,
THE NATIONAL OPERA
WILL GIVE TO DAY, 6 PLUVIOSE, YEAR II., OF THE REPUBLIC,
MILTIADES AT MARATHON,
THE SIEGE OF THIONVILLE,
THE OFFERING TO LIBERTY.

The Opera under the Republic was directed, until 1792, by four distinguished *sans culottes*—Henriot, Chaumette, Le Rouxand Hébert, the last named of whom had once been check-taker at the Académie! The others know nothing whatever of operatic affairs. The management of the theatre was afterwards trans- ferred to Francœur, one of the former directors, associated with Cellérier, an architect; but the dethroned *impresarii,* accompanied by Danton and other republican amateurs, constantly made their appearance behind the scenes, and very frequently did the chief members of the company the honour of supping with them. In these cases the invitations, as under the ancient régime, proceeded, not from the artists, but from the artists' patrons; with this difference, however, that under the republic, the latter never paid the bill. There was no Duke de Bouillon now testifying his admiration of the vocal art to the tune of 900,000 francs;* there was no Prince de Soubise, to receive from the united ballet letters of condolence, thanks, and proposed pecuniary assistance; and if there *had* been such an impossible phenomenon as a Count de Lauragais, what, I wonder, would he not have given to have been able to clear the *coulisses* of such abominable intruders as the before named republican chiefs? " The chiefs of the republic, one and indivisible," says M. Castil Blaze, " were very fond of moistening their throats. Henriot, Danton, Hébert, Le Roux, Chaumette, had hardly taken a turn in the *coulisses* or in the *foyer,* before they said to such an actor or actress : We are going to your room, see that we are received properly." A superb collation was brought in. When the repast was finished and the bottles were empty, the national convention, the commune of Paris beat a retreat with-

* There was a Marquis de Louvois, but he was employed as a scene-shifter.

out troubling itself about the expense. You think, perhaps, that the dancer or the singer paid for the representatives of the people? Not at all; honest Mangin, who kept the refreshment room of the theatre, knew perfectly well that the actors of the Opera were not paid, that they had no sort of money, not even a rag of an assignat; he made a sacrifice; from delicacy he did not ask from the artists what he would not have dared to claim from the sans culottes for fear of the guillotine."

Sometimes the executioner, who, as a public official, had a right to his entrées, made his appearance behind the scenes, and it is said that in a facetious mood, he would sometimes express his opinion about the " execution " of the music. So, I am told, the London hangman went one night to the pit of Her Majesty's Theatre to hear Jenny Lind, and on seeing the Swedish nightingale, exclaimed, breathless with admiration and excitement, "What a throat to scrag!"

Operatic kings and queens were suppressed by the republic. Not only were they forbidden to appear on the stage, but even their names were not to be pronounced behind the scenes, and the expressions *côté du roi, côté de la reine,* were changed into *côté jardin, côté cour,* which at the theatre of the Tuileries indicated respectively the left and right of the stage, from the stage point of view. At first all pieces in which kings and queens appeared, were prohibited, but the dramas of *sans culottes* origin were so stupid and disgusting, that the republic was absolutely obliged to return to the old monarchical *répertoire*. The kings, however, were turned into chiefs; princes and dukes became representatives of the people; seigneurs subsided into mayors; and substitutes more or less synonymous, were found for such offensive words as crown, throne, sceptre, &c. In a new republican version of a lyrical work represented at the Opera Comique, *le roi* in one well known line was replaced by *la loi*, and the vocalist had to declaim *La loi passait, et le tambour battait aux champs.* A certain voluble executant, however, is said to have preferred the following emendation: *Le pouvoir exécutif passait, et le tambour battait aux champs.*

The scenes of most of the new operas were laid in Italy, Prussia, Portugal,—anywhere but in France, where it would have been indispensable, from a political, and impossible from a poetical, point of view to make the lovers address one another as *citoyen, citoyenne.*

On the 19th of June, 1793, the directors of the Opera having objected to give a gratuitous performance of *The Siege of Thionville*, the commune of Paris issued the following edict:

"Considering that for a long time past the aristocracy has taken refuge in the administration of various theatres;

"Considering that these gentlemen corrupt the public mind by the pieces they represent;

"Considering that they exercise a fatal influence on the revolution;

It is decreed that the *Siege of Thionville* shall be represented gratis and solely for the amusement of the *sans culottes*, who, to this moment have been the true defenders of liberty and supporters of democracy."

Soon afterwards it was proposed to shut up the Opera, but Hébert, the ferocious Hébert, better known as *le père Duchèsne*, undertook its defence on the ground that it procured subsistence for a number of families, and "caused the agreeable arts to flourish."

It was thereupon resolved "that the Opera should be encouraged and defended against its enemies." At the same time the managers Cellérier and Francœur were arrested as *suspects*. Neither of them was executed.

The Opera was now once more placed under the direction of a committee chosen from among the singers and dancers, who were selected this time, not by reason of their artistic merit, but solely with reference to their political principles. Lays, one of the chief managers, was a furious democrat, and on one occasion insisted on Mademoiselle Maillard (Gluck's "Armida!") appearing in a procession as the Goddess of Reason.

Mademoiselle Maillard having refused, Chaumette was appealed to. The arguments he employed were simple but convincing. "Well, *citoyenne*," he said, "since you refuse to be a divinity, you must not be astonished if we treat you *as a mortal*." Fortunately for the poor prima donna, Mormoro, a member of the Commune of Paris, and a raging "Maratiste" (which has not quite the same meaning now as in the days of the "Todistes") claimed the obnoxious part for his unhappy wife. The beautiful Madame Mormoro was forced to appear in the streets of Paris in the light and airy costume of an antique Goddess, with the thermometer at twenty degrees below freezing point! "Reason" not unreasonably wept with annoyance throughout the ceremony.

Léonard Bourdon, called by those who knew him *Léopard* Bourdon, used all his influence, as a distinguished member of the Mountain, to get a work he had prepared for the Opera produced. His piece was called the *Tomb of the Impostors*, or *the Inauguration of the Temple of Truth*. It was printed at the expense of the Republic, but never brought out. In the first scene the stage represents a church, built with human skulls. In the sanctuary there is to be a fountain of blood. A woman enters to confess, the priest behaves atrociously in the confessional, &c., &c. The scenes and incidents throughout the drama are all in the same style, and the whole is dedicated in an uncomplimentary epistle to the Pope. Léopard tormented the directors, actors, and actresses, night and day, to produce his master-piece, and threatened, that if they were not quick about it, he would have a guillotine erected on the stage.

This threat was not quite so vain as it might seem. A list of twenty-two persons engaged at the Opera (twenty-two—the fatal number during the Reign of Terror), had been already drawn up by Hébert, as a sort of executioner's memorandum. When he was in a good humour he would show it to the singers and dancers, and say to them with easy familiarity: " I shall have to send you all to the guillotine some day. Two reasons have prevented me hitherto; in the first place you are not worth the trouble, in the second I want you for my amusement." These reasons were not considered quite satisfactory by the proscribed artists, and Beaupré, a comic dancer of great talent, contrived by various humorous strata-gems (one of which, and doubtless the most readily forgiven, consisted in intoxicating Hébert), to gain possession of the fatal list; but the day afterwards the republican *dilettante* was always sufficiently recovered from the effects of his excessive potations to draw up another one exactly like it.

At the head of the catalogue of suspected ones figured the name of Lainez, whom the republicans could not pardon for the energy and expression with which he had sung the air *Chantez, célébrez votre reine*, at the last performances of *Iphigénie en Aulide;* and that of Mademoiselle Maillard, whose crime has been already mentioned. At this period it was dangerous not only to sing the words, but even to hum or whistle the music of such airs as the aforesaid *Chantez, célébrez votre reine, O Richard o mon roi! Charmante Gabrielle*, and many others, among which may be mentioned *Pauvre Jacques*—an adaptation of Dibdin's *Poor Jack*, in which allusions had been discovered to the fate of Louis XVI. Indeed, to perform any kind of music might be fatal to the executant, and thus Mesdemoiselles de Saint Léger, two young ladies living in Arras, were executed for having played the piano the day that Valenciennes fell into the hands of the enemy.

Mademoiselle Maillard, much as she detested the republicans, was forced, on one occasion, to sing a republican hymn. When Lainez complimented her on the warmth of her expression, the vigour of her execution, she replied, " I was burning with rage at having to sing to such monsters."

Vestris, the Prince de Guéméné of the Vestris family, he who had been accused by his father of wishing to produce a misunderstanding between the Vestrises and the Bourbons, had to dance in a *pas de trois* as a *sans culottes*, between two nuns !

Sophie Arnould, accused (and not quite unreasonably), of aristocratic sympathies, pointed indignantly to a bust of Gluck in her room, and asked the intelligent agents of the Republic, if it was likely she would keep the bust of Marat were she not a true republican?

The vocalists of a revolutionary turn of mind would have succeeded better if they had possessed more talent; but the Parisian public, even in 1793, was not prepared to accept correctness in politics as an excuse for inaccuracy in singing. Lefèvre, a sixth tenor, but a bloodthirsty republican, insisted on being promoted to first characters, and threatened those whom he wished to replace with denunciations and the guillotine, if they kept him in a subordinate position any longer. Lefèvre had his wish gratified in part, but not altogether. He appeared as *primo tenore*, but was violently hissed by his friends, the *sans culottes*. He then came out as first bass, and was hissed again. In his rage he attributed his *fiasco* to the machinations of the counter-revolution, and wanted the soldiers to come into the theatre, and fire upon the infamous accomplices of " Pitt and Coburg."

This bad singer, and worse man, was one of the twelve chiefs of the National Guard of Paris, and on certain days had the command of the city. As his military rule was most oppressive, the Parisians used to punish him for his tyranny as a soldier, by ridiculing his monstrous defects as a vocalist.

Though the Reign of Terror was a fearful time for artists and art, the number of playhouses in Paris increased enormously. There were sixty-three theatres open, and in spite of war, famine, and the guillotine, they were always full.

In 1794, the opera was transferred to the Rue de la Loi (afterwards Rue de Richelieu), immediately opposite the National Library. With regard to this change of locality, let us hear what M. Castil Blaze has to say, in his own words.

" How was it that the opera was moved to a building exactly opposite the National Library, so precious and so combustible a repository of human knowledge. The two establishments were only separated by a street, very much too narrow : if the theatre caught fire, was it not sure to burn the library ? That is what a great many persons still ask ; this question has been re-produced a hundred times in our journals. Go back to the time when the house was built by Mademoiselle Montansier ; read the *Moniteur Universel*, and you will see that it was precisely in order to expose this same library to the happy chances of a fire, that the great lyrical entertainment was transferred to its neighbourhood. The opera hung over it, and threatened it constantly. At this time enlightenment abounded to such a point, that the judicious Henriot, convinced in his innermost conscience that all reading was henceforth useless, had made a motion to burn the library. To move the opera to the Rue Richelieu—the opera, which twice in eighteen years had been a prey to the flames—to place it exactly opposite our literary treasures, was to multiply to infinity the chances of their being burnt.'

Mercier, in reference to the literary views of the Committee of Public Safety, writes in the *Nouveau Paris*, as follows :—

" The language of Omar about the Koran was not more terrible than those uttered by the members of the committee of public safety when they expressed their intentions formally, as follows :—' Yes, we will burn all the libraries, for nothing will be needed but the history of the Revolution and its laws." If the motion of Henriot had been carried, David, the great Conventional painter was ready to propose that the same service should be rendered to the masterpieces in the Louvre, as to the literary wealth of the National Library. Republican subjects, according to David, were alone worthy of being represented.

At one of the sittings of the very council in which Henriot had already brought forward his motion for burning the Library, Mademoiselle Montansier was accused of having built the theatre in the Rue Richelieu with that very design. On the 14th of

November, 1793, Chaumette at the sitting of the Commune of Paris, said—

"I denounce the *Citoyenne* Montansier. The money of the Englishman* has been largely employed in raising this edifice, and the former queen gave fifty thousand crowns towards it. I demand that this theatre be closed on account of the dangers which would result from its catching fire." Adopted.

Hébert. "I denounce *la demoiselle* Montansier, personally; I have information against her. She offered me a box at her new theatre to procure my silence. I demand that la Montansier be arrested as a suspicious person." Adopted.

Chaumette. "I demand, moreover, that the actors, actresses and directors of the Parisian theatres be subjected to the censorship of the council." Adopted.

After deciding that the theatre in the Rue de la Loi could not be kept open without imperilling the existence of the National Library, and after imprisoning Mademoiselle Montansier for having built it, the Commune of Paris deliberately opened it as an opera house! Mademoiselle Montansier was, nevertheless, still kept in prison, and remained there ten months, until after the death of Robespierre.

Mademoiselle Montansier's nocturnal assemblies in the Palais Royal were equally renowned · before and after her arrest. Actors and actresses, gamblers, poets, representatives of the people, republican gene-

* It was built chiefly with the money of Danton and Sébastian Lacroix.

rals, retired aristocrats, conspicuous *sans culottes*, and celebrities of all kinds congregated there. Art, pleasure, politics, the new opera, the last execution were alike discussed by Dugazon and Barras, le père Duchesne and the Duke de Lauzun, Robespierre and Mademoiselle Maillard, the Chevalier de Saint Georges and Danton, Martainville and the Marquis de Chauvelin, Lays and Marat, Volange and the Duke of Orleans. From the names just mentioned, it will be understood that some members of this interesting society were from time to time found wanting. Their absence was not much remarked, and fresh notorieties constantly came forward to fill the places of those claimed by the guillotine.

After Mademoiselle Montansier's liberation from prison, Napoleon Bonaparte was introduced to her by Dugazon and Barras. His ambition had not yet been excited, and Barras—who may, nevertheless, have looked upon him as a possible rival, and one to be dreaded—wished to get up a marriage between him and the fashionable but now somewhat antiquated syren of the Palais Royal. Everything went on well for some time. Then a magnificent dinner was given with the view of bringing the affair to a conclusion ; but Bonaparte was very reserved, and Barras now saw that his project was not likely to succeed. At a banquet given by Mademoiselle Montansier, to celebrate the success of the thirteenth Vendémiaire, Bonaparte proposed a toast in honour of his venerable "intended," and soon afterwards she married Neuville.

Mademoiselle Montansier who had been shamefully cheated, indeed robbed, by the Convention, hoped to have her claims recognised by the Directory. Barras offered her one million, six hundred thousand francs. She refused it, the indemnity she demanded for the losses which she had sustained by the seizure of her theatre at the hands of the Convention amounting to seven millions. Napoleon, when first consul, caused the theatre to be estimated, when its value was fixed at one million three hundred thousand francs. After various delays, Mademoiselle Montansier received a partial recognition of her claim, accompanied by an order for payment, signed by the Emperor at Moscow.

Some readers have, probably, been unable to reconcile two facts mentioned above with respect to the Opera under the Convention :—1. That the performers were not paid; and 2. That the public attended the representations in immense numbers. The explanation is very simple. The money was stolen by the Commune of Paris. Gardel, the ballet-master, required fifty thousand francs for the production of a work composed by himself, on the subject of *William Tell.* Twice was the sum amassed from the receipts and professedly set apart for the unfortunate *William Tell,* and twice the money disappeared. It had been devoted to the requirements of patriots in real life.

Danton, Hébert, Chaumette, Henriot, Robespierre,

all administrators of the Opera; Dubuisson, Fabre d'Eglantine, librettists writing for the Opera, and both republicans had been executed during the Reign of Terror. Chamfort, a republican, killed himself to avoid the same fate.

Coquéau, architect, musician, and writer, the author of a number of musical articles produced during the Gluck and Piccinni contests, was guillotined in the year II. of the republic.

The musician, Edelman, after bringing a number of persons to the scaffold, including his patron and benefactor, the Baron de Diétrich, arrived there himself in 1794, accompanied by his brother.

In the same year Despréaux, leader of the first violins at the opera in 1782, and member of the Revolutionary Tribunal in 1793, killed himself from remorse.

Altogether, sixteen persons belonging to the opera in various ways killed themselves, or were executed in 1792, '93, and '94.

After the fall of Robespierre, the royalists for a time ruled the theatres, and avenged themselves on all actors who had made themselves conspicuous as revolutionists. Trial, a comic tenor, who had made a very serious accusation against Mademoiselle Buret, of the Comédie Italienne, which led to her execution, was forced to sing the *Réveil du Peuple* on his knees, amid the execrations of the audience. He sang it, but was thrown into such a state of agitation that he died from the effects.

Lays, whose favourite part was that of "Oreste," in *Iphigénie en Tauride*, had, in the course of the opera, to declaim these verses :—

> " J'ai trahi l'amitié,
> J'ai trahi la nature ;
> Des plus noirs attentats
> J'ai comblé la mesure."

The audience of the Bordeaux theatre considered this confession so becoming in the mouth of the singer who had to utter it, that Lays took care not to give them an opportunity a second time of manifesting their views on the subject. Lays made his next appearance in *Œdipe à Colone*. As in this opera he had to represent the virtuous Theseus, he felt sure that the public would not be able to confound him in any manner with the character he was supporting ; but he had to submit to all sorts of insults during the performance, and at the fall of the curtain was compelled to begin the *Réveil du Peuple*. After the third verse, he was told he was unworthy to sing such a song, and was driven from the stage.

On the 23rd of January, 1796, Mademoiselle Guimard re-appeared at a performance given for the benefit of aged and retired artists. A number of veteran connoisseurs came forward on this occasion to see how the once charming Madeleine looked at the age of fifty-nine. After the ballet an old *habitué* of Louis the Fifteenth's time called for a coach, drove to his lodging, and on getting out, proceeded naturally to pay the driver the amount of his fare.

" You are joking, my dear Count," said the coach-man.   "Whoever heard of Lauragais paying the Chevalier de Ferrière for taking him home in his car-riage ? "

" What ! is it you ? " said the Count de Lauragais.

" Myself ! " replied the Chevalier.

The two friends embraced, and the Chevalier de Ferrière then explained that, when all the royalists were concealing themselves or emigrating, he had determined to do both.   He had assumed the great coat of his coachman, painted a number over the arms on his carriage, and emigrated as far as the Boule-vard, where he found plenty of customers, and passed uninjured and unsuspected through the Reign of Terror.

" Where do you live ? " said the Count.

" Rue des Tuileries," replied the Chevalier, "and my horses with me.   The poor beasts have shared all my misfortunes."

" Give me the whip and reins, and get inside," cried de Lauragais.

" What for ? " inquired the Chevalier.

" To drive you home.   It is an act which, as a gentleman, I insist on performing ; a duty I owe to my old companion and friend.   Your day's work is over.   To-morrow morning we will go to Sophie's, who expects me to breakfast."

" Where ? "

" At the Hotel d'Angivillier, a caravansary of painters and musicians, where Fouché has granted her, on the part of the Republic, an apartment and a pension of two thousand four hundred francs—we should have said a hundred *louis* formerly. This is called a national reward for the eminent services rendered by the *citoyenne* Arnould to the country, and to the sovereign people at the Opera. The poor girl was greatly in need of it."

Fouché had once been desperately in love with Sophie Arnould, and now pitied her in her distress. Thanks to her influence with the minister, the Chevalier Ferrière obtained an order, authorizing him to return to France, though he had never left Paris, except occasionally to drive a fare to one of the suburbs.

The natural effect of Napoleon's campaigns in Italy was to create among the French army a taste for Italian music. The First Consul and many of his generals were passionately fond of it; and a hint from the Tuileries in 1801 was sufficient to induce Mademoiselle Montansier to engage an Italian company, which performed for the first time in Paris on the 1st of May in the same year. The enterprise, however, was not successful; and in 1803 the directress, who had been arrested before because money was owing to her, was put in prison for owing money.

If, by taking his troops to Italy, Napoleon was the means of introducing a taste for Italian music among the French, he provided his country with Italian

singers in a far more direct manner.   At Dresden,
in 1806, he was delighted with the performance of
Brizzi and Madame Paer in the opera of *Achille,*
composed by the prima donna's husband.

" You sing divinely, Madame Paer," said the
emperor.   What do they give you at this theatre? "

" Fifteen thousand francs, Sire."

" You shall receive thirty.   M. Brizzi, you shall
follow me on the same terms."

" But we are engaged."

" With me.   You see the affair is quite settled.
The Prince of Benevento will attend to the diplomatic part of it."

Napoleon took away *Achille,* and everything belonging to it; music, composer, and the two principal singers.   The engagement by which the emperor engaged Paer as composer of his chamber
music, was drawn up by Talleyrand, and bore his
signature, approved by Napoleon, and attested by
Maret, the secretary of state.   Paer, who had been
four years at Dresden, and who, independently of his
contract, was personally much attached to the king
of Saxony, did all in his power to avoid entering
into Napoleon's service.   Perhaps, too, he was not
pleased at the prospect of having to follow the
emperor about from one battle-field to another,
though by a special article in the engagement offered
to him, he was guaranteed ten francs a post, and
thirty-four francs a day for his travelling expenses.
As Paer, in spite of the compliments, and the liberal

terms* offered to him by Napoleon, continued to object, General Clarke told the emperor that he had an excellent plan for getting over all difficulties, and saving the maestro from any reproaches of ingratitude which the king of Saxony might otherwise address to him. This plan consisted in placing Paer in the hands of *gens d'armes*, and having him conducted from camp to camp wherever the emperor went. No violence, however, was done to the composer. The king of Saxony liberated him from his engagement at the Dresden opera, and, moreover, signified to him that he must either follow Napoleon, or quit Saxony immediately. It is said that Paer was ceded by a secret treaty between the two sovereigns, like a fortress, or rather like a province, as provinces were transferred before the idea of nationality was invented; that is to say, without the wishes of the inhabitants being in any way taken into account. The king of Saxony was only too glad that Napoleon took nothing from him but his singers and musicians.

Brizzi, the tenor, Madame Paer, the prima donna, and her husband, the composer, were ordered to start at once for Warsaw. In the morning, the emperor would attend to military and state affairs, and perhaps preside at a battle, for fighting was now going on in the neighbourhood of the Polish capital. In

* Twenty-eight thousand francs a year, to which Napoleon always added twelve thousand in presents, with an annual *congé* of four months.

the evening, he had a concert at head quarters, the programme of which generally included several pieces by Paisiello.   Napoleon was particularly fond of Paisiello's music, and Paer, who, besides being a composer, was a singer of high merit, knew a great deal of it by heart.

Paisiello had been Napoleon's chapel-master since 1801, the emperor having sent for him to Naples after signing the Concordat with the Pope.   On arriving in Paris, the cunning Italian, like an experienced courtier, was no sooner introduced to Napoleon than he addressed him as ' sire !'

" ' Sire,' what do you mean ?" replied the first consul ; " I am a general, and nothing more."

" Well, General," continued the composer, " I have come to place myself at your majesty's orders."

" I must really beg you," continued Napoleon, " not to address me in this manner."

" Forgive me, General," answered Paisiello, " but I cannot give up the habit I have contracted in addressing sovereigns who, compared with you, seem but pigmies.   However, I will not forget your commands, sire ; and if I have been unfortunate enough to offend, I must throw myself upon your Majesty's indulgence."

Paisiello received ten thousand francs for the mass he wrote for Napoleon's coronation.   Each of the masses for the imperial chapel brought him one thousand francs.   Not much, certainly ; but then it must be remembered that he produced as many as fourteen in two years. They were for the most part made up of pieces of church music, which the maestro had written for Italy, and when this fruitful source failed him, he had recourse to his numerous serious and comic operas. Thus, an air from the *Nittetti* was made to do duty as a *Gloria*, another from the *Scuffiara* as an *Agnus Dei*. Music depends so much upon association that, doubtless, only those persons who had already heard these melodies on the stage, found them at all inappropriate in a church. Figaro's air in the *Barber of Seville* would certainly not sound well in a mass; but there are plenty of love songs, songs expressive of despair (if not of too violent a kind), songs, in short, of a sentimental and slightly passionate cast, which only require to be united to religious words to be at once and thereby endowed with a religious character. Gluck, himself, who is supposed by many to have believed that music was capable of conveying absolute, definite ideas, borrowed pieces from his old Italian operas to introduce into the scores he was writing, on entirely different subjects, for the Académie Royale of Paris. Thus, he has employed an air from his *Telemacco* in the introduction to the overture of *Iphigénie en Aulide*. The chorus in the latter work, *Que d'attraits que de majesté*, is founded on the air, *Al mio spirto*, in the same composer's *Clemenza di Tito*. The overture to Gluck's *Telemacco* became that of his *Armide*. Music serves admirably to heighten the effect of a dramatic situation, or to give force and intensity to the expression of words; but the same music may often be allied with equal advantage to words of very different shades of meaning. Thus, the same melody will depict equally well the rage of a baffled conspirator, the jealousy of an injured and most respectable husband, and various other kinds of agitation; the grief of lovers about to part, the joy of lovers at meeting again, and other emotions of a tender nature; the despondency of a man firmly bent on suicide, the calm devotion of a pious woman entering a convent, and other feelings of a solemn class. The signification we discover in music also depends much upon the circumstances under which it is heard, and to some extent also on the mood we are in when hearing it.

Under the republic, consulate, and empire, music did not flourish in France, and not even the imperial Spontini and Cherubini, in spite of the almost European reputation they for some time enjoyed, produced any works which will bear comparison with the masterpieces of their successors, Rossini, Auber, and Meyerbeer. During the dark artistic period which separates the fall of the monarchy from the restoration, a few interesting works were produced at the Opera Comique; but until Napoleon's advent to power, France neglected more than ever the music of Italy, and did worse than neglect that of Germany, for, in 1793, the directors of the Academy brought out a version of Mozart's *Marriage of Figaro*, in five acts, without recitative and with all the prose dialogue of Beaumarchais introduced. In 1805, too, a *pasticcio* by Kalkbrenner, formed out of the music of Mozart's *Don Juan,* with improvements and additions by Kalkbrenner himself, was performed at the same theatre. Both these medleys met with the fate which might have been anticipated for them.

CHAPTER XIV.

OPERA IN ITALY, GERMANY AND RUSSIA, DURING AND
IN CONNECTION WITH THE REPUBLICAN AND NAPO-
LEONIC WARS. PAISIELLO, PAER, CIMAROSA, MOZART.
THE MARRIAGE OF FIGARO. DON GIOVANNI.

NOTHING shows better the effect on art of the long
continental wars at the end of the eighteenth and
beginning of the nineteenth century than the fact
that Mozart's two greatest works, written for Vienna
and Prague immediately before the French Revolution, did not become known in England and France
until about a quarter of a century after their production.   Fortunate Austria, before the great break
up of European territories and dynasties, possessed
the two first musical capitals in Europe.   Opera had
already declined in Berlin, and its history, even under
the direction of the flute-playing Frederic, possesses
little interest for English readers after the departure
or rather flight of Madame Mara.   Italy was still
the great nursery of music, but her maestri composed

their greatest works for foreign theatres, and many
of them were attached to foreign courts. Thus,
Paisiello wrote his *Barbiere di Siviglia* for St. Petersburgh, whither he had been invited by the Empress
Catherine, and where he was succeeded by Cimarosa.
Cimarosa, again, on his return from St. Petersburgh,
wrote his masterpiece, *Il Matrimonio Segretto*, for the
Emperor Leopold II., at Vienna. Of the Opera at
Stockholm, we have heard nothing since the time of
Queen Christina. The Dresden Opera, which, in the
days of Handel, was the first in Europe, still main-
tained its pre-eminence at the beginning of the
second half of the eighteenth century, when Rousseau
published his "Musical Dictionary," and described
at length the composition of its admirable orchestra.
But the state and the resources of the kings of
Saxony declined with the power of Poland, and the
Dresden Opera, though, thanks to the taste which
presided at the court, its performances were still excellent, had quite lost its peculiar celebrity long before
Napoleon came, and carried away its last remaining
glories in the shape of the composer, Paer, and
Madame Paer and Brizzi, its two principal singers.

The first great musical work produced in Russia,
Paisiello's *Barbiere di Siviglia*, was performed for the
first time at St. Petersburgh, in 1780. In this opera
work, of which the success soon became European,
the composer entered thoroughly into the spirit of all
Beaumarchais's best scenes, so admirably adapted for
musical illustration. Of the solos, the three most

admired were Almaviva's opening romance, Don
Basil's *La Calomnia,* and the air for Don Bartholo ;
the other favourite pieces being a comic trio, in
which La Jeunesse sneezes, and L'Eveillé yawns in
the presence of the tutor (I need scarcely remark
that the personages just named belong to Beaumarchais's comedy, and that they are not introduced in
Rossini's opera), another trio, in which Rosina gives
the letter to Figaro, a duet for the entry of the tenor
in the assumed character of Don Alonzo, and a
quintett, in which Don Basil is sent to bed, and in
which the phrase *buona sera* is treated with great
felicity.

Pergolese rendered a still greater service to Russia
than did Paisiello by writing one of his masterpieces for
its capital, when he took the young Bortnianski with
him from St. Petersburgh to Italy, and there educated
the greatest religious composer that Russia, not by
any means deficient in composers, has yet known.

We have seen that Paisiello, some years after his
return to Italy, was engaged by Napoleon as chapel-
master, and that the services of Paer were soon afterwards claimed and secured by the emperor as composer
of his chamber music. This was not the first time
that Paer had been forced to alter his own private
arrangements in consequence of the very despotic
patronage accorded to music by the victorious leaders
of the French army. In 1799 he was at Udine,
where his wife was engaged as *prima donna.* Portogallo's *la Donna di genio volubile* was about to be

represented before a large number of the officers under the command of Bernadotte, when suddenly it appeared impossible to continue the performance owing to the very determined indisposition of the *primo basso*. This gentleman had gone to bed in the middle of the day disguised as an invalid. He declared himself seriously unwell in the afternoon, and in the evening sent a message to the theatre to excuse himself from appearing in Portogallo's opera. Paer and his wife understood what this meant. The performance was for Madame Paer's benefit; and Olivieri, the perfidious basso, from private pique, had determined, if possible, to prevent it taking place. Paer's spirit was roused by the attitude of the *primo buffo*, which was still that of a man confined to his bed; and he resolved to frustrate his infamous scheme, which, though simple, appeared certain of success, inasmuch as no other comic *basso* was to be found anywhere near Udine. The audience was impatient, Madame Paer in tears, the manager in despair, when Paer desired that the performance might begin; saying, that Providence would send them a basso who would at least know his part, and that in any case Madame Paer must get ready for the first scene. Madame Paer obeyed the marital injunction, but in a state of great trepidation; for she had no confidence in the capabilities of the promised basso, and was not by any means sure that he even existed. The curtain was about to rise, when the singer who was to have fallen from the clouds walked quietly on to the stage, perfectly dressed for the part he was about to undertake, and without any sign of hesitation on his countenance. The *prima donna* uttered a cry of surprise, burst into a fit of laughter, and then rushed weeping into the arms of her husband,—for it was Paer himself who had undertaken to replace the treacherous Olivieri.

"No," said Madame Paer; "this is impossible! It shall never be said that I allowed you, a great composer, who will one day be known throughout Europe, to act the buffoon. No! the performance must be stopped!"

At this moment the final chords of the overture were heard. Poor Madame Paer resigned herself to her fate, and went weeping on to the stage to begin a comic duet with her husband, who seemed in excellent spirits, and commenced his part with so much *verve* and humour, that the audience rewarded his exertions with a storm of applause. Paer's gaiety soon communicated itself to his wife. If Paer was to perform at all, it was necessary that his performance should outshine that of all possible rivals, and especially that of the miscreant Olivieri, who was now laughing between his sheets at the success which he fancied must have already attended his masterly device. The *prima donna* had never sung so charmingly before, but the greatest triumph of the evening was gained by the new *basso*. Olivieri, who previously had been pronounced unapproachable in Portogallo's opera, was now looked upon as quite an inferior singer compared

to the *buffo caricato* who had so unexpectedly presented himself before the Udine public. Paer, in
addition to his great natural histrionic ability, knew
every note of *la Donna*. Olivieri had studied only
his own part. Paer, in directing the rehearsals, had
made himself thoroughly acquainted with all of them,
and gave a significance to some portions of the music
which had never been expressed or apprehended by
his now defeated, routed, utterly confounded rival.

At present comes the dark side of the picture.
Olivieri, dangerously ill the night before, was perfectly
well the next morning, and quite ready to resume his
part in *la Donna di genio volubile*. Paer, on the other
hand, was quite willing to give it up to him; but both
reckoned without the military connoisseurs of Udine,
and above all without Bernadotte, who arrived the
day after Paer's great success, when all the officers
of the staff were talking of nothing else. Olivieri
was announced to appear in his old character; but
when the bill was shown to the General, he declared
that the original representative might go back to
bed, for that the only buffo he would listen to was
the illustrious Paer. In vain the director explained
that the composer was not engaged as a singer,
and that nothing but the sudden indisposition of
Olivieri would have induced him to appear on the
stage at all. Bernadotte swore he would have Paer,
and no one else; and as the unfortunate *impresario*
continued his objections, he was ordered into arrest,
and informed that he should remain in prison until

the *maestro* Paer undertook once more the part of
" Pippo " in Portogallo's opera.

The General then sent a company of grenadiers to
surround Paer's house ; but the composer had heard
of what had befallen the manager, and, foreseeing his
own probable fate, if he remained openly in Udine,
had concealed himself, and spread a report that he
was in the country.   Lancers and hussars were dis-
patched in search of him, but naturally without effect.
In the supposed absence of Paer, the army was obliged
to accept Olivieri ; and when six or seven representations of the popular opera had taken place and the
military public had become accustomed to Olivieri's
performance of the part of " Pippo," Paer came forth
from his hiding place and suffered no more from the
warlike dilettanti-ism of Bernadotte.

There would be no end to my anecdotes if I were
to attempt to give a complete list of all those in
which musicians and singers have been made to figure
in connection with all sorts of events during the last
great continental war.   The great vocalists, and many
of the great composers of the day, continued to travel
about from city to city, and from court to court, as
though Europe were still in a state of profound peace.
Sometimes, as happened once to Paer, and was nearly
happening to him a second time, they were taken
prisoners ; or they found themselves shut up in a be-
sieged town ; and a great *cantatrice*, Madame Fodor,
who chanced to be engaged at the Hamburg opera
when Hamburg was invested, was actually the cause

of a *sortie* being made in her favour.   On one occasion, while she was singing, the audience was disturbed by a cannon ball coming through the roof of the theatre and taking its place in the gallery ; but the performances continued nevertheless, and the officers and soldiers of the garrison continued to be delighted with their favourite vocalist.   Madame Fodor, however, on her side, was beginning to get tired of her position ; not that she cared much about the bombardment which was renewed from time to time, but because the supply of milk had failed, cows and oxen having been alike slaughtered for the sustenance of the beleaguered garrison. Without milk, Madame Fodor was scarcely able to sing ; at least, she had so accustomed herself to drink it every evening during the intervals of performance, that she found it inconvenient and painful to do without it.   Hearing in what a painful situation their beloved vocalist found herself, the French army gallantly resolved to remedy it without delay.   The next evening a *sortie* was effected, and a cow brought back in triumph.   This cow was kept in the property and painting room in the theatre, above the stage, and was lowered like a drop scene, to be milked whenever Madame Fodor was thirsty.   So, at least, says the operatic anecdote on the subject, though it would perhaps have been a more convenient proceeding to have sent some trustworthy person to perform the milking operation up stairs.   In any case, the cow was kept carefully shut up and under guard.   Otherwise the

animal's life would not have been safe, so great was
the scarcity of provision in Hamburg at the time,
and so great the general hunger for beef of any kind.

Madame Huberti, after flying from Paris during
the Reign of Terror, married the Count d'Entraigues,
and would seem to have terminated her operatic
career happily and honourably; but she was destined
some years afterwards to die a horrible death. The
countess always wore the order of St. Michael,
which had been given to her by the then unacknowledged Louis XVIII., in token of the services
she had rendered to the royalist party, by enabling her
husband to escape from prison and preserving his port-
folio which contained a number of political papers of
great importance. The Count afterwards entered
the service of Russia, and was entrusted by the government with several confidential missions. Hitherto he had been working in the interest of the
Bourbons against Napoleon; but when the French
emperor and the emperor Alexander formed an alliance, after the battles of Eylau and Friedland, he
seems to have thought that his connexion with Russia
ought to terminate. However this may have been,
he found means to obtain a copy of the secret articles
contained in the treaty of Tilsit* and hastened to
London to communicate them to the English govern-

* According to M. Thiers, the pretended copies of the secret
articles, sold to the English Government, were not genuine, and the
money paid for them was " *mal gagné.*"

ment. For this service he is said to have received a
pension, and he now established himself in England,
where he appears to have had continual relations with
the foreign office. The French police heard how the
Count d'Entraigues was employed in London, and
Fouché sent over two agents to watch him and inter-
cept his letters. These emissaries employed an Italian
refugee, to get acquainted with and bribe Lorenzo,
the Count's servant, who allowed his compatriot to
read and even to take copies of the despatches frequently entrusted to him by his master to take to
Mr. Canning. He, moreover, gave him a number
of the Count's letters to and from other persons.
One evening a letter was brought to M. d'Entraigues
which obliged him to go early the next morning from
his residence at Barnes to London. Lorenzo had
observed the seal of the foreign office on the envelope,
and saw that his treachery would soon be discovered.
Everything was ready for the journey, when he stabbed
his master, who fell to the ground mortally wounded.
The Countess was getting into the carriage. To prevent her charging him with her husband's death, the
servant also stabbed her, and a few moments afterwards, in confusion and despair, blew his own brains
out with a pistol which he in the first instance appears to have intended for M. d'Entraigues. This
horrible affair occurred on the 22nd of July, 1812.

Nothing fatal happened to Madame Colbran, though
she was deeply mixed up with politics, her name being
at one time quite a party word among the royalists

at Naples. Those who admired the king made a point of admiring his favourite singer. A gentleman from England asked a friend one night at the Naples theatre how he liked the vocalist in question.

"Like her? I am a royalist," was the reply.

When the revolutionists gained the upper hand, Madame Colbran was hissed; but the discomfiture of the popular party was always followed by renewed triumphs for the singer.

Madame Colbran must not lead us on to her future husband, Rossini, whose epoch has not yet arrived. The mention of Paer's wife has already taken us far away from the composers in vogue at the end of the eighteenth century.

Two of the three best comic operas ever produced, *Le Nozze di Figaro* and *Il Matrimonio Segretto* (I need scarcely name Rossini's *Il Barbiere di Siviglia* as the third), were written for Vienna within six years (1786—1792), and at the special request of emperors of Germany. Cimarosa was returning from St. Petersburgh when Leopold II., Joseph the Second's successor, detained him at Vienna, and invited him to compose something for his theatre. The *maestro* had not much time, but he did his best, and the result was, *Il Matrimonio Segretto*. The Emperor was delighted with the work, which seemed almost to have been improvised, and gave the composer twelve thousand francs, or, as some say, twelve thousand florins; in either case, a very liberal sum for the period when Cimarosa, Paisiello and Gug-

Kelmi had mutually agreed, whatever more they might receive for their operas, never to take less than two thousand four hundred francs.

The libretto of *Il Matrimonio Segretto*, by Bertatti, is imitated from that of a forgotten French operetta, *Sophie ou le Mariage Caché*, which is again founded on Garrick and Coleman's *Clandestine Marriage* The Emperor Leopold was unable to be present at the first performance of Cimarosa's new work, but he heard of its enormous success, and determined not to miss a note at the second representation. He was in his box before the commencement of the overture, and listened to the performance throughout with the greatest attention, but without manifesting any opinion as to the merits of the music. As the Sovereign did not applaud, the brilliant audience who had assembled to hear *Il Matrimonio* a second time, were obliged, by court etiquette, to remain silent without giving the slightest expression to the delight the music afforded them. This icy reception was very different to the one obtained by the opera the night before, when the marks of approbation from all parts of the house had been of the most enthusiastic kind. However, when the piece was at an end, the Emperor rose and said aloud—

"Bravo, Cimarosa, bravissimo! The whole opera is admirable, delightful, enchanting. I did not applaud that I might not lose a single note of this masterpiece. You have heard it twice, and I must have the same pleasure before I go to bed. Singers and

musicians, pass into the next room ! Cimarosa will
come too, and will preside at the banquet prepared
for you.   When you have had sufficient rest we
will begin again.   I *encore* the whole opera, and, in
the mean while, let us applaud it as it deserves."
Leopold clapped his hands, and for some minutes the
whole theatre resounded with plaudits.   After the
banquet, the entire opera was repeated.

The only other example of such an occurrence as
the above is to be found in the career of Terence,
whose *Eunuchus* on its first production, was performed
twice the same day, or, rather, once in the morning,
and once in the evening.

A similar amount of success obtained by Paer's
Laodicea had quite an opposite result ; for, as nearly
the whole opera was encored, piece by piece, it was
found impossible to conclude it the same evening,
and the performance of the last act was postponed
until the next night.

Mozart's *Nozze di Figaro*, produced six years
before the *Matrimonio Segretto*, was far less justly
appreciated,—indeed, at Vienna, was not appreciated
at all.   This admirable work, so full of fresh spon-
taneous melody, and of rich, varied harmony was actually hissed by the Viennese !   They even hissed
Non piu andrai, which seems equally calculated to
delight the educated and the most uneducated ear.
Mozart has made allusion to this almost incredible
instance of bad taste very happily and ingeniously in
the supper scene of *Don Giovanni*.

Joseph II. cared only for Italian music, and never gave his entire approbation to anything Mozart produced, though the musicians of the period acknowledged him to be the greatest composer in Europe.

" It is too fine for our ears," said the presumptuous Joseph, speaking to Mozart of the *Seraglio*. " Seriously, I think there are too many notes."

"Precisely the proper number," replied the composer.

The Emperor rewarded his frankness by giving him only fifty ducats for his opera.*

Nevertheless, the *Seraglio* had caused the success of one of the emperor's favourite enterprises. It was the first work produced at the German Opera, established by Joseph II., at Vienna. Until that time, Italian opera predominated everywhere; indeed, German opera, that is to say, lyric dramas in the German language, set to music by German composers, and sung by German singers, could not be said to exist. There were a number of Italian musicians living at Vienna who were quite aware of Mozart's superiority, and hated him for it; the more so, as by taking such an important part in the establishment of the German Opera, he threatened to diminish the reputation of the Italian school. The *Entführung aus dem Serail* was the first blow to the supremacy of Italian opera. *Der Schauspiel-director* was the second, and when, after the produc-

* Alexander II. gives Verdi an honorarium of 80,000 roubles for the opera he is now writing for St. Petersburg. The work, of course, remains Signor Verdi's property.

tion of this latter work at the new German theâtre of Vienna, Mozart proceeded to write the *Nozze di Figaro* for the Italians, he simply placed himself in the hands of his enemies. At the first representation, the two first acts of the *Nozze* were so shamefully executed, that the composer went in despair to the emperor to denounce the treachery of which he was being made the victim. Joseph had detected the conspiracy and was nearly as indignant as Mozart himself. He sent a severe message round to the stage, but the harm was now done, and the remainder of the opera was listened to very coldly. *Le Nozze di Figaro* failed at Vienna, and was not appreciated, did not even get a fair hearing, until it was produced some months afterwards at Prague. The Slavonians of Bohemia showed infinitely more good taste and intelligence than the Germans (led away and demoralized, however, by an Italian clique) at Vienna. At Prague, *le Nozze di Figaro* caused the greatest enthusiasm, and Mozart replied nobly to the sympathy and admiration of the Bohemians. "These good people," he said, "have avenged me. They know how to do me justice, I must write something to please them." He kept his word, and the year afterwards gave them the immortal *Don Giovanni*.

At the head of the clique which had sworn eternal enmity to Mozart, was Salieri, a musician with a sort of Pontius Pilate reputation, owing his infamous celebrity to the fact that his name is now inseparably coupled with that of the sublime composer whom he would have destroyed. Salieri (whom we have met with before in Paris as the would-be successor of Gluck) was the most learned of the Italian composers at that time residing in Vienna; and, therefore, must have felt the greatness of Mozart's genius more profoundly than any of the others. When *Don Giovanni*, after its success at Prague, was produced at Vienna, it was badly put on the stage, imperfectly rehearsed, and represented altogether in a very unsatisfactory manner. Nor, with improved execution did the audience show any disposition to appreciate its manifold beauties. Mozart's *Don Giovanni* was quite eclipsed by the *Assur* of his envious and malignant rival.

"I will leave it to psychologists to determine," says M. Oulibicheff,* "whether the day on which Salieri triumphed publicly over Mozart, was the happiest or the most painful of his life. He triumphed, indeed, thanks to the ignorance of the Viennese, to his own skill as a director, (which enabled him to render the work of his rival scarcely recognisable), and to the entire devotion of his subordinates. He must have been pleased; but Salieri was not only envious, he was also a great musician. He had read the score of *Don Giovanni*, and you know that the works one reads with the greatest attention are those of one's enemies. With what admiration and despair it must have filled the heart of an artist who was even more ambitious of true glory than of mere renown! What must he have felt in

* Nouvelle Biographie de Mozart. Moscou, 1843.

his inmost soul!   And what serpents must again have
crawled and hissed in the wreath of laurel which
was placed on his head!   In spite of the fiasco of
his opera, which he seems to have foreseen, and to
which, at all events, he resigned himself with great
calmness, Mozart, doubtless, more happy than his
conqueror, added a few 'numbers,' each a master-
piece to his score.   Four new pieces were written for
it, at the request of the Viennese singers."

M.Oulibicheff's compatriot Poushkin has written
an admirable study on the subject presented above
in a few suggestive phrases by Mozart's biographer.
Unfortunately, it is impossible in these volumes to
find a place for the Russian poet's "Mozart and
Salieri."

After the failure of *Don Giovanni* at Vienna, a
number of persons were speaking of it in a room
where Haydn and the principal connoisseurs of the
place were assembled.   Every one agreed in pronounc-
ing it a most estimable work, but, also, every one had
something to say against it.   At last, Haydn, who,
hitherto, had not spoken a word, was asked to give
his opinion.

" I do not feel myself in a position to decide this
dispute," he answered.   "All I know and can assure
you of is that Mozart is the greatest composer of our
time."

As Salieri's *Assur* completely eclipsed *Don Giovanni*, so, previously, did Martini's *Cosa Rara*, the
Nozze di Figaro.   Both these phenomena manifested

themselves at Vienna, and the reader has already been reminded that the fate of the *Nozze di Figaro* is alluded to in *Don Giovanni*. All the airs played by the hero's musicians in the supper scene are taken from the operas which were most in vogue when Mozart produced his great work; such as *La Cosa Rara, Frà due Litiganti terzo gode*, and *I Pretendenti Burlati*. Leporello calls attention to the melodies as the orchestra on the stage plays them, and when, to terminate the series, the clarionets strike up *Non piu andrai*, he exclaims *Questo lo conosco pur troppo!* "I know this one only too well!" With the exception of *Non piu andrai*, which the Viennese could not tolerate the first time they heard it, none of the airs introduced in the *Don Giovanni* supper scene would be known in the present day, but for *Don Giovanni*.

Don Giovanni, composed by Mozart to *Da Ponte's* libretto (which is founded on Molière's *Festin de Pierre*, which is imitated from Tirso di Molina's *El Burlador di Siviglia*, which seems to have had its origin in a very ancient legend*), was produced at Prague, on the 4th of November, 1787. The subject had already been treated in a ballet, in four acts, for which Gluck wrote the music (produced at

---

* There are numerous analogies between the various Spanish legends of Don Juan, the Anglo-Saxon and German legends of Faust, and the Polish legend of Twardowski. It might be shown that they were all begotten by the legend of Theophilus of Syracuse, and that their latest descendant is *Punch* of London.

Parma in 1758; and long before the production of
Mozart's *Don Giovanni*, it had been dramatised in
some shape or other in almost every country in
Europe, and especially in Spain, Italy, and France,
where several versions of the Italian *Il Convitato di
Pietra* were being played, when Molière first brought
out his so-called *Festin de Pierre*. The original cast
of *Don Giovanni* at Prague was as follows :—

Donna Anna, Teresa Saporiti.
Elvira, Catarina Micelli.
Zerlina, Madame Bondini (Catarina Saporiti).
Don Giovanni, Bassi (Luigi).
Ottavio, Baglioni (Antonio).
Leporello, Ponziani (Felice).
Don Pedro, Lolli (Guiseppe).
Masetto, the same.

Righini, of Bologna, had produced his opera of
Don Giovanni, ossia il Convitato di Pietra, at Prague,
only eight years before, for which reason the title
of *Il Dissoluto Punito* was given to Mozart's work.
It was not until some years afterwards that it received the name by which it is now universally
known.

Although the part of *Don Giovanni* was written
for a baritone, tenors, such as Tacchinardi and
Garcia, have often played it, and frequently with
greater success than the majority of baritones have
obtained. But no individual success of a favourite
singer can compensate for the transpositions and
changes that have to be effected in Mozart's master-

piece, when the character of the hero is assigned to a vocalist who cannot execute the music which of right belongs to it. It has been said that Mozart wrote the part of *Don Giovanni* for a baritone, because it so happened that the baritone at the Prague theatre, Bassi, was the best singer of the company; but it is not to be imagined that the musical characterization of the personages in the most truly dramatic opera ever written, was the result of anything but the composer's well-considered design. " *Don Giovanni* was not intended for Vienna, but for Prague," Mozart is reported to have said. " The truth, however, is," he added, " that I wrote it for myself, and a few friends." Accordingly, the great composer was not thinking of Bassi at the time. It would be easy, moreover, to show, that though the most feminine of male voices may suit the ordinary *jeune premier*, or *premier amoureux*, there is nothing tenor-like in the temperament of a *Don Giovanni;* deceiving all women, defying all men, breaking all laws, human and divine, and an unbeliever in everything—even in the power of equestrian statues to get off their horses, and sit down to supper.

But, let us not consider whether or not *Fin ch' han dal vino* is improved by being sung (as tenor *Don Giovannis* sometimes sing it) a fourth higher than it was written by Mozart; or whether it is tolerable that the concerted pieces in which *Don Giovanni* takes part should be, not transposed (for that would be insufficient, or, rather, would increase the difficulties

F 2

of execution) but so altered, that in some passages the original design of the composer is entirely perverted. Let us simply repeat the maxim, on which it is impossible to lay too much stress, that the work of a great master should not be touched, re-touched, or in any manner interfered with, under any pretext. There is, absolutely, no excuse for managers mutilating *Don Giovanni*; not even the excuse that in its original form this inexhaustible opera does not "draw." It has already lived, and with full, unfailing life, for three-quarters of a century. It has survived all sorts of revolutions in taste, and especially in musical taste. There are now no Emperors of Germany. Prague has become a third-rate city. That German Opera, which Mozart originated with his *Entführung aus dem Serail*, has attained a grand development, and among its composers has numbered Beethoven, Weber, and the latter's follower, and occasional imitator, Meyerbeer. Rossini has appeared with his seductive melody, and his brilliant, sonorous orchestra. But justice is still—more than ever—done to Mozart. The verdict of Prague is maintained; and this year, as ten, twenty, forty years ago, if the manager of the Italian Opera of London, Paris, or St. Petersburgh, has had for some time past a series of empty houses, he takes an opera, seventy-four years of age, and which, according to all ordinary musical calculations, ought long since to have had, at least, one act in the grave, dresses it badly, puts it badly on the stage, with such scenery as would be thought unworthy of Verdi, and hazardous for Meyerbeer, announces *Don Giovanni*, and every place in the theatre is taken !

Although Mozart's genius was fully acknowledged by the greatest musicians, among his contemporaries (the reader already knows what Haydn said of him, and what Cimarosa replied when he was addressed as his superior), his music found an echo in the hearts of only a very small portion of the ordinary public. Admired at Prague, condemned at Vienna, unknown in the rest of Europe, it may be said, with only too much truth, that Mozart's master-pieces, speaking generally, met with no recognition until after his death ; with no fitting recognition until long afterwards. From the slow, strong, oak-like growth of Mozart's fame, now flourishing, and still increasing every day, we may see, not for his name alone, but for his music, a continued celebrity and popularity, which will probably endure as long as our modern civilization. I have already spoken of the effects of the last general war in checking literary and artistic communication between the nations of Europe. This will, in part, account for Mozart's master-piece not having been performed at the Italian Opera of Paris until 1811, nor in London until after the peace, in 1817. In the Paris cast, the part of *Don Giovanni* was assigned to a tenor, Tacchinardi ; and when the opera was revived at the same theatre (which was not until nine years afterwards), Tacchinardi was replaced by Garcia.

The first "Don Giovanni" who appeared in London, was the celebrated baritone, Ambrogetti. Among the other distinguished singers who have appeared as "Don Giovanni," with great success, may be mentioned Nourrit, the tenor; Lablache (in 1832), before he had identified himself with the part of "Leporello;" Tamburini, and I suppose I must now add, Mario; though this great artist has been seen and heard to more advantage in other characters. The last great "Don Giovanni" known to the present generation was Signor Tamburini. It is a remarkable fact, well worth the consideration of managers, who are inclined to take liberties with Mozart's master-piece, that when Garcia, the tenor, appeared in London as "Don Giovanni," after Ambrogetti, the baritone, he produced comparatively but little effect; though Garcia was one of the most accomplished musicians, and, probably, the very best singer of his day.

Without going back again to the original cast, I may notice among the most celebrated Donna Annas, Madame Ronzi de Begnis, Mademoiselle Sontag, Madame Grisi, Mademoiselle Sophie Cruvelli, and Mademoiselle Titiens.

Among the Zerlinas, Madame Fodor, Madame Malibran, Madame Persiani*, and Madame Bosio.

* Madame Alboni has appeared as Zerlina, and sings the music

Among the Don Ottavios, Rubini and Mario.

Porto is said to have been particularly admirable as Masetto, and Angrisani and Angelini as the commandant.

Certainly, no one living has heard a better Leporello than Lablache.

Mr. Ebers tells us, in his "Seven Years of the King's Theatre," that *Don Giovanni* was brought out by Mr. Ayrton in 1817, "in opposition to a vexatious cabal," and "in despite of difficulties of many kinds which would have deterred a less decided and persevering manager." Nevertheless, "it filled the boxes and benches of the theatre for the whole season, and restored to a flourishing condition the finances of the concern, which were in an almost exhausted state."

The war, so injurious to the Opera, had a still more disastrous effect on the ballet, a fact for which we have the authority of the manager and author from whom I have just quoted. "The procrastinated war," says Mr. Ebers, "which, until the treaty of Aix-la-Chapelle, had kept England and France in hostilities, had rendered the importation of dancers from the latter country almost impracticable." Mr. Waters, Mr. Ebers' predecessor, had repeatedly endeavoured to prevail on French dancers to come to England, "either with the *congés*, if attainable, or by such clan-

of this, as of every other part that she undertakes, to perfection; but she is not so intimately associated with the character as the other vocalists mentioned above.

destine means as could be carried into effect." He failed; and we are told that his want of success in this respect was one cause of the disagreement between himself and the committee of the theatre, which led soon afterwards to his abandoning the management. Mr. Ebers, however, testifies from his own experience to the almost insuperable difficulty of inducing the directors of the French Opera to cede any of their principal performers even for a few weeks to the late enemies of their country. When the dancers were willing to accept the terms offered to them, it was impossible to obtain leave from the minister entrusted with the supreme direction of operatic affairs; if the minister was willing, then objections came from the ballet itself. It was necessary to secure the aid of the highest diplomatists, and the engagement of a few first dancers and *coryphées* was made as important an affair as the signing of a treaty of commerce. The special envoy, the Cobden of the affair, was Monsieur Boisgerard, an ex-officer in the French army under the Bourbons, and actually the second balletmaster of the King's Theatre; but all official correspondence connected with the negotiation had to be transmitted through the medium of the English ambassador at Paris to the Baron de la Ferté. Boisgerard arrived in Paris furnished with letters of introduction from the five noblemen who at that time formed a " committee of superintendence " to aid Mr. Ebers in the management of the King's Theatre, and directed all his attention and energy towards forming

an engagement with Bigottini and Noblet, the principal *danseuses*, and Albert, the *premier danseur* of
the French Opera. In spite of his excellent recom-
mendations, of the esteem in which he was himself
held by his numerous friends in Paris, and of the interest of a dancer named Deshayes, who appears to
have readily joined in the conspiracy, and who was
afterwards rewarded for his aid with a lucrative engagement as first ballet-master at the London Opera
House—in spite of all these advantages it was impossible, for some time, to obtain any concessions
from the Académie. To begin with, Bigottini, Noblet
and Albert refused point blank to leave Paris. M.
Boisgerard, however, as a ballet-master and a man of
the world, understood that this was intended only as
an invitation for larger offers; and finally all three
were engaged, conditionally on their *congés* being
obtained from the directors of the theatre. Now the
real difficulty began; now the influence of the five
English noblemen was brought to bear; now despatches were interchanged between the British ambassador in Paris and the Baron de la Ferté, intendant of the royal theatres; now consultations took
place between the said intendant and the Viscount de
la Rochefoucault, aide-de-camp of the king, entrusted
with the department of fine arts in the ministry of
the king's household; and between the said artistic
officer of the king's household and Duplanty, the ad-
ministrator of the Royal Academy of Music, and of
the Italian Opera. The result of all this negotiation

was, that the administration first hesitated and finally refused to allow Mademoiselle Bigottini to visit England on any terms; but, after considerable trouble, the French agents in the service of Mr. Ebers obtained permission for Albert and Noblet to accept engagements for two months,—it being further arranged that, at the expiration of that period, they should be replaced by Coulon and Fanny Bias. Albert was to receive fifty pounds for every night of performance, and twenty-five pounds for his travelling expenses. Noblet's terms were five hundred and fifty pounds for the two months, with twenty-five pounds for expenses. Coulon and Bias were each to receive the same terms as Noblet. Three other dancers, Montessu, Lacombe, and Mademoiselle de Varennes, were at the same time given over to Mr. Ebers for an entire season, and he was allowed to retain all his prisoners—that is to say, those members of the Académie, with Mademoiselle Mélanie at their head, whom previous managers had taken from the French prior to the friendly and pacific embassy of M. Boisgerard. An attempt was made to secure the services of Mademoiselle Elisa, but without avail. M. and Mademoiselle Paul entered into an agreement, but the administration refused to ratify it; otherwise, with a little encouragement, Mr. Ebers would probably have engaged the entire ballet of the Académie Royale.

Male dancers have, I am glad to think, never been much esteemed in England; and Albert, though successful enough, produced nothing like the same impression in London which he was in the habit of causing in Paris. Mademoiselle Noblet's dancing, on the other hand, excited the greatest enthusiasm, and the subscribers made all possible exertions to obtain a prolongation of her *congé* when the time for her return to the Académie arrived. Noblet's performance in the ballet of *Nina* (of which the subject is identical with that of Paisiello's opera of the same name) is said to have been particularly admirable, especially for the great dramatic talent which she exhibited in pourtraying the heroine's melancholy madness. *Nina* was announced for Mademoiselle Noblet's benefit, on a night not approved by the Lord Chamberlain—either because it interfered with some of the court regulations, or for some other reason not explained. The secretary to the committee of the Opera was directed to address a letter to the Chamberlain, representing to him how inconvenient it would be to postpone the benefit, as the *congé* of the *bénéficiaire* was now on the point of expiring. Lord Hertford, with becoming politeness, wrote the following letter, which shows with what deep interest the graceful dancer inspired even those who knew her only by reputation. The letter was addressed to the Marquis of Ailesbury, one of the members of the operatic committee.

" MY DEAR LORD,—I have this moment (eleven o'clock) received your letter, which I have sent to the Chamberlain's office to Mr. Mash; and as Mademoiselle Noblet is a very pretty woman as I am told,

I hope she will call there to assist in the solicitation which interests her so much. Not having been for many years at the opera, except for the single purpose of attending his majesty, I am no judge of the propriety of her request or the objections which may arise to the postponement of her benefit for one day at so short a notice. I hope the fair solicitress will be prepared with an answer on this part of the subject, as it is always my wish to accommodate you ; and I remain most sincerely your very faithful servant,

"INGRAM HERTFORD."

"Manchester Square,
    April 29th, 1821."

Mademoiselle Noblet's benefit having taken place, the subscribers, horrified at the notion that they had now, perhaps, seen her for the last time, determined, in spite of all obstacles, in spite even of the very explicit agreement between the director of the King's Theatre and the administration of the Académie Royale, that she should remain in London. The *danseuse* was willing enough to prolong her stay, but the authorities at the French Opera protested. The Academy of Music was not going to be deprived in this way of one of the greatest ornaments of its ballet, and the Count de Caraman, on behalf of the Academy, called on the committee to direct Mr. Ebers to send over to Paris, without delay, the performers whose *congés* were now at an end. The members of the committee replied that they had only power to interfere as regarded the choice of operas and ballets, and that they had nothing to do with agreements between the manager and the performers. They added, "that they had certainly employed their influence with the English ambassador at Paris at the commencement of the season, to obtain the best artists from that city; but it appearing that the Academy was not disposed to grant *congés* for London, even to artists, for whose services the Academy had no occasion, the committee had determined not again to meddle in that branch of the management."

The French now sent over an ambassador extraordinary, the Baron de la Ferté himself, to negotiate for the restoration of the deserters. It was decided, however, that they should be permitted to remain until the end of the season; and, moreover, that two first and two second dancers should be allowed annually to come to London, but only under the precise stipulations contained in the following treaty, which was signed between Mr. Ebers, on the one hand, and M. Duplantys on the part of Viscount de la Rochefoucault, on the other.

"The administration of the Theatre of the Royal Academy of music, wishing to facilitate to the administration of the theatre of London, the means of making known the French artists of the ballet without this advantage being prejudicial to the Opera of Paris;

"Consents to grant to Mr. Ebers for each season, the first commencing on the 10th of January, and

ending the 20th of April, and the second ending the
1st of August, two first dancers, two *figurants*, and
two *figurantes*; but in making this concession, the
administration of the Royal Academy of Music re-
serves the right of only allowing those dancers to
leave Paris to whom it may be convenient to grant
a *congé*; this rule applies equally to the *figurants*
and *figurantes*. None of them can leave the Paris
theatre except by the formal permission of the authorities.

"And in return for these concessions, Mr. Ebers
promises to engage no dancer until he has first obtained the necessary authorization in accordance with
his demand.

"He engages not under any pretext to keep the
principal dancers a longer time than has been agreed
without a fresh permission, and above all, to make
them no offers with the view of enticing them from
their permanent engagements with the French authorities.

"The present treaty is for the space of   .

"In case of Mr. Ebers failing in one of the articles
of the said treaty, the whole treaty becomes null and
void."

The prime mover in the diplomatic transactions
which had the effect of securing Mademoiselle Noblet
for the London Opera was, as I have said, the ballet
master, Boisgerard, formerly an officer in the French
army. In a chapter which is intended to show to some
extent the effect on opera of the disturbed state of

Europe consequent on the French Revolution, it will, perhaps, not be out of place to relate a very daring exploit performed by the said M. Boisgerard, which was the cause of his adopting an operatic career. "This gentleman," says Mr. Ebers, in the account published by him of his administration of the King's Theatre from 1821 to 1828, " was a Frenchman of good extraction, and at the period of the French Revolution, was attached to the royal party. When Sir Sidney Smith was confined in the Temple, Boisgerard acted up to his principles by attempting, and with great personal risk, effecting the escape of that distinguished officer, whose friends were making every effort for his liberation. Having obtained an impression of the seal of the Directorial Government, he affixed it to an order, forged by himself, for the delivery of Sir Sidney Smith into his care. Accompanied by a friend, disguised like himself, in the uniform of an officer of the revolutionary army, he did not scruple personally to present the fictitious document to the keeper of the Temple, who, opening a small closet, took thence some original document, with the writing and seal of which, he carefully compared the forged order. Desiring the adventurers to wait a few minutes, he then withdrew, and locked the door after him. Giving themselves up for lost, the confederate determined to resist, sword in hand, any attempt made to secure them. The period which thus elapsed, may be imagined as one of the most horrible suspense to Boisgerard and his companion ;

his own account of his feelings at the time was extremely interesting. Left alone, and in doubt whether each succeeding moment might not be attended by a discovery involving the safety of his life, the acuteness of his organs of sense was heightened to painfulness; the least noise thrilled through his brain, and the gloomy apartment in which he sat seemed filled with strange images. They preserved their self-possession, and, after the lapse of a few minutes, their anxiety was determined by the re-appearance of the gaoler, accompanied by his captive, who was delivered to Boisgerard. But here a new and unlooked for difficulty occurred; Sir Sidney Smith, not knowing Boisgerard, refused, for some time, to quit the prison; and considerable address was required on the part of his deliverers to overcome his scruples. At last, the precincts of the Temple were cleared; and, after going a short distance in a fiacre, then walking, then entering another carriage, and so on, adopting every means of baffling pursuit, the fugitives got to Havre, where Sir Sidney was put on board an English vessel. Boisgerard, on his return to Paris (for he quitted Sir Sidney at Havre) was a thousand times in dread of detection; tarrying at an *auberge*, he was asked whether he had heard the news of Sir Sidney's escape; the querist adding, that four persons had been arrested on suspicion of having been instrumental in it. However, he escaped all these dangers, and continued at Paris until his visit to England, which took place after the peace of Amiens. A pension had been granted to Sir Sidney Smith for his meritorious services; and, on Boisgerard's arrival here, a reward of a similar nature was bestowed on him through the influence of Sir Sidney, who took every opportunity of testifying his gratitude."

We have already seen that though the international character of the Opera must always be seriously interfered with by international wars, the intelligent military amateur may yet be able to turn his European campaigning to some operatic advantage. The French officers acquired a taste for Italian music in Italy. So an English officer serving in the Peninsula, imbibed a passion for Spanish dancing, to which was due the choregraphic existence of the celebrated Maria Mercandotti,—by all accounts one of the most beautiful girls and one of the most charming dancers that the world ever saw. This inestimable treasure was discovered by lord Fife—a keen-eyed connoisseur, who when Maria was but a child, foretold the position she would one day occupy, if her mother would but allow her to join the dancing school of the French Academy. Madame Mercandotti brought her daughter to England when she was fifteen. The young Spaniard danced a bolero one night at the Opera, repeated it a few days afterwards at Brighton, before Queen Charlotte, and then set off to Paris, where she joined the Académie. After a very short period of study, she made her *début* with success, such as scarcely any dancer had obtained at the French Opera, since the time of La Camargo —herself, by the way, a Spaniard.

Mademoiselle Mercandotti came to London, was received with the greatest enthusiasm, was the fashionable theme of one entire operatic season, had a number of poems, valuable presents, and offers of undying affection addressed to her, and ended by marrying Mr. Hughes Ball.

The production of this *danseuse* appears to have seen the last direct result of that scattering of the amateurs of one nation among the artists of another, which was produced by the European convulsions of from 1789 to 1815.

CHAPTER XV.

MANNERS AND CUSTOMS AT THE LONDON OPERA, HALF A CENTURY SINCE.

A COMPLETE History of the Opera would include a history of operatic music, a history of operatic dancing, a history of the chief operatic theatres, and a history of operatic society. I have made no attempt to treat the subject on such a grand scale; but though I shall have little to say about the principal lyrical theatres of Europe, or of the habits of opera-goers as a European class, there is one great musical dramatic establishment, to whose fortunes I must pay some special attention, and concerning whose audiences much may be said that will at least interest an English reader. After several divided reigns at the Lincoln's Inn Theatre, at Covent Garden, at the Pantheon, and at the King's Theatre, Italian Opera found itself, in 1793, established solely and majestically at the last of these houses, which I need hardly remind the reader was its first home in England. The management was now exercised by Mr. Taylor, the proprietor. This gentleman, who was originally a banker's clerk, appears to have had no qualification for his more exalted position, beyond the somewhat questionable one of a taste for speculation. He is described as having had "all Sheridan's deficiency of financial arrangement, without that extraordinary man's resources." Nevertheless he was no bad hand at borrowing money. All the advances, however, made to him by his friends, to enable him to undertake the management of the Opera, are said to have been repaid. Mr. Ebers, his not unfriendly biographer, finds it difficult to account for this, and can only explain it by the excellent support the Opera received at the period. Mr. Taylor was what in the last century; was called a humorist." Not that he possessed much humour, but he was a queer, eccentric man, and given to practical jokes, which, in the present day, would not be thought amusing even by the friends of those injured by them. On one occasion, Taylor having been prevailed upon to invite a number of persons to breakfast, spread a report that he intended to set them down to empty plates. He, moreover, recommended each of the guests, in an anonymous letter, to turn the tables on the would-be ingenious Taylor, by taking to the *déjeuner* a supply of suitable provisions, so that the inhospitable inviter might be shamed and the invited enabled to feast in company, notwithstanding his machinations to the contrary. The manager enjoyed such a reputation for liberality that no one doubted the statement contained in the anonymous letter.

Each of the guests sent or took in his carriage a certain quantity of eatables, and when all had arrived, the happy Taylor found his room filled with all the materials for a monster pic nic. Breakfast *had* been prepared, the guests sat down to table, some amused, others disgusted at the hoax which had been practised upon them, and Taylor ordered the game, preserved meats, lobsters, champagne, &c., into his own larder and wine cellar.

Even while directing the affairs of the Opera, Taylor passed a considerable portion of his time in the King's Bench, or within its " rules."

" How can you conduct the management of the King's Theatre, a friend asked him one day, " perpetually in durance as you are?"

" My dear fellow," he replied, "how could I possibly conduct it if I were at liberty? I should be eaten up, sir—devoured. Here comes a dancer,—' Mr. Taylor, I want such a dress;' another, ' I want such and such ornaments.' One singer demands to sing in a part not allotted to him; another, to have an addition to his appointments. No, let me be shut up and they go to Masterson (Taylor's secretary); he, they are aware, cannot go beyond his line; but if they get at *me*—pshaw! no man at large can manage that theatre; and in faith," he added, " no man that undertakes it ought to go at large."

Though Mr. Taylor lived within the " rules," the " rules " in no way governed him. He would frequently go away for days together into the country and amuse himself with fishing, of which he appears to have been particularly fond. At one time, while living within the "rules," he inherited a large sum of money, which he took care not to devote to the payment of his debts. He preferred investing it in land, bought an estate in the country (with good fishing), and lived for some months the quiet, peaceable life of an ardent, enthusiastic angler, until at last the sheriffs broke in upon his repose and carried him back captive to prison.

But the most extraordinary exploit performed by Taylor during the period of his supposed incarceration, was of a political nature. He went down to Hull at the time of an election and actually stood for the borough. He was not returned—or rather he was returned to prison.

One way and another Mr. Taylor seems to have made a great deal of money out of the Opera; and at one time he hit upon a plan which looked at first as if it had only to be pursued with boldness to increase his income to an indefinite amount. This simple expedient consisted in raising the price of the subscribers' boxes. For the one hundred and eighty pound boxes he charged three hundred pounds, and so in proportion with all the others. A meeting of subscribers having been held, at which, although the expensive Catalani was engaged, it was decided that the proposed augmentation was not justified by the rate of the receipts and disbursements, and this decision having been communicated to Taylor, he replied, that if the subscribers resisted his just demands he would shut up their boxes.· In consequence of this defiant conduct on the part of the manager, many of the subscribers withdrew from the theatre and prevailed upon Caldas, a Portuguese wine merchant, to re-open the Pantheon for the performance of concerts and all such music as could be executed without infringing the licence of the King's Theatre. The Pantheon speculation prospered at first, but the seceders 'from the King's Theatre missed their operas, and doubtless also their ballets. A sort of compromise was effected between them and Taylor, who persisted, however, in keeping up the price of his boxes ; and the unfortunate Caldas, utterly deserted by those who had dragged him from his wine-cellars to expose him to the perils of musical speculation, became a bankrupt.

Taylor was now in his turn brought to account. Waters, his partner in the proprietorship of the King's Theatre, had been proceeding against him in Chancery, and it was ordered that the partnership should be dissolved and the house sold. To the great annoyance of the public, the first step taken in the affair was to close the theatre,—the chancellor, who is said to have had no ear for music, having refused to appoint a manager.

It was proposed by private friends that Taylor should cede his interest in the theatre to Waters ; but it was difficult to bring them to any understanding on the subject, or even to arrange an interview

between them. Waters prided himself on the de-
corum of his conduct, while Taylor appears to have
aimed at quite a contrary reputation.   All business
transactions, prior to Taylor's arrest, had been rendered nearly impossible between them; because one
would attend to no affairs on Sunday, while the
other, with a just fear of writs before him, objected
to show himself in London on any other day.   The
sight of Waters, moreover, is said to have rendered
Taylor "passionate and scurrilous;" and while the
negociations were being carried on, through interme-
diaries, between himself and his partner, he entered
into a treaty with the lessee of the Pantheon, with
the view of opening it in opposition to the King's
Theatre.   •

Ultimately, the management of the theatre was
confided, under certain restrictions, to Mr. Waters;
but even now possession was not given up to him
without a struggle.

When Mr. Waters' people were refused admittance
by Mr. Taylor's people, words led to blows.   The ad-
herents of the former partners, and actual enemies
and rivals, fought valiantly on both sides, but luck
had now turned against Taylor, and his party were
defeated and ejected.   That night, however, when the
Watersites fancied themselves secure in their strong-
hold, the Taylorites attacked them; effected a breach
in the stage door, stormed the passage, gained admittance to the stage, and finally drove their enemies
out into the Haymarket.   The unmusical chancellor,

whose opinion of the Opera could scarcely have been improved by the lawless proceeding of those connected with it, was again appealed to; and Waters established himself in the theatre by virtue of an order from the court.

The series of battles at the King's Theatre terminated with the European war. Napoleon was at Elba, Mr. Taylor still in the Bench, when Mr. Waters opened the Opera, and, during the great season which followed the peace of 1814, gained seven thousand pounds.

Taylor appears to have ended his days in prison; profiting freely by the "rules," and when at head quarters enjoying the society of Sir John and Lady Ladd. The trio seem, on the whole, to have led a very agreeable prison life (and, though strictly forbidden to wander from the jail beyond their appointed tether, appear in many respects to have been remarkably free. Taylor's great natural animal spirits increased with the wine he consumed; and occasionally his behaviour was such as would certainly have shocked Waters. On one occasion, his elation is said to have carried him so beyond bounds, that Lady Ladd found it expedient to empty the tea-kettle over him.

In 1816 the Opera, by direction of the Chancellor, (it was a fortunate thing that this time he did not order it to be pulled down,) was again put up for sale, and purchased out and out by Waters for seven thousand one hundred and fifty pounds. As the now sole proprietor was unable to pay into court even the first instalment of the purchase money,* he mortgaged the theatre, with a number of houses belonging to him, to Chambers the banker.   Taylor, who had no longer any sort of connection with the Opera, at present amused himself by writing anonymous letters to Mr. Chambers, prophesying the ruin of Waters, and giving dismal but grotesque pictures of the manager's penniless and bailiff-persecuted position. Mr. Ebers, who was a great deal mixed up with operatic affairs before assuming the absolute direction of the Opera, also came in for his share of these epistles, which every one seems to have instantly recognised as the production of Taylor.   "If Waters is with you at Brompton," he once wrote to Mr. Ebers, "for God's sake send him away instantly, for the bailiffs (alias bloodhounds) are out after him in all directions; and tell Chambers not to let him stay at Enfield, because that is a suspected place; and so is Lee's in York Street, Westminster, and Di Giovanni, in Smith Street, and Reed's in Flask Lane—both in Chelsea.   It was reported he was seen in the lane near your house an evening or two ago, with his eye blacked, and in the great coat and hat of a Chelsea pensioner."   At another time, Mr. Chambers was informed that Michael Kelly, the singer, was at an hotel at Brighton, on the point of death, and desirous while he yet lived to communicate something very

* Waters appears to have spent nearly all the money he made, during the seasons of 1814 and 1815, in improving the house.

important respecting Waters. The holder of Waters' mortgage took a post chaise and four and hurried in great alarm to Brighton, where he found Michael Kelly sitting in his balcony, with a pine apple and a bottle of claret before him.

Taylor's prophecies concerning Waters, after all, came true. His embarrassments increased year by year, and in 1820 an execution was put into the theatre at the suit of Chambers. Ten performances were yet due to the subscribers, when, on the evening of the 15th of August, bills were posted on the walls of the theatre, announcing that the Opera was closed. Mr. Waters did not join his former partner in the Bench, but retired to Calais.

Mr. Ebers's management commenced in 1821. He formed an excellent company, of which several singers, still under engagement to Mr. Waters, formed part, and which included among the singers, Madame Camporese, Madame Vestris, Madame Ronzi de Begnis; and M. M. Ambrogetti, Angrisani, Begrez, and Curioni. The chief dancers (as already mentioned in the previous chapter), were Noblet, Fanny Bias, and Albert. The season was a short one, it was considered successful, though the manager but lost money by it. The selection of operas was admirable, and consisted of Paer's *Agnese*, Rossini's *Gazza Ladra*, *Tancredi* and *Turco* in *Italia*, with Mozart's *Clemenza di Tito*, *Don Giovanni*, and *Nozze di Figaro*. The manager's losses were already seven thousand pounds. By way of encouraging him,

G 2

Mr. Chambers increased his rent the following year from three thousand one hundred and eighty pounds to ten thousand. It is right to add, that in the meanwhile Mr. Chambers had bought up Water's entire interest in the Opera for eighty thousand pounds. Altogether, by buying and selling the theatre, Waters had cleared no less than seventy-three thousand pounds. Not contented with this, he no sooner heard of the excellent terms on which Mr. Chambers had let the house, than he made an application (a fruitless one), to the ever-to-be-tormented Chancellor, to have the deed of sale declared invalid.

During Mr. Ebers's management, from the beginning of 1821 to the end of 1827, he lost money regularly every year; the smallest deficit in the budget of any one season being that of the last, when the manager thought himself fortunate to be minus only three thousand pounds (within a few sovereigns).

After Mr. Ebers's retirement, the management of the Opera was undertaken by Messrs. Laporte and Laurent. Mr. Laporte was succeeded by Mr. Lumley, the history of whose management belongs to a much later period than that treated of in the present chapter.

During the early part of the last century, the character of the London Opera House, as a fashionable place of entertainment, and in some other respects, appears to have considerably changed. Before the fire in 1789, the subscription to a box for fifty representations was at the rate of twenty guineas a seat. The charge for pit tickets was at this time ten shillings and sixpence ; so that a subscriber who meant to be a true habitué, and visited the Opera every night, saved five guineas by becoming a subscriber. At this time, too, the theatre was differently constructed, and there were only thirty-six private boxes, eighteen arranged in three rows on each side of the house. " The boxes," says Lord Mount Edgcumbe, in his " Musical Reminiscences," " were then much larger and more commodious than they are now, and could contain with ease more than their allotted subscribers ; far different from the miserable pigeon-holes of the present theatre, into which six persons can scarcely be squeezed, whom, in most situations, two-thirds can never see the stage. The front," continues Lord Mount Edgcumbe, " was then occupied by open public boxes, or *amphitheatre* (as it is called in French theatres), communicating with the pit. Both of these were filled, exclusively, with the highest classes of society ; all, without exception, in full dress, then universally worn. The audiences thus assembled were considered as indisputably presenting a finer spectacle than any other theatre in Europe, and absolutely astonished the foreign performers, to whom such a sight was entirely new. At the end of the performance, the company of the pit and boxes repaired to

the coffee-room, which was then the best assembly in
London ; private ones being rarely given on opera
nights ; and all the first society was regularly to be
seen there.   Over the front box was the five shilling
gallery ; then resorted to by respectable persons not
in full dress : and above that an upper gallery, to
which the admission was three shillings.   Subsequently the house was encircled with private boxes ;
yet still the prices remained the same, and the pit
preserved its respectability, and even grandeur, till
the old house was burnt down in 1789."

When the Opera was rebuilt, the number of representations for the season, was increased to sixty,
and the subscription was at the same time raised to
thirty guineas, so that the admission to a box still
did not exceed the price of a pit ticket.   During the
second year of Catalani's engagement, however, when
she obtained a larger salary than had ever been paid
to a singer before, the subscription for a whole box
with accommodation for six persons, was raised from
one hundred and eighty to three hundred guineas.
This, it will, perhaps, be remembered, was to some
extent a cunning device of Taylor's ; at least, it was
considered so at the time by the subscribers, though
the expenses of the theatre had much increased, and
the terms on which Catalani was engaged, were
really enormous.*   Dr. Veron, in his interesting

* After receiving, the first year she sang in London, two thousand guineas, (five hundred more than was paid to Banti,) she

memoirs (to which, by the way, I may refer all those who desire full particulars respecting the management of the French Opera during the commencement of the Meyerbeer period) tells us that, at the end of the continental war, the price of the *demi-tasse* in the cafés of Paris was raised from six to eight *sous*, and that it has never been lowered. So it is in taxation. An impost once established, unless the people absolutely refuse to pay it, is never taken off; and so it has been with the boxes at the London Opera House. The price of the best boxes once raised from one hundred and eighty to three hundred guineas, was never, to any considerable extent, diminished, and hence the custom arose of halving and sub-dividing the subscriptions, so that very few persons have now the sole ownership of a box. Hence, too, that of letting them for the night. and selling the tickets when the proprietor does not want them. This latter practice must have had the effect of lessening considerably the profits directly resulting from the high sums charged for the boxes. The price of admission to the pit being ten shillings and six-pence, the subscribers, through the librarians, and the librarians, who had themselves speculated in boxes, found it necessary in order to get rid of the box-tickets singly, to sell them at a reduced price. This explains why, for many years past, the ordinary

declared that her price was ridiculously low, and that to retain her "*ci voglioni molte mila lire sterline.*" She demanded and ob-tained five thousand.

price of pit tickets at the libraries and at shops of all kinds in the vicinity of the Opera, has been only eight shillings and six-pence. No one but a foreigner or a countryman, inexperienced in the ways of London, would think of paying ten shillings and six-pence at the theatre for admission to the pit; indeed, it is a species of deception to continue that charge at all, though it certainly does happen once or twice in a great many years that the public profit by the establishment of a fixed official price for pit tickets. Thus, during the great popularity of Jenny Lind, the box tickets giving the right of entry to the pit, were sold for a guinea, and even thirty shillings, and thousands of persons were imbecile enough to purchase them, whereas, at the theatre itself, anyone could, as usual, go into the pit by paying ten shillings and six-pence.

"Formerly," to go back to Lord Mount Edgcumbe's interesting remarks on this subject, "every lady possessing an opera box, considered it as much her home as her house, and was as sure to be found there, few missing any of the performances. If prevented from going, the *loan* of her box and the gratuitous use of the tickets was a favour always cheerfully offered and thankfully received, as a matter of course, without any idea of payment. Then, too, it was a favour to ask gentlemen to belong to a box, when subscribing to one was actually advantageous. Now, no lady can propose to them to give her more than double the price of the admission at the door, so that having paid so exorbitantly, every one is glad to be re-imbursed a part, at least, of the great expense which she must often support alone. Boxes and tickets, therefore, are no longer given; they are let for what can be got; for which traffic the circulating libraries afford an easy accommodation. Many, too, which are not taken for the season, are disposed of in the same manner, and are almost put up to auction. Their price varying from three to eight, or even ten guineas, according to the performance of the evening, and other accidental circumstances." From these causes the whole style of the opera house, as regards the audience, has become changed. " The pit has long ceased to be the resort of ladies of fashion, and, latterly, by the innovations introduced, is no longer agreeable to the former male frequenters of it." This state of things, however, has been altered, if not remedied, from the opera-goers' point of view, by the introduction of stalls where the manager compensates himself for the slightly reduced price of pit tickets, by charging exactly double what was paid for admission to the pit under the old system.

On the whole, the Opera has become less aristocratic, less respectable, and far more expensive than of old. Those who, under the ancient system, paid ten shillings and six-pence to go to the pit, must now, to obtain the same amount of comfort, give a guinea for a stall, while " most improper company is sometimes to be seen even in the principal tiers; and tickets bearing the names of ladies of the highest class have been presented by those of the lowest, such as used to be admitted only to the hindmost rows of the gallery." The last remark belongs to Lord Mount Edgcumbe, but it is, at least, as true now as it was thirty years ago. Numbers of objectionable persons go to the Opera as to all other public places, and I do not think it would be fair to the respectable lovers of music who cannot afford to pay more than a few shillings for their evening's entertainment, that they should be all collected in the gallery. It would, moreover, be placing too much power in the hands of the operatic officials, who already show themselves sufficiently severe censors in the article of dress. I do not know whether it is chiefly a disgrace to the English public or to the English system of operatic management; but it certainly is disgraceful, that a check-taker at a theatre should be allowed to exercise any supervision, or make the slightest remark concerning the costume of a gentleman choosing to attend that theatre, and conforming generally in his conduct and by his appearance to the usages of decent society. It is not found necessary to enforce any regulation as to dress at other opera houses, not even in St. Petersburgh and Moscow, where, as the theatres are directed by the Imperial Government, one might expect to find a more despotic code of laws in force than in a country like England. When an Englishman goes to a morning or evening concert, he does not present himself in the attire of a scavenger, and there is no reason for supposing that he would appear in any unbecoming garb, if liberty of dress were permitted to him at the Opera. The absurdity of the present system is that, whereas, a gentleman who has come to London only for a day or two, and does not happen to have a dress-coat in his portmanteau; who happens even to be dressed in exact accordance with the notions of the operatic check-takers, except as to his cravat, which we will suppose through the eccentricity of the wearer, to be black, with the smallest sprig, or spray, or spot of some colour on it; while such a one would be regarded as unworthy to enter the pit of the Opera, a waiter from an oyster-shop, in his inevitable black and white, reeking with the drippings of shell-fish, and the fumes of bad tobacco, or a drunken undertaker, fresh from a funeral, coming with the required number of shillings in his dirty hands, could not be refused admission. If the check-takers are empowered to inspect and decide as to the propriety of the cut and colour of clothes, why should they not also be allowed to examine the texture? On the same principle, too, the cleanliness of opera goers ought to be enquired into. No one, whose hair is not properly brushed, should be permitted to enter the stalls, and visitors to the pit should be compelled to show their nails.

I will conclude this chapter with an extract from an epistle from a gentleman, who, during Mr. Ebers's management of the King's Theatre, was a victim to

the despotic (and, in the main, unnecessary) regulations of which I have been speaking.   I cannot say
I feel any sympathy for this particular sufferer; but
his letter is amusing.   " I was dressed," he says, in
his protest forwarded to the manager the next morning, " in a *superfine blue coat*, with *gold buttons*, a
white waistcoat, fashionable tight drab pantaloons,
white silk stockings, and dress shoes; *all worn but
once a few days before at a dress concert at the Crown
and Anchor Tavern !*" The italics, and mark of admiration, are the property of the gentleman in the
superfine blue coat, who next proceeds to express his
natural indignation at the idea of the manager pre-
suming to " enact sumptuary laws without the inter-
vention of the legislature," and threatens him with
legal proceedings, and an appeal to British jury.   " I
have mixed," he continues, " too much in genteel society, not to know that black breeches, or pantaloons,
with black silk stockings, is a very prevailing full
dress; and why is it so?   Because it is convenient
and economical, *for you can wear a pair of white
silk stockings but once without washing, and a pair
of black is frequently worn for weeks without ablution.*
P.S. I have no objection to submit an inspection of
my dress of the evening in question to you, or any
competent person you may appoint."

If this gentleman, instead of being excluded, had
been admitted into the theatre, the silent ridicule to
which his costume would have exposed him, would
have effectually prevented him from making his

appearance there in any such guise again. It might also have acted as a terrible warning to others in-clined to sin in a similar manner.

CHAPTER XVI.

INNOVATORS in art, whether corrupters or improvers, are always sure to meet with opposition from a certain number of persons who have formed their tastes in some particular style which has long been a source of delight to them, and to interfere with which is to shock all their artistic sympathies. How often have we seen poets of one generation not ignored, but condemned and vilified by the critics and even by the poets themselves of the generation preceding it. Musicians seem to suffer even more than poets from this injustice of those who having contracted a special and narrow admiration for the works of their own particular epoch, will see no merit in the productions of any newer school that may arrive. Byron, Shelley, Keats, Tennyson have one and all been attacked, and their poetic merit denied by those who in several instances had given excellent proofs of their ability to appreciate poetry. Almost every distinguished composer of the last fifty years has met with the same fate, not always at the hands of the ignorant public, for it is this ignorant public with its naïve, uncritical admiration, which has sometimes been the first to do justice to the critic-reviled poets and composers, but at those of musicians and of educated amateurs. Ignorance, prejudice, malice, are the causes too often assigned for the non-appreciation of the artist of to-day by the art-lover, partly of to-day, but above all of yesterday. It should be remembered however, that there is a conservatism in taste as in politics, and that both have their advantages, though the lovers of noise and of revolution may be unable to see them; that the extension of the suffrage, the excessive use of imagery, the special cultivation of brilliant orchestral effects, may, in the eyes of many, really seem injurious to the true interests of government, poetry and music; finally that as in old age we find men still keeping more or less to the costumes of their prime, and as the man who during the best days of his life has habituated himself to drink port, does not suddenly acquire a taste for claret, or *vice versâ*,—so those who had accustomed their musical stomachs to the soft strains of Paisiello and Cimarosa, *could not* enjoy the sparkling, stimulating music of Rossini. So afterwards to the Rossinians, Donizetti poured forth nothing but what was insipid and frivolous; Bellini was languid and lackadaisical; Meyerbeer with his restlessness and violence, his new instruments, his drum songs, trumpet songs, fencing and pistol songs, tinder-box music, skating scenes and panoramic effects, was a noisy *charlatan*; Verdi, with his abruptness, his occasional vulgarity and his general melodramatic style, a mere musical Fitzball.

It must not be supposed, however, that I believe
in the constant progress of art; that I look upon
Meyerbeer as equal to Weber, or Weber as superior
to Mozart.   It is quite certain that Rossini has not
been approached in facility, in richness of invention,
in gaiety, in brilliancy, in constructiveness, or in
true dramatic power by any of the Italian, French,
or German theatrical composers who have succeeded
him, though nearly all have imitated him one way or
another: I will exclude Weber alone, an original
genius, belonging entirely to Germany* and to himself.   It is, at least, quite certain that Rossini is by
far the greatest of the series of Italian composers,
which begins with himself and seems to have ended
with Verdi; and yet, while neither Verdi nor Bellini,
nor Donizetti, were at all justly appreciated in this
country when they first made their appearance,
Rossini was—not merely sneered at and pooh-poohed;
he was for a long time condemned and abused every
where, and on the production of some of his finest
works was hissed and hooted in the theatres of his
native land.   But the human heart is not so black as
it is sometimes painted, and the Italian audiences
who whistled and screeched at the *Barber of Seville*
did so chiefly because they did not like it.   It was
not the sort of music which had hitherto given them
pleasure, and therefore they were not pleased.

* There is a scientific German mind and a romantic German mind,
and I perhaps need scarcely say, that Weber's music appears to me
thoroughly German, in the sense in which the legends and ballads
of Germany belong thoroughly to that country.

Rossini had already composed several operas for various Italian theatres (among which may be particularly mentioned *L'Italiana in Algeri*, written for Venice in 1813, the composer having then just attained his majority) when the *Barbiere di Siviglia* was produced at Rome for the Carnival of 1816. The singers were Vitarelli, Boticelli, Zamboni, Garcia and Mesdames Giorgi-Righetti, and Rossi. A number of different versions of the circumstances which attended, preceded, and followed the representation of this opera, have been published, but the account furnished by Madame Giorgi-Righetti, who introduced the music of Rossini to the world, is the one most to be relied upon and which I shall adopt. I may first of all remind the reader that a very interesting life of Rossini, written with great *verve* and spirit, full of acute observations, but also full of misstatements and errors of all kinds,* has been published by Stendhal, who was more than its translator, but not its author. Stendhal's "Vie de Rossini" is founded on a work by the Abbé Carpani. To what extent the ingenious author of the treatise *De l'Amour*, and of the admirable novel *La Charteuse de Parme*, is indebted to the Abbé, I cannot say; but if he borrowed from him his supposed facts, and his opinions as a musician, he owes him all the worst portion of his book. The brothers Escudier have also published a "Vie de

---

* As for instance where *Semiramide* is described as an opera written in the German style!

Rossini," which is chiefly valuable for the list of his works, and the dates of their production.

To return to the *Barber of Seville*, of which the subject was suggested to Rossini by the author of the *libretto*, Sterbini. Sterbini proposed to arrange it for music in a new form; Rossini acquiesced, and the librettists went to work. The report was soon spread that Rossini was about to reset Paisiello's libretto. For this some accused Rossini of presumption, while others said that in taking Paisiello's subject he was behaving meanly and unjustly. This was absurd, for all Metastasio's lyrical dramas have been set to music by numbers of composers; but this fact was not likely to be taken into consideration by Rossini's enemies. Paisiello himself took part in the intrigues against the young composer, and wrote a letter from Naples, begging one of his friends at Rome to leave nothing undone that could contribute to the failure of the second *Barber*. When the night of representation, at the Argentina Theatre, arrived, Rossini's enemies were all at their posts, declaring openly what they hoped and intended should be the fate of the new opera. His friends, on the other hand, were not nearly so decided, remembering, as they did, the uncomplimentary manner in which Rossini's *Torvaldo* had been received only a short time before. The composer, says Madame Giorgi Righetti " was weak enough to allow Garcia to sing beneath Rosina's balcony a Spanish melody of his own arrangement. Garcia maintained, that as the scene was in Spain the Spanish melody would give the drama an appropriate local colour; but, unfortunately, the artist who reasoned so well, and who was such an excellent singer, forgot to tune his guitar before appearing on the stage as "Almaviva." He began the operation in the presence of the public. A string broke. The vocalist proceeded to replace it; but before he could do so, laughter and hisses were heard from all parts of the house. The Spanish air, when Garcia was at last ready to sing it, did not please the Italian audience, and the pit listened to it just enough to be able to give an ironical imitation of it afterwards.

The introduction to Figaro's air seemed to be liked; but when Zamboni entered, with another guitar in his hand, a loud laugh was set up, and not a phrase of *Largo al factotum* was heard. When Rosina made her appearance in the balcony, the public were quite prepared to applaud Madame Giorgi-Righetti in an air which they thought they had a right to expect from her; but only hearing her utter a phrase which led to nothing, the expressions of disapprobation recommenced. The duet between "Almaviva" and "Figaro" was accompanied throughout with hissing and shouting. The fate of the work seemed now decided.

At length Rosina came on, and sang the *cavatina* which had so long been looked for. Madame Giorgi-Righetti was young, had a fresh beautiful voice, and was a great favourite with the Roman public. Three long rounds of applause followed the conclusion of her air, and gave some hope that the opera might yet be saved. Rossini, who was at the orchestral piano, bowed to the public, then turned towards the singer, and whispered " *oh natura !* "

This happy moment did not last, and the hisses recommenced with the duet between Figaro and Rosina. The noise increased, and it was impossible to hear a note of the finale. When the curtain fell Rossini turned towards the public, shrugged his shoulders and clapped his hands. The audience were deeply offended by this openly-expressed contempt for their opinion, but they made no reply at the time.

The vengeance was reserved for the second act, of which not a note passed the orchestra. The hubbub was so great, that nothing like it was ever heard at any theatre. Rossini in the meanwhile remained perfectly calm, and afterwards went home as composed as if the work, received in so insulting a manner, had been the production of some other musician. After changing their clothes, Madame Giorgi-Righetti, Garcia, Zamboni, and Botticelli, went to his house to console him in his misfortune. They found him fast asleep.

The next day he wrote the delightful *cavatina, Ecco ridente il cielo,* to replace Garcia's unfortunate Spanish air. The melody of the new solo was borrowed from the opening chorus of *Aureliano* in *Palmira,* written by Rossini in 1814, for Milan, and produced without success ; the said chorus having

itself figured before in the same composer's *Ciro* in
Babilonia, also unfavourably received. Garcia read
his *cavatina* as it was written, and sang it the same
evening. Rossini, having now made the only alteration he thought necessary, went back to bed, and pretended to be ill, that he might not have to take his
place in the evening at the piano.

At the second performance, the Romans seemed
disposed to listen to the work of which they had
really heard nothing the night before. This was all
that was needed to ensure the opera's triumphant
success. Many of the pieces were applauded; but
still no enthusiasm was exhibited. The music, however, pleased more and more with each succeeding
representation, until at last the climax was reached, and
Il Barbiere produced those transports of admiration
among the Romans with which it was afterwards received in every town in Italy, and in due time throughout Europe. It must be added, that a great many connoisseurs at Rome were struck from the first moment
with the innumerable beauties of Rossini's score,
and went to his house to congratulate him on its
excellence. As for Rossini, he was not at all surprised at the change which took place in public
opinion. He was as certain of the success of his
work the first night, when it was being hooted, as he
was a week afterwards, when every one applauded it
to the skies.

In Paris, more than three years afterwards, with
Garcia still playing the part of " Almaviva,". and with

Madame Ronzi de Begnis as "Rosina," *Il Barbiere*
was not much better received than on its first production at Rome.   It was less astonishing that it should
fail before an audience of Parisians (at that time quite
unacquainted with Rossini's style) than before a highly
musical public like that of Rome.   In each case, the
work of Paisiello was made the excuse for condemn-
ing that of Rossini; but Rossini's *Barber* was not
treated with indignity at the Italian Theatre of Paris.
It was simply listened to very coldly.   Every one was
saying, that after Paisiello's opera it was nothing, that
the two were not to be compared, &c., when, fortunately, some one proposed that Paisiello's *Barber*
should be revived.   Paer, the director of the music,
and who is said to have been rendered very uneasy by
Rossini's Italian successes, thought that to crush Rossini by means of his predecessor, was no bad idea.   The
St. Petersburgh *Barber* of 1788 was brought out;
but it was found that he had grown old and feeble;
or, rather, the simplicity of the style was no longer
admired, and the artists who had already lost the traditions of the school, were unable to sing the music
with any effect.   Rossini's *Barber* has now been
before the world for nearly half a century, and we
all know whether it is old-fashioned; whether the
airs are tedious; whether the form of the concerted
pieces, and of the grand finale, leaves anything to
be desired; whether the instrumentation is poor;
whether, in short, on any one point, any subsequent
work of the same kind even by Rossini himself, has

surpassed, equalled, or even approached it. But the thirty years of Paisiello's Barber bore heavily upon the poor old man, and he was found sadly wanting in that gaiety and brilliancy which have given such celebrity to Rossini's hero, and after which Beaumarchais's sparkling epigrammatic dialogue appears almost dull.* Paisiello's opera was a complete failure. And when Rossini's *Barbiere* was brought out again, every one was struck by the contrast. It profited by the very artifice which was to have destroyed it, and Rossini's enemies took care for the future not to establish comparisons between Rossini and Paisiello. Madame Ronzi de Begnis, too, had been replaced very advantageously by Madame Fodor. With two such admirable singers as Fodor and Garcia in the parts of " Rosina " and " Almaviva," with Pellegrini as " Figaro," and Begnis as " Basil," the suc-

---

* It would be absurd to say that if Rossini had set the *Marriage of Figaro* to music, he would have produced a finer work than Mozart's masterpiece on the same subject ; but Rossini's genius, by its comic side, is far more akin to that of Beaumarchais, than is Mozart's. Mozart has given a tender poetic character to many portions of his *Marriage of Figaro*, which the original comedy does not possess at all. In particular, he has so elevated the part of "Cherubino" by pure and beautiful melodies, as to have completely transformed it. It is surely no disparagement to Mozart, to say, that he took a higher view of life than Beaumarchais was capable of ?

I may add, that, in comparing Rossini with Beaumarchais, it must always be remembered that the former possesses the highest dramatic talent of a serious, passionate kind—witness *Otello* and *William Tell ;* whereas Beaumarchais's serious dramatic works, such as *La Mère Coupable, Les Deux Amis,* and *Eugénie* (the best of the three), are very inferior productions.

cess of the opera increased with each representation :
and though certain musical *quid-nuncs* continued to
shake their heads when Rossini's name was mentioned in a drawing-room, his reputation with the
great body of the theatrical public was now fully
established.

The *tirana* composed by Garcia *Se il mio nome
saper voi bramate,* which he apppears to have abandoned after the unfavourable manner in which it was
received at Rome, was afterwards re-introduced into
the *Barber* by Rubini.

The whole of the *Barber of Seville* was composed
from beginning to end in a month. *Ecco ridente il
cielo* (the air adapted from *Aureliano* in *Palmira*) was,
as already mentioned, added after the first representation. The overture, moreover, had been previously written for *Aureliano in Palmira,* and (after
the failure of that work) had been prefixed to *Elizabetta regina d'Inghilterra* which met with some success, thanks to the admirable singing of Mademoiselle
Colbran, in the principal character.

Rossini took his failures very easily, and with the
calm confidence of a man who knew he could do
better things and that the public would appreciate
them. When his *Sigismondo* was violently hissed at
Venice he sent a letter to his mother with a picture
of a large *fiasco,* (bottle). His *Torvaldo e Dorliska,*
which was brought out soon afterwards, was also
hissed, but not so much.

This time Rossini sent his mother a picture of a *fiaschetto* (little bottle).

The motive of the *allegro* in the trio of the last act of (to return for a moment to) the *Barber of Seville*, is, as most of my readers are probably aware, simply an arrangement of the bass air sung by " Simon," in *Haydn's Seasons*. The comic air, sung by " Berta," the duenna, is a Russian dance tune, which was very fashionable in Rome, in 1816. Rossini is said to have introduced it into the *Barber of Seville*, out of compliment to some Russian lady.

Rossini's first opera *la Pietra del Paragone*, was written when he was seventeen years of age, for the Scala at Milan, where it was produced in the autumn of 1812. He introduced the best pieces out of this work into the *Cenerentola*, which was brought out five years afterwards at Rome. Besides *la Pietra del Paragone*, he laid *il Turco in Italia*, and *la Gazzetta* under contribution to enrich the score of *Cinderella*. The air *Miei rampolli*, the duet *un Soave non so chè*, the drinking chorus and the burlesque proclamation of the baron belonged originally to *la Pietra del Paragone*; the *sestett*, the *stretta* of the finale, the duet *zitto, zitto*, to the *Turco in Italia*, (produced at Milan in 1814), *Miei rampolli* had also been inserted in *la Gazzetta*.

The principal female part in the *Cenerentola*, though written for a contralto, has generally, (like those of

Rosina and Isabella, and also written for contraltos), been sung by sopranos, such as Madame Fodor, Madame Cinti, Madame Sontag, &c. When sung by Mademoiselle Alboni, these parts are executed in every respect in conformity with the composer's intentions.

Rossini's first serious opera, or at least the first of those by which his name became known throughout Europe, was *Tancredi*, written for Venice in 1813, the year after *la Pietra del Paragone*. In this opera, we find indicated, if not fully carried out, all those admirable changes in the composition of the lyric drama which were imputed to him by his adversaries as so many artistic crimes. Lord Mount Edgcumbe, in his objections to Rossini's music, strange and almost inexplicable as they appear, yet only says in somewhat different language what is advanced by Rossini's admirers, in proof of his great merit. The connoisseur of a past epoch describes the changes introduced by Rossini into dramatic music, for an enemy, fairly enough; only he regards as detestable innovations what others have accepted as admirable reforms. It appeared to Rossini that the number of airs written for the so-called lyric dramas of his youth, delayed the action to a most wearisome extent. In *Tancredi*, concerted pieces in which the dramatic action is kept up, are introduced in situations where formerly there would have been only monologues. In *Tancredi* the bass has little to do, but more than in the operas of the old-school, where he was kept quite in the back ground, the *ultima parte* being seldom heard except in *ensembles*. By degrees the bass was brought forward, until at last he became an indispensable and frequently the principal character in all tragic operas. In the old opera the number of characters was limited and choruses were seldom introduced. Think, then, how an amateur of the simple, quiet old school must have been shocked by a thoroughly Rossinian opera, such as *Semiramide*, with its brilliant, sonorous instrumentation, its prominent part for the bass or baritone, its long elaborate finale, and above all its military band on the stage ! Mozart had already anticipated every resource that has since been adopted by Rossini, but to Rossini belongs, nevertheless, the merit of having brought the lyric drama to perfection on the Italian stage, and forty and even thirty years ago it was to Rossini that its supposed degradation was attributed.

"So great a change," says Lord Mount Edgcumbe, "has taken place in the character of the (operatic) dramas, in the style of the music and its performance, that I cannot help enlarging on that subject before I proceed further. One of the most material alterations is, that the grand distinction between serious and comic operas is nearly at an end, the separation of the singers for their performance, entirely so.* Not only do the same sing in both, but a new

* The serious opera consisted of the following persons : the *prima uomo (soprano)*, *prima donna*, and tenor; the *secondo uomo (soprano)*, *seconda donna* and *ultima parte*, (bass), The company for the comic

species of drama has arisen, a kind of mongrel between them called *semi seria*, which bears the same analogy to the other two that that nondescript melodrama does to the legitimate tragedy and comedy of the English stage."

And of which style specimens may be found in Shakespeare's plays and in Mozart's *Don Giovanni!* The union of the serious and the comic in the same lyric work was an innovation of Mozart's, like almost all the innovations attributed by Lord Mount Edgcumbe to Rossini. Indeed, nearly all the operatic reforms of the last three-quarters of a century that have endured, have had Mozart for their originator.

"The construction of these newly invented pieces," continues Lord Mount Edgcumbe, "is essentially different from the old. The dialogue which used to be carried on in recitative, and which in Metastasio's operas, is often so beautiful and interesting, is now cut up (and rendered unintelligible, if it were worth listening to), into *pezzi concertati*, or long singing conversations, which present a tedious succession of unconnected, ever-changing motivos, having nothing to do with each other : and if a satisfactory air is for a moment introduced, which the ear would like to dwell upon, to hear modulated, varied and again returned to, it is broken off before it is well understood,

---

opera consisted of the *primo buffo* (tenor), *prima buffa, buffo caricato* (bass), *seconda buffa* and *ultima parte* (bass). There were also the *uomo serio* and *donna seria*, generally the second man and woman of the serious opera.

by a sudden transition into a totally different melody, time and key, and recurs no more; so that no impression can be made or recollection of it preserved. Single songs are almost exploded . . . . even the *prima donna* who would formerly have complained at having less than three or four airs allotted to her, is now satisfied with one trifling *cavatina* for a whole opera."

Lord Mount Edgcumbe has hitherto given a tolerably true account of the reforms introduced by Rossini into the operatic music of Italy; only, instead of calling Rossini's concerted pieces and finales, "a tedious succession of unconnected, ever-changing motivos," he ought to describe them as highly interesting, well connected and eminently dramatic. He goes on to condemn Rossini for his new distribution of characters, and especially for his employment of bass voices in chief parts "to the manifest injury of melody and total subversion of harmony, in which the lowest part is their peculiar province." Here, however, it occurs to Lord Mount Edgcumbe, and he thereupon expresses his surprise, "that the principal characters in two of Mozart's operas should have been written for basses."

When the above curious, and in its way valuable, strictures on Rossini's music were penned, not only *Tancredi,* but also *Il Barbiere, Otello, La Cenerentola, Mosè in Egitto, La Gazza Ladra,* and other of his works had been produced. *Il Barbiere* succeeded at once in England, and Lord Mount Edgcumbe tells us that for many years after the first introduction of Rossini's works into England "so entirely did he engross the stage, that the operas of no other master were ever to be heard, with the exception of those of Mozart ; and of his only *Don Giovanni* and *le Nozze di Figaro* were often repeated . . . . Every other composer, past and present, was totally put aside, and these two alone named or thought of." Rossini, then, if wrongly applauded, was at least applauded in good company. It appears from Mr. Ebers's "Seven years of the King's Theatre," that of all the operas produced from 1821 to 1828, nearly half were Rossini's, or in exact numbers fourteen out of thirty-four, but it must be remembered that the majority of these were constantly repeated, whereas most of the others were brought out only for a few nights and then laid aside. During the period in question the composer whose works, next to Rossini, were most often represented, was Mozart with *Don Giovanni*, *Le Nozze*, *La Clemenza di Tito*, and *Cosi fan Tutti*. The other operas included in the repertoire were by Paer, Mayer, Zingarelli, Spontini, (*la Vestale*), Mercadante, Meyerbeer, (*Il Crociato in Egitto*) &c.

Our consideration of the causes of Rossini's success, and want of success, has led us far away from the first representation of *Tancredi* at the theatre of La Fenice. Its success was so great, that each of its melodies became for the Venetians a second "Carnival of Venice;" and even in the law courts, the judges are said to have been obliged to direct the ushers to stop the singing of *Di tanti palpiti*, and *Mi rivedrai te rivedrò*.

"I thought after hearing my opera, that the Venetians would think me mad," said Rossini. "Not at all; I found they were much madder than I was." *Tancredi* was followed by *Aureliano*, produced at Milan in 1814, and, as has already been mentioned, without success. The introduction, however, containing the chorus from which Almaviva's *cavatina* was adapted, is said to have been one of Rossini's finest pieces. *Otello*, the second of Rossini's important serious operas, was produced in 1816 at Naples (Del Fondo Theatre). The principal female part, as in the now-forgotten *Elizabetta*, and as in a great number of subsequent works, was written for Mademoiselle Colbran. The other parts were sustained by Benedetti, Nozzari, and the celebrated Davide.

In *Otello*, Rossini continued the reforms which he had commenced in *Tancredi*. He made each dramatic scene one continued piece of music, used recitative but sparingly, and when he employed it, accompanied it for the first time in Italy, with the full band. The piano was now banished from the orchestra, forty-two years after it had been banished by Gluck from the orchestras of France.

Davide, in the part of "Otello," created the greatest enthusiasm.   The following account of his performance is given by a French critic, M. Edouard Bertin, in a letter from Venice, dated 1823 :—

" Davide excites among the *dilettanti* of this town an enthusiasm and delight which could scarcely be conceived without having been witnessed.   He is a singer of the new school, full of mannerism, affectation, and display, abusing, like Martin, his magnificent voice with its prodigious compass (three octaves comprised between four B flats).   He crushes the principal motive of an air beneath the luxuriance of his ornamentation, and which has no other merit than that of difficulty conquered.   But he is also a singer full of warmth, *verve*, expression, energy, and musical sentiment ; alone he can fill up and give life to a scene ; it is impossible for another singer to carry away an audience as he does, and when he will only be simple, he is admirable; he is the Rossini of song.   He is a great singer; the greatest I ever heard.   Doubtless, the manner in which Garcia plays and sings the part of "Otello" is preferable, taking it altogether, to that of Davide.   It is purer, more severe, more constantly dramatic ; but with all his faults Davide produces more effect, a great deal more effect.   There is something in him, I cannot say what, which, even when he is ridiculous, commands, enhances attention.   He never leaves you cold ; and when he does not move you, he astonishes you ; in a word, before hearing him, I did not know what the power of singing really was. The enthusiasm he excites is without limits. In fact, his faults are not faults for Italians, who in their *opera seria* do not employ what the French call the tragic style, and who scarcely understand us, when we tell them that a waltz or quadrille movement is out of place in the mouth of a Cæsar, an Assur, or an Otello. With them the essential thing is to please: they are only difficult on this point, and their indifference as to all the rest is really inconceivable: here is an example of it. Davide, considering apparently that the final duet of *Otello* did not sufficiently show off his voice, determined to substitute for it a duet from *Armida* (Amor possente nome), which is very pretty, but anything rather than severe. As it was impossible to kill Desdemona to such a tune, the Moor, after giving way to the most violent jealousy, sheathes his dagger, and begins in the most tender and graceful manner his duet with Desdemona, at the conclusion of which he takes her politely by the hand, and retires, amidst the applause and bravos of the public, who seem to think it quite natural that the piece should finish in this manner, or, rather, that it should not finish at all: for after this beautiful *dénouement*, the action is about as far advanced as it was in the first scene. We do not in France carry our love of music so far as to tolerate such absurdities as these, and perhaps we are right."

Lord Byron saw *Otello* at Venice, soon after its first production. He speaks of it in one of his letters, dated 1818, in which he condemns the libretto, but expresses his admiration of the music.

La Gazza Ladra was written for Milan, and brought out at the theatre of "La Scala," in 1817. Four years afterwards it was produced in London in the spring, and Paris in the autumn. The part of " Ninetta," afterwards so favourite a character with Sontag, Malibran, and Grisi, was sung in 1821 by Madame Camporese in London, by Madame Fodor in Paris. Camporese's performance was of the greatest merit, and highly successful. Fodor's is said to have been perfection. The part of "Pippo," originally written for a contralto, used at one time to be sung at the English and French theatres by a baritone or bass. It was not until some years after *La Gazza Ladra* was produced, that a contralto (except for first parts), was considered an indispensable member of an opera company.

Madame Fodor was not an Italian, but a Russian. She was married to a Frenchman, M. Mainvielle, and, before visiting Italy, and, until her *début*, had studied chiefly in Paris. Her Italian tour is said to have greatly improved her style, which, when she first appeared in London, in 1816, left much to be desired. Camporese was of good birth, and was married to a member of the Guistiniani family. She cultivated singing in the first instance only as an accomplishment; but was obliged by circumstances to make it her profession. In Italy she sang only at concerts, and it was not until her arrival in England that she appeared on the stage. She seems to have possessed very varied powers; appearing at one time as "Zerlina" to Ronzi's "Donna Anna;" at another, as "Donna Anna," to Fodor's "Zerlina."

La Gazza Ladra is known to be founded on a French melo-drama, *La Pie Voleuse*, of which the capabilities for operatic "setting," were first discovered by Paer. Paer had seen Mademoiselle Jenny Vertpré in *La Pie Voleuse*. He bought the play, and sent it to his librettist in ordinary at Milan, with marginal notes, showing how it ought to be divided for musical purposes. The opera book intended by Paer for himself was offered to Rossini, and by him was made the groundwork of one of his most brilliant productions.

La Gazza Ladra marks another step in Rossini's progress as a composer, and accordingly we find Lord Mount Edgcumbe saying, soon after its production in England:—"Of all the operas of Rossini that have been performed here, that of *la Gazza Ladra* is most peculiarly liable to all the objections I have made to the new style of drama, of which it is the most striking example." The only opera of Rossini's which Lord Mount Edgcumbe seems really to have liked was *Aureliano in Palmira*, written in the composer's earliest style, and which failed.

" Its finales," (Lord Mount Edgcumbe is speaking of *La Gazza Ladra*) " and many of its very numerous *pezzi concertati*, are uncommonly loud, and the lavish use made of the noisy instruments, appears, to my judgment, singularly inappropriate to the subject; which, though it might have been rendered touching, is far from calling for such warlike accompaniments. Nothing can be more absurd than the manner in which this simple story is represented in the Italian piece, or than to be a young peasant servant girl, led to trial and execution, under a guard of soldiers, with military music." The quintett of *La Gazza Ladra*, is, indeed, open to a few objections from a dramatic point of view. "Ninetta" is afraid of compromising her father; but "Fernando" has already given himself up to the authorities, in order to save his daughter— in whose defence he does not say a word. An explanation seems necessary, but then the drama would be at an end. There would be no quintett, and we should lose one of Rossini's finest pieces. Would it be worth while to destroy this quintett, in order to make the opera end like the French melo-drama, and as the French operatic version of *La Gazza Ladra* also terminates?

I have already spoken of *La Cenerentola*, produced in 1817 at Rome. This admirable work has of late years been much neglected. The last time it was heard in England at Her Majesty's Theatre, Madame Alboni played the principal part, and excited the greatest enthusiasm by her execution of the final air, *Non piu mesta* (the model of so many solos for the *prima donna*, introduced with or without reason, at the end of subsequent operas); but the cast was a very imperfect one, and the performance on the whole (as usual, of late years, at this theatre) very unsatisfactory.

Mosè in Egitto was produced at the San * Carlo Theatre, at Naples, in 1818; the principal female part being written again for Mademoiselle Colbran. In this work, two leading parts, those of " Faraoni " and "Mosè," were assigned to basses. The once proscribed, or, at least contemned basso, was, for the first time brought forward, and honoured with full recognition in an Italian *opera seria*. The story of the Red Sea, and of the chorus sung on its banks, has often been told; but I will repeat it in a few words, for the benefit of those readers who may not have met with it before. The Passage of the Red Sea was intended to be particularly grand; but, instead of producing the effect anticipated, it was received every night with laughter. The two first acts were always applauded; but the Red Sea was a decided obstacle to the success of the third. Tottola, the librettist, came to Rossini one morning, with a prayer for the Israelites, which he fancied, if the composer would set it to music, might save the conclusion of the opera. Rossini, who was in bed at the time, saw at once the importance of the suggestion, wrote on the spur of the moment, and in a few minutes, the magnificent *Del tuo stellato soglio*. It was performed the same evening, and excited transports of admiration. The scene of the Red Sea,

* The San Carlo, Benedetti Theatre, &c., are named after the parishes in which they are built.

instead of being looked forward to as a source of hilarity, became now the chief "attraction" of the opera. The performance of the prayer produced a sort of frenzy among the audience, and a certain Neapolitan doctor, whose name has not transpired, told either Stendhal or the Abbé Carpani (on whose *Letters*, as before mentioned, Beyle's "Vie de Rossini par Stendhal" is founded), that the number of nervous indispositions among the ladies of Naples was increased in a remarkable manner by the change of key, from the minor to the major, in the last verse.

Mosè was brought out in London, as an oratorio, in the beginning of 1822. Probably, dramatic action was absolutely necessary for its success; at all events, it failed as an oratorio. The same year it was produced as an opera at the King's Theatre; but with a complete transformation in the libretto, and under the title of *Pietro l' Eremita*. The opera attracted throughout the season, and no work of Rossini's was ever more successful on its first production in this country. The subscribers to the King's Theatre were in ecstacies with it, and one of the most distinguished supporters of the theatre, after assuring the manager that he deserved well of this country, offered to testify his gratitude by proposing him at White's !

In the autumn of the same year *Mosè* was produced at the Italian Opera of Paris, and in 1827, a French version of it was brought out at the Académie. The

Red Sea appears to have been a source of trouble everywhere. At the Aeadémie, forty-five thousand francs were sunk in it, and to so little effect, or rather with such bad effect, that the machinists' and decorators' waves had to be suppressed after the first evening. In London the Red Sea became merely a river. The river, however, failed quite as egregiously as the larger body of water, and had to be drained off before the second performance took place.

Mosè is quite long enough and sufficiently complete in its original form. Several pieces, however, out of other operas, by Rossini, were added to it in the London version of the work. In Paris, in accordance with the absurd custom (if it be not even a law) at the Académie, *Mosè* could not be represented without the introduction of a ballet. The necessary dance music was taken from *Ciro in Babilonia* and *Armida,* and the opera was further strengthened as it was thought (weakened as it turned out), by the introduction of a new air for Mademoiselle Cinti, and several new choruses.

The *Mosè* of the Académie, with its four acts of music (one more than the original opera) was found far too long. It was admired, and for a little while applauded; but when it had once wearied the public, it was in vain that the directors reduced its dimensions. It became smaller and smaller, until it at last disappeared.

Zelmira, written originally for Vienna, and which

is said to have contained Madame Colbran Rossini's best part, was produced at Naples in 1822. The composer and his favourite *prima donna* were married in the spring of the same year at Castelnaso, near Bologna.

"The recitatives of *Zelmira*," says Carpani, in his *Le Rossinane ossia lettere musico-teatrali*, "are the best and most dramatic that the Italian school has produced; their eloquence is equal to that of the most beautiful airs, and the spectator, equally charmed and surprised, listens to them from one end to the other. These recitatives are sustained by the orchestra; *Otello, Mosè in Egitto,* are written after the same system, but I will not attribute to Rossini the honour of a discovery which belongs to our neighbours. Although the French Opera is still barbarous from a vocal point of view, there are some points about it which may be advantageously borrowed. The introduction of accompanied recitative is of the greatest importance for our *opera seria*, which, in the hands of the Mayers, Paers, the Rossinis, has at last become dramatic."

Zelmira was brought out in London in 1824, under the direction of Rossini himself, and with Madame Colbran Rossini in the principal part. The reception of the composer, when he made his appearance in the orchestra, was most enthusiastic, and at the end of the opera, he was called on to the stage, which, in England, was, then, quite a novel compliment.

At the same time, all possible attention was paid to

Rossini, in private, by the most distinguished persons in the country. He was invited by George IV. to the Pavilion at Brighton, and the King gave orders that when his guest entered the music room, his private band should play the overture to the *Barber of Seville*. The overture being concluded, his Majesty asked Rossini what piece he would like to hear next. The composer named *God save the King*.

The music of *Zelmira* was greatly admired by connoisseurs, but made no impression on the public, and though Madame Colbran-Rossini's performance is said to have been admirable, it must be remembered that she had already passed the zenith of her powers. Born in Madrid, in 1785, she appears to have retired from the stage, as far as Italy was concerned, in 1823, after the production of *Semiramide*. At least, I find no account of her having sung anywhere after the season of 1824, in London, though her name appears in the list of the celebrated company assembled the same year by Barbaja, at Vienna. Mademoiselle Colbran figures among the sopranos with Mesdames Mainvielle-Fodor, Féron, Esther Mombelli,* Dardanelli, Sontag, Unger, Giuditta, Grisi, and Grimbaun. The contraltos of this unrivalled *troupe* were Mesdames Cesare-Cantarelli and Eckerlin; the tenors, Davide, Nozzari, Donzelli, Rubini, and Cicimarra; the basses, Lablache, Bassi,

---

* Particularly celebrated for her performance of the brilliant part of the heroine in *La Cenerentola*, which, however, was not written for her.

Ambroggi, Tamburini, and Bolticelli. Rossini had undertaken to write an opera entitled *Ugo rè d' Italia,* for the King's Theatre. The engagement had been made at the beginning of the season, in January, and the work was repeatedly announced for performance, when, at the end of May, it was said to be only half finished. He had, at this time, quarrelled with the management, and accepted the post of director at the Italian Opera of Paris. The end of *Ugo rè d'Italia* is said by Mr. Ebers to have been, that the score, as far as it was written, was deposited with Messrs. Ransom, the bankers. Messrs. Ransom, however, have informed me, that they never had a score of Rossini's in their possession.

After Rossini's departure from London, his *Semiramide,* produced at Venice only the year before, was brought out with Madame Pasta, in the principal character. The part of "Semiramide" had been played at the *Fenice* Theatre, by Madame Colbran; it was the last Rossini wrote for his wife, and *Semiramide* was the last opera he composed for Italy. When we meet with Rossini again, it will be at the Académie Royale of Paris, as the composer of *the Siege of Corinth, Count Ory,* and *William Tell.*

The first great representative of "Semiramide" was Pasta, who has probably never been surpassed in that character. After performing it with admirable success in London, she resumed in it the year afterwards, 1825, at the Italian Opera of Paris. Madame

Pasta had already gained great celebrity by her representation of "Tancredi" and of "Romeo," but in *Semiramide*, she seems, for the first time, to have exhibited her genius in all its fulness.*

The original "Arsace" was Madame Mariani, the first great "Arsace," Madame Pisaroni.

Since the first production of *Semiramide*, thirty years ago, all the most distinguished sopranos and contraltos of the day have loved to appear in that admirable work.

Among the "Semiramides," I may mention in particular Pasta, Grisi, Viardot-Garcia, and Cruvelli. Although not usually given to singers who particularly excel in the execution of light delicate music, the part of "Semiramide" was also sung with success by Madame Sontag (Paris, 1829), and Madame Bosio (St. Petersburgh, 1855).

Among the "Arsaces," may be cited Pisaroni, Brambilla, and Alboni.

Malibran, with her versatile comprehensive genius, appeared both as "Arsace" and as "Semiramide," and was equally fortunate in each of these very different impersonations.

I will now say a few words respecting those of the singers just named, whose names are more especially associated with Rossini's earliest successes in England.

* When Madame Pasta sang at concerts, after her retirement from the stage, her favourite air was still Tancredi's *Di tanti palpiti.*

Madame Pasta having appeared in Paris with success in 1816, was engaged with her husband, Signor Pasta (an unsuccessful tenor), for the following season at the King's Theatre. She made no great impression that year, and was quite eclipsed by Fodor and Camporese, who were members of the same company. The young singer, not discouraged, but convinced that she had much to learn, returned to Italy, where she studied unremittingly for four years. She reappeared at the Italian Opera of Paris in 1821, as "Desdemona," in Rossini's *Otello*, then for the first time produced in France. Her success was complete, but her performance does not appear to have excited that enthusiasm which was afterwards caused by her representation of "Medea," in Mayer's opera of that name. In *Medea*, however, Pasta was everything ; in *Otello*, she had to share her triumph with Garcia, Bordogni, and Levasseur. From this time, the new tragic vocalist gained constantly in public estimation. *Medea* was laid aside ; but Pasta gained fresh applause in every new part she undertook, and especially in *Tancredi* and *Semiramide*.

Pasta made her second appearance at the King's Theatre in 1824, in the character of "Desdemona." Her performance, from a histrionic as well as from a vocal point of view, was most admirable ; and the habitués could scarcely persuade themselves that this was the singer who had come before them four years previously, and had gone away without leaving a regret behind. When Rossini's last Italian opera

was produced, the same season, the character of " Semiramide " was assigned to Madame Pasta, who now
sang it for the first time. She had already represented the part of " Tancredi," and her three great
Rossinian impersonations raised her reputation to the
highest point. In London, Madame Pasta did not
appear as "Medea" until 1826, when she already
enjoyed the greatest celebrity. It was found at the
King's Theatre, as at the Italian Opera of Paris, that
Mayer's simple and frequently insipid music was not
tolerable, after the brilliant dramatic compositions of
Rossini; but Pasta's delineation of "Medea's" thirst
for vengeance and despair, is said to have been sublime.

A story is told of a distinguished critic persuading
himself, that with such a power of pourtraying
"Medea's" emotions, Madame Pasta must possess "Medea's" features; but for some such natural conformity
he seems to have thought it impossible that she could
at once, by intuition, enter profoundly and sympa-
thetically into all " Medea's" inmost feelings. Much
might be said in favour of the critic's theory; it is
unnecessary to say a word in favour of a performance
by which such a theory could be suggested. We are
told, that the believer in the personal resemblance
between Pasta and " Medea " was sent a journey of
seventy miles to see a visionary portrait of " Medea,"
recovered from the ruins of Herculaneum. To rush
off on such a journey with such an object, may not
have been very reasonable; to cause the journey to be

undertaken, was perfectly silly.   Probably, it was a joke of our friend Taylor's.

Madame Pisaroni made her début in Italy in the year 1811, when she was eighteen years of age.   She at first came out as a soprano, but two years afterwards, a severe illness having changed the nature of her voice, she appeared in all the most celebrated parts, written for the musicos or sopranists, who were now beginning to die out, and to be replaced by ladies with contralto voices.   Madame Pisaroni was not only not beautiful, she was hideously ugly; I have seen her portrait, and am not exaggerating.   Lord Mount Edgcumbe tells us, that another favourite contralto of the day Mariani (Rossini's original Arsace) was Pisaroni's rival " in voice, singing, and ugliness ;" adding, that " in the two first qualities, she was certainly her inferior ; though in the last it was difficult to know to which the preference should be given."   But the anti-pathetic, revolting, almost insulting features of the great contralto, were forgotten as soon as she began to sing.   As the hideous Wilkes boasted that he was " only a quarter of an hour behind the handsomest man in Europe," so Madame Pisaroni might have said, that she had only to deliver one phrase of music to place herself on a level with the most personally prepossessing vocalist of the day.   This extraordinary singer on gaining a contralto, did not lose her original soprano voice.   After her illness, she is said to have possessed three octaves (between four C's), but her best notes were now in the contralto register. In airs, in concerted pieces, in recitative, she was equally admirable. To sustain a high note, and then dazzle the audience with a rapid descending scale of two octaves, was for her an easy means of triumph. Altogether, her execution seems never to have been surpassed. After making her début in Paris as "Arsace," Madame Pisaroni resumed that part in 1829, under great difficulties. The frightfully ugly "Arsace" had to appear side by side with a charmingly pretty "Semiramide,"—the soprano part of the opera being taken by Mademoiselle Sontag. But in the hour of danger the poor contralto was saved by her thoroughly beautiful singing, and Pisaroni and Sontag, who as a vocalist also left nothing to desire, were equally applauded. In London, Pisaroni appears to have confined herself intentionally to the representation of male characters, appearing as "Arsace," "Malcolm," in *La Donna del Lago*, and "Tancredi;" but in Paris she played the principal female part in *L'Italiana in Algeri*, and what is more, played it with wonderful success.

The great part of "Arsace" was also that in which Mademoiselle Brambilla made her début in England in the year 1827. Brambilla, who was a pupil of the conservatory of Milan, had never appeared on any stage; but though her acting is said to have been indifferent, her lovely voice, her already excellent style, her youth and her great beauty, ensured her success.

" She has the finest eyes, the sweetest voice, and the best disposition in the world," said a certain cardinal of the youthful Brambilla, " if she is discovered to possess any other merits, the safety of the Catholic Church will require her excommunication." After singing in London several years, and revisiting Italy, Brambilla was engaged in Paris, where she again chose the part of " Arsace," for her début.

Many of our readers will probably remember that " Arsace " was also the character in which Mademoiselle Alboni made her first appearance in England, and on this side of the Alps. Until the opening night of the Royal Italian Opera, 1847, the English public had never heard of Mademoiselle Alboni; but she had only to sing the first phrase of her part, to call forth unanimous applause, and before the evening was at an end, she had quite established herself in the position which she has ever since held.

Sontag and Malibran both made their first appearance in England as " Rosina," in the *Barber of Seville*. Several points of similarity might be pointed out between the romantic careers of these two wonderfully successful and wonderfully unfortunate vocalists. Madeimoselle Garcia first appeared on the stage at Naples, when she was eight years old. Mademoiselle Sontag was in her sixth year when she came out at Frankfort. Each spent her childhood and youth in singing and acting, and each, after obtaining a full measure of success, made an apparently brilliant marriage, and was thought to have quitted the stage. Both, however, re-appeared, one after a very short interval, the other, after a retirement of something like twenty years. The position of Mademoiselle Garcia's husband, M. Malibran, was as nothing, compared to that of Count Rossi, who married Mademoiselle Sontag; the former was a French merchant, established (not very firmly, as it afterwards appeared) at New York; the latter was the Sardinian Ambassador at the court of Vienna; but on the other hand, the Countess Rossi's end was far more tragic, or rather more miserable and horrible than that of Madame Malibran, itself sufficiently painful and heart-rending.

Though Rosina appears to have been one of Mademoiselle Sontag's best, if not absolutely her best part, she also appeared to great advantage during her brief career in London and Paris, in two other Rossinian characters. "Desdemona" and "Semiramide." In her own country she was known as one of the most admirable representatives of " Agatha," in *Der Freischütz*, and she sang " Agatha's " great *scena* frequently, and always with immense success, at concerts, in London. She also appeared as " Donna Anna," in *Don Giovanni*, (from the pleasing, graceful character of her talent, one would have fancied the part of " Zerlina" better suited to her), but in Italian opera all her triumphs were gained in the works of Rossini.

When Marietta Garcia made her début in London, in the *Barber of Seville*, she was, seriously, only just beginning her career, and was at that time but seventeen years of age. She appeared the same year in Paris, as the heroine in *Torvaldo e Dorliska* (Rossini's *"fiaschetto,"* now quite forgotten) and was then taken by her father on that disastrous American tour which ended with her marriage. Having crossed the Atlantic, Garcia converted his family into a complete opera company, of which he himself was the tenor and the excellent musical director (if there had only been a little more to direct). The daughter was the *prima donna*, the mother had to content herself with secondary parts, the son officiated as baritone and bass. In America, under a good master, but with strange subordinates, and a wretched *entourage*, Mademoiselle Garcia accustomed herself to represent operatic characters of every kind. One evening, when an uncultivated American orchestra was massacring Mozart's master-piece, Garcia, the "Don Giovanni" of the evening, became so indignant that he rushed, sword in hand, to the foot lights, and compelled the musicians to re-commence the finale to the first act, which they executed the second time with care, if not with skill. This was a severe school in which poor Marietta was being formed; but without it we should probably never have heard of her appearing one night as "Desdemona" or as "Arsace," the next as "Otello," or as "Semiramide;" nor of her gaining fresh laurels with equal certainty in the *Sonnambula* and in *Norma*. But we have at present only to do with that period of operatic history, during which, Rossini's supremacy on the Italian stage was unquestioned. Towards 1830, we find two new composers appearing, who, if they, to some extent, displaced their great predecessor, at the same time followed in his steps. For some dozen years, Rossini had been the sole support, indeed, the very life of Italian opera. Naturally, his works were not without their fruit, and a great part of Donizetti's and Bellini's music may be said to belong to Rossini, inasmuch as Rossini was clearly Donizetti's and Bellini's progenitor.

CHAPTER XVII.

OPERA IN FRANCE UNDER THE CONSULATE, EMPIRE, AND RESTORATION.

THE History of the Opera, under the Consulate and the Empire, is perhaps more remarkable in connexion with political than with musical events. Few persons at present know much of Spontini's operas, though *la Vestale* in its day was celebrated in Paris, London and especially in Berlin; nor of Cherubini's, though the overtures to *Anacreon* and *les Abencerrages* are still heard from time to time at "classical" concerts; but every one remembers the plot to assassinate the First Consul which was to have been put into execution at the Opera, and the plot to destroy the Emperor, the Empress and all their retinue, which was to take effect just outside its doors. Then there is the appearance of the Emperor at the Opera, after his hasty arrival in Paris from Moscow, on the very night before his return to meet the Russians with the allies who had now joined them, at Bautzen and Lutzen—the same night by the way on which *les Abencerrages* was produced, with no great success. Then again there is the evening of the 29th of March, 1814, when *Iphigénie en Aulide* was performed to an accompaniment of cannon which the Piccinnists, if they could only have heard it, would have declared very appropriate to Gluck's music; that of the 1st of April, when by desire, of the Russian emperor and the Prussian king, *la Vestale* was represented; and finally that of the 17th of May, 1814, when *Œdipe à Colone* was played before Louis XVIII., who had that morning made his triumphal entry into Paris.

On the 10th of October, 1800, a band of republicans had sworn to assassinate the First Consul at the Opera. A new work was to be produced that evening composed by Porta to a libretto founded on Corneille's tragedy of *les Horaces*. The most striking scene in the piece, that in which the Horatii swear to conquer or perish, was to be the signal for action; all the lights were to be put out at the same moment, fireworks and grenades were to be thrown into the boxes, the pit and on to the stage; cries of "fire" and "murder" were to be raised from all parts of the house, and in the midst of the general confusion the First Consul was to be assassinated in his box. The leaders of the plot, to make certain of their cue, had contrived to be present at the rehearsal of the new opera, and everything was prepared for the next evening and the post of each conspirator duly assigned to him; when one of the number, conscience smitten and unable to sleep during the night of the 9th, went at daybreak the next morning to the Prefect of Police and informed him of all the details of the plot.

The conspiracy said Bonaparte, some twenty years afterwards at St. Helena, " was revealed by a captain in the line.* What limit is there," he added, " to the combinations of folly and stupidity ! This officer had a horror of me as Consul but adored me as general. He was anxious that I should be torn from my post, but he would have been very sorry that my life should be taken. I ought to be made prisoner, he said, in no way injured, and sent to the army to continue to defeat the enemies of France. The other conspirators laughed in his face, and when he saw them distribute daggers, and that they were going beyond his intentions, he proceeded at once to denounce the whole affair."

Bonaparte, after the informer had been brought before him, suggested to the officers of his staff, the Prefect of Police and other functionaries whom he had assembled, that it would be as well not to let him appear at the Opera in the evening ; but the general opinion was, that on the contrary, he should be forced to go, and ultimately it was decided that until the commencement of the performance everything should be allowed to take place as if the conspiracy had not been discovered.

In the evening the First Consul went to the Opera, attended by a number of superior officers, all in plain

* Mémorial de Sainte Hélène.

clothes. The first act passed off quietly enough—in all probability, far too quietly to please the composer, for some two hundred persons among the audience, including the conspirators, the police and the officers attached to Bonaparte's person, were thinking of anything but the music of *les Horaces*. It was necessary, however, to pay very particular attention to the music of the second act in which the scene of the oath occurred.

The sentinels outside the Consul's box had received orders to let no one approach who had not the pass word, issued an hour before for the opera only; and as a certain number of conspirators had taken up their positions in the corridors, to extinguish the lights at the signal agreed upon, a certain number of Bonaparte's officers were sent also into the corridors to prevent the execution of this manœuvre. The scene of the oath was approaching, when a body of police went to the boxes in which the leaders of the plot were assembled, found them with fireworks and grenades in their hands, notified to them their arrest in the politest manner, cautioned them against creating the slightest disturbance, and led them so dexterously and quietly into captivity, that their disappearance from the theatre was not observed, or if so, was doubtless attributed to the badness of Porta's music. The officers in the corridors carried pistols, and at the proper moment seized the appointed lamp-extinguishers. Then the old Horatius came forward and exclaimed—

" Jurez donc devant moi, par le ciel qui m'écoute.
Que le dernier de vous sera mort où vainqueur."

The orchestra " attacked " the introduction to the
quartett.   The fatal prelude must have sounded somewhat unmusical to the ear of the First Consul ; but
the conspirators were now all in custody and assembled
in one of the vestibules on the ground floor.

On the 24th of December, 1800, the day on which
the " infernal machine " was directed against the
First Consul on his way to the Opera, a French version of Haydn's *Creation* was to be executed.   Indeed,
the performance had already commenced, when, during
the gentle *adagio* of the introduction, the dull report
of an explosion, as if of a cannon, was heard, but without the audience being at all alarmed.   Immediately
afterwards the First Consul appeared in his box with
Lannes, Lauriston, Berthier, and Duroc.   Madame
Bonaparte, as she was getting into her carriage, thought
of some alteration to make in her dress, and returned
to her apartments for a few minutes.   But for this
delay her carriage would have passed before the infernal
machine at the moment of its explosion.   Ten minutes
afterwards she made her appearance at the Opera
with her daughter, Mademoiselle Hortense Beau-
harnais, Madame Murat, and Colonel Rapp.   The
performance of the *Creation* continued as if nothing
had happened ; and the report, which had interfered
so unexpectedly with the effect of the opening *adagio*,

was explained in various ways; the account generally received in the pit being, that a grocer going into his cellar with a candle, had set light to a barrel of gunpowder. Two houses were said to have been blown up. This was at the beginning of the first part of the *Creation*; at the end of the second, the number had probably increased to half a dozen.

Under the consulate and the empire, the arts did not flourish greatly in France; not for want of direct encouragement on the part of the ruler, but rather because he at the same time encouraged far above everything else the art of war. Until the appearance of Spontini with *la Vestale,* the Académie, under Napoleon Bonaparte, whether known as Bonaparte or Napoleon, was chiefly supported by composers who composed without inventing, and who, with the exception of Cherubini, were either very feeble originators or mere plagiarists and spoliators. Even Mozart did not escape the French arrangers. His *Marriage of Figaro* had been brought out in 1793, with all the prose dialogue of Beaumarchais's comedy substituted for the recitative of the original opera. *Les Mystères d'Isis*, an adaptation, perversion, disarrangement of *Die Zauberflötte,* with several pieces suppressed, or replaced by fragments from the *Nozze di Figaro, Don Giovanni,* and Haydn's symphonies, was produced on the 23rd of August, 1801, under the auspices of Morel the librettist, and Lachnith the musician.

Les Misères *d'Isis* was the appropriate name given

to this sad medley by the musicians of the orchestra.
Lachnith was far from being ashamed of what he
had done.   On the contrary, he gloried in it, and
seemed somehow or other to have persuaded himself
that the pieces which he had stolen from Mozart and
Hadyn were his own compositions.   One evening,
when he was present at the representation of *Les
Mystères d'Isis*, he was affected to tears, and exclaimed, " No, I will compose no more !   I could
never go beyond this !"

Don Giovanni, in the hands of Kalkbrenner, fared
no better than the *Zauberflötte* in those of Lachnith.
It even fared worse ; for Kalkbrenner did not content
himself with spoiling the general effect of the work,
by means of pieces introduced from Mozart's other
operas, and from Haydn's symphonies : he mutilated
it so as completely to alter its form, and further de-
based it by mixing with its pure gold the dross of his
own vile music.

In Kalkbrenner's *Don Giovanni*, the opera opened
with a recitative, composed by Kalkbrenner himself.
Next came Leporello's solo, followed by an interpolated romance, in the form of a serenade, which was
sung by Don Juan, under Donna Anna's window.
The struggle of Don Juan with Donna Anna, the
entry of the commandant, his combat with Don
Juan, the trio for the three men and all the rest of
the introduction, was cut out. The duet of Donna Anna
and Ottavio was placed at the end of the act, and as
Don Juan had killed the commandant off the stage,

it was of course deprived of its marvellous recitative, which, to be duly effective, must be declaimed by Donna Anna over the body of her father. The whole of the opera was treated in the same style. The first act was made to end as it had begun, with a few phrases of recitative of Kalkbrenner's own production. The greater part of the action of Da Ponte's libretto was related in dialogue, so that the most dramatic portion of the music lost all its significance. The whole opera, in short, was disfigured, cut to pieces, destroyed, and further defiled by the musical weeds which the infamous Kalkbrenner introduced among its still majestic ruins. At this period the supreme direction of the Opera was in the hands of a jury, composed of certain members of the Institute of France. It seems never to have occurred to this learned body that there was any impropriety in the trio of masques being executed by three men, and in the two soprano parts being given to tenors,—by which arrangement the part of Ottavio, Mozart's tenor, instead of being the lowest in the harmony, was made the highest. The said trio was sung by three archers, of course to entirely new words! Let us pass on to another opera, which, if not comparable to *Don Giovanni*, was at least a magnificent work for France in 1807, and which had the advantage of being admirably executed under the careful direction of its composer.

Spontini had already produced *La Finta Filosofa*,

which, originally brought out at Naples, was afterwards performed at the Italian Theatre of Paris,
without success; *La Petite Maison*, written for the
Opéra Comique, and violently hissed; and *Milton*
also composed for the Opéra Comique, and favourably received.   When *La Vestale* was submitted to
the jury of the Académie, it was refused unani-
mously on the ground of the extravagance of its
style, and of the audacity of certain innovations in
the score.   Spontini appealed to the Empress Jose-
phine, and it was owing to her influence, and through
a direct order of the court that *La Vestale* was put
upon the stage.   The jury was inexorable, however,
as regarded certain portions of the work, and the
composer was obliged to submit it to the orchestral
conductor, who injured it in several places, but without spoiling it.   Spontini wished to give the part of
the tenor to Nourrit; but Lainez protested, went to
the superintendant of the imperial theatres, represented that he had been first tenor and first lover at
the Opera for thirty years, and finally received full permission to make love to the Vestal of the Académie.

The Emperor Napoleon had the principal pieces in
La Vestale executed by his private band, nearly a
year before the opera was brought out at the Académie.   He had sufficient taste to admire the music,
and predicted to Spontini the success it afterwards
met with.   He is said, in particular, to have praised
the finale, the first dramatic finale written for the
French Opera.

La Vestale was received by the public with enthusiasm.   It is said to have been admirably executed,
and we know that Spontini was difficult on this point,
for we are told by Mr. Ebers that he objected to the
performance of *La Vestale*, in London, on the ground
" that the means of representation there were inade-
quate to do justice to his composition."   This was
twenty years after it was first brought out in Paris,
when all Rossini's finest and most elaborately constructed operas (such as *Semiramide*, for instance),
had been played in London, and in a manner which
quite satisfied Rossini.   Probably. however, it was in
the spectacular department that Spontini expected
the King's Theatre would break down.   However
that may have been, *La Vestale* was produced in
London, and met with very little success.   The part
of " La Vestale " was given to a Madame Biagioli,
who objected to it as not sufficiently good for her.
From the accounts extant of this lady's powers, it is
quite certain that Spontini, if he had heard her,
would have considered her not nearly good enough
for his music.   It would, of course, have been far
better for the composer, as for the manager and the
public, if Spontini had consented to superintend the
production of his work himself; but failing that, it
was scandalous in defiance of his wishes to produce it
at all.   Unfortunately, this is a kind of scandal from
which operatic managers in England have seldom
shrunk.

Spontini's *Fernand Cortez*, produced at the Académie in 1809, met with less success than *La Vestale*. In both these works, the spectacular element played an important part, and in *Fernand Cortez*, it was found necessary to introduce a number of Franconi's horses. A journalist of the period proposed that the following inscription should be placed above the doors of the theatre :—*Içi on joue l'opéra à pied et à cheval.*

Spontini, as special composer for the Académie of grand operas with hippic and panoramic effects, was the predecessor of M. M. Meyerbeer, and Halévy; and Heine, in his " Lutèce " * has given us a very witty, and perhaps, in the main, truthful account of Spontini's animosity towards Meyerbeer, whom he is said to have always regarded as an intriguer and interloper. I may here, however, mention as a proof of the attractiveness of *La Vestale* from a purely musical point of view, that it was once represented with great success, not only without magnificent or appropriate scenery, but with the scenery belonging to another piece ! This was on the 1st of April, 1814, the day after the entry of the Russian and Prussian troops into Paris. *Le Triomphe de Trajan* had been announced ; the allied sovereigns, however, wished to hear *La Vestale,* and the performance was changed. But there was not time to prepare the scenery for Spontini's opera, and that of the said *Triomphe* was made to do duty for it.

* " Lutèce " par Henri Heine (a French version, by Heine himself, of his letters from Paris to the *Allgemeine Zeitung*).

Le Triomphe de Trajan was a work in which Napoleon's clemency to a treacherous or patriotic German prince was celebrated, and it has been said that the programme of the 1st of April was changed, because the allied sovereigns disliked the subject of the opera. But it was perfectly natural that they should wish to hear Spontini's master-piece, and that they should not particularly care to listen to a *pièce d'occasion*, set to music by a French composer of no name.

I have said that Cherubini's *Abencerrages*, of which all but the overture is now forgotten, was produced in 1813, and that the emperor attended its first representation the night before his departure from Paris, to rejoin his troops, and if possible, check the advance of the victorious allies. No other work of importance was produced at the French Académie until Rossini's *Siège de Corinthe* was brought out in 1825. This, the first work written by the great Italian master specially for the French Opera, was represented at the existing theatre in the Rue Lepelletier, the opera house in the Rue Richelieu having been pulled down in 1820.

In the year just mentioned, on the 13th of February, being the last Sunday of the Carnival, an unusually brilliant audience had assembled at the Académie Royale. *Le Rossignol*, an insipid, and fortunately, very brief production, was the opera ; but the great attraction of the evening consisted in two ballets, *La Carnaval de Venise*, and *Les Noces de Gamache.* The Duke and Duchess de Berri were present, and when *Le Carnaval de Venise, Le Rossignol,* and the first act of *Les Noces de Gamache,* had been performed, the duchess rose to leave the theatre. Her husband accompanied her to the carriage, and was taking leave of her, intending to return to the theatre for the last act of the ballet, when a man crept up to him, placed his left arm on the duke's left side, pulled him violently towards him, and as he held him in his grasp, thrust a dagger through his body. The dagger entered the duke's right side, and the pressure of the assassin's arm, and the force with which the blow was given, were so great, that the weapon went through the lungs, and pierced the heart, a blade of six inches inflicting a wound nine inches long. The news of the duke's assassination spread through the streets of Paris as if by electricity ; and M. Alexandre Dumas, in his interesting Memoirs, tells us almost the same thing that Balzac says about it in one of his novels ; that it was known at the farther end of Paris, before a man on horseback, despatched at the moment the blow was struck, could possibly have reached the spot. On the other hand, M. Castil Blaze shows us very plainly that the terrible occurrence was not known within the Opera ; or, at least, only to a few officials, until after the conclusion of the performance, which went on as if nothing had happened. The duke was carried into the director's room, where he was attended by Blancheton, the surgeon of the Opera, and at once bled in both arms. He, himself, drew the dagger from the wound, and observed at the same time that he felt it was mortal. The Count d'Artois, and the Duke and Duchess d'Angoulême arrived soon afterwards. There lay the unhappy prince, on a bed hastily arranged, and already inundated, soaked with blood, surrounded by his father, brother, sister, and wife, whose poignant anguish was from time to time alleviated by some faint ray of hope, destined, however, to be quickly dispelled.

Five of the most celebrated doctors in Paris, with Dupuytren among the number, had been sent for; and as the patient was now nearly suffocating from internal hæmorrhage, the orifice of the wound was widened. This afforded some relief, and for a moment it was thought just possible that a recovery might be effected. Another moment, and it was evident that there was no hope. The duke asked to see his daughter, and embraced her several times; he also expressed a desire to see the king. Now the sacrament was administered to him, but, on the express condition exacted by the Archbishop of Paris, that the Opera House should afterwards be destroyed. Two other unacknowledged daughters of his youth were brought to the dying man's bedside, and received his blessing. He had already recommended them to the duchess's care.

"Soon you will have no father," she said to them, "and I shall have three daughters."

In the meanwhile the Spanish ballet was being continued, amidst the mirth and applause of the audience, who testified by their demeanour that it was Carnival time, and that the *jours gras* had already commenced. The house was crowded, and the boleros and sequidillas with which the Spaniards of the Parisian ballet astonished and dazzled Don Quixote and his faithful knight, threw boxes, pit, and gallery, into ecstasies of delight.

Elsewhere, in the room next his victim, stood the assassin, interrogated by the ministers, Decazes and Pasquier, with the bloody dagger before them on the table. The murderer simply declared that he had no accomplices,* and that he took all the responsibility of the crime on himself.

At five in the morning, Louis XVIII. was by the side of his dying nephew. An attempt had been made, the making of which was little less than an insult to the king, to dissuade him from being present at the duke's last moments.

" The sight of death does not terrify me," replied His Majesty, " and I have a duty to perform." After begging that his murderer might be forgiven, and entreating the duchess not to give way to despair,

---

* He persisted in this declaration, in spite of his judges, who were not ashamed to resort to torture, in the hope of extracting a full confession from him. The thumb-screw and the rack were not, it is true, employed ; but sentinels were stationed in the wretched man's cell, with orders not to allow him a moment's sleep, until he confessed.

the Duke de Berri breathed his last in the arms of the king, who closed his eyes at half-past six in the morning.

Opera was now to be heard no more in the Rue Riche-lieu. The holy sacrament had crossed the threshold of a profane building, and it was necessary that this profane building should be destroyed; indeed, a promise to that effect had been already given. All the theatres were closed for ten days, and the Opera, now homeless, did not re-commence its performances until upwards of two months afterwards, when it took possession for a time of the Théâtre Favart. In the August of the same year the erection of the theatre in the Rue Lepelletier was commenced. The present Théâtre d l'Opéra, (the absurd title of Académie having recently been abandoned), was intended when it was first built, to be but a temporary affair. Strangely enough it has lasted forty years, during which time it has seen solidly constructed opera-houses perish by fire in all parts of Europe. May the new opera-house about to be erected in Paris, under the auspices of Napoleon III., be equally fortunate.

I am here reminded that both the Napoleons have proved themselves good and intelligent friends to the Opera. In the year eleven of the French republic, the First Consul and his two associates, the Minister of the French republic, the three Consuls, the Ministers of the interior and police, General Junot, the Secretary of State, and a few more officials occupied among them as many as seventeen boxes at the opera, containing altogether ninety-four places.   Bonaparte had a report drawn up from which it appeared that the value of these boxes to the administration, was sixty thousand four hundred francs per annum, including fifteen thousand francs for those kept at his own disposition.   Thereupon he added to the report the following brief, but on the whole satisfactory remark.

" A datter du premier nivose toutes ces loges seront payées par ceux qui les occupent."

The error in orthography is not the printers', but Napoleon Bonaparte's, and the document in which it occurs, is at present in the hands of M. Regnier of the Comédie Française.

A month afterwards, Napoleon, or at least the consular trio of which he was the chief, assigned to the Opera a regular subsidy of 600,000 francs a year; he at the same time gave it a respectable name. Under the Convention it had been entitled " Théâtre de la République et des Arts ;" the First Consul called it simply, " Théâtre des Arts," an appellation it had borne before.*

Hardly had the new theatre in the Rue Lepelletier

* The Académie Royale became the Opéra National ; the Opéra National, after its establishment in the abode of the former Théâtre National, became the Théâtre des Arts ; and the Théâtre des Arts, the Théâtre de la République et des Arts.   Napoleon's Théâtre des Arts became soon afterwards the Académie Impériale, the Académie Impériale the Académie Royale, the Académie Royale the Académie Nationale, the Académie Nationale once more the Académie Impériale, and the Académie Impériale simply the Théâtre de l'Opera, by far the best title that could be given to it.

opened its doors, when a singer of the highest class, a tenor of the most perfect kind, made his appearance. This was Adolphe Nourrit, a pupil of Garcia, who, on the 10th of September, 1821, made his first appearance with the greatest success as "Pylade" in *Iphigénie en Tauride*. It was not, however, until Auber's *Muette de Portici* was produced in 1828, that Nourrit had an opportunity of distinguishing himself in a new and important part.

La Muette was the first of those important works to which the French Opera owes its actual celebrity in Europe. *Le Siège de Corinthe*, translated and adapted from *Maometto II.*, with additions (including the admirable blessing of the flags) written specially for the Académie, had been brought out eighteen months before, but without much success. *Maometto II.* was not one of Rossini's best works, the drama on which it was constructed was essentially feeble and uninteresting, and the manner in which the whole was "arranged" for the French stage, was unsatisfactory in many respects. *Le Siège de Corinthe* was greatly applauded the first night, but it soon ceased to have any attraction for the public. Rossini had previously written *Il Viaggio a Reims* for the coronation of Charles X., and this work was re-produced at the Academy three years afterwards, with several important additions (such as the duet for "Isolier" and the "Count," the chorus of women, the unaccompanied quartett, the highly effective drinking chorus, and the beautiful trio of the last act), under the title of *le Comte Ory*. In the meanwhile *La Muette* had been brought out, to be followed the year afterwards by *Guillaume Tell*, which was to be succeeded in its turn by Meyerbeer's *Robert le Diable*, *Les Huguenots* and *Le Prophète*, (works which belong specially to the Académie and with which its modern reputation is intimately associated), by Auber's *Gustave III.*, Donizetti's *la Favorite*, &c.

La Muette di Portici had the great advantage of enabling the Académie to display all its resources at once. It was brought out with magnificent scenery and an excellent *corps de ballet*, with a *première danseuse*, Mademoiselle Noblet as the heroine, with the new tenor, Nourrit, in the important part of the hero, and with a well taught chorus capable of sustaining with due effect the prominent *rôle* assigned to it. For in the year 1828 it was quite a novelty at the French Opera to see the chorus taking part in the general action of the drama.

If we compare *La Muette* with the "Grand Operas" produced subsequently at the Académie, we find that it differs from them all in some important respects. In the former, instead of a *prima donna* we have a *prima ballerina* in the principal female part. Of course the concerted pieces suffer by this, or rather the number of concerted pieces is diminished, and to the same cause may, perhaps, be attributed the absence of finales in *La Muette*. It chiefly owed its success (which is still renewed from time to time whenever it is re-produced) to the intrinsic beauty of its melodies and to the dramatic situations provided by the ingenious librettist, M. Scribe, and admirably taken advantage of by the composer. But the part of Fenella had also great attractions for those unmusical persons who are found in almost every audience in England and France, and for whom the chief interest in every opera consists in the skeleton-drama on which it is founded. To them the graceful Fenella with her expressive pantomime is no bad substitute for a singer whose words would be unintelligible to them, and whose singing, continued throughout the Opera, would perhaps fatigue their dull ears. These ballet-operas seem to have been very popular in France about the period when *La Muette* was produced, the other most celebrated example of the style being Auber's *Le Dieu et la Bayadère*. In the present day it would be considered that a *prima ballerina*, introduced as a principal character in an opera, would interfere too much with the combinations of the singing personages.

I need say nothing about the charming music of *La Muette*, which is well known to every frequenter of the Opera, further than to mention, that the melody of the celebrated barcarole and chorus, "*Amis, amis le soleil va paraitre*" had already been heard in a work of Auber's, called *Emma;* and that the brilliant overture had previously served as an instrumental preface to *Le Maçon*.

La Muette de Portici was translated and played with great success in England. But shameful liberties were taken with the piece; recitatives were omitted, songs were interpolated: and it was not until *Masa- niello* was produced at the Royal Italian Opera that the English public had an opportunity of hearing Auber's great work without suppressions or addi- tions.

The greatest opera ever written for the Académie, and one of the three or four greatest operas ever pro- duced, was now about to be brought out. *Guillaume Tell* was represented for the first time on the 3rd of August, 1829. It was not unsuccessful, or even coldly received the first night, as has often been stated; but the result of the first few representations was on the whole unsatisfactory. Musicians and connoisseurs were struck by the great beauties of the work from the very beginning; but some years passed before it was fully appreciated by the general public. The success of the music was certainly not assisted by the libretto—one of the most tedious and insipid ever put together; and it was not until Rossini's masterpiece had been cut down from five to three acts, that the Parisians, as a body, took any great interest in it.

Guillaume Tell is now played everywhere in the three act form. Some years ago a German doctor, who had paid four francs to hear *Der Freischütz* at the French Opera, proceeded against the directors for the recovery of his money, on the plea that it had been obtained from him on false pretences, the work advertised as *Der Freischütz* not being precisely the

Der Freischütz * which Karl Maria von Weber composed. The doctor might amuse himself (the authorities permitting) by bringing an action against the managers of the Berlin theatre every time they produce Rossini's *Guillaume Tell*—which is often enough, and always in three acts.

The original cast of *Guillaume Tell* included Nourrit, Levasseur, Dabadie, A. Dupont, Massol, and Madame Cinti-Damoreau. The singers and musicians of the Opera were enthusiastic in their admiration of the new work, and the morning after its production assembled on the terrace of the house where Rossini lived and performed a selection from it in his honour. One distinguished artist who took no part in this ceremony had, nevertheless, contributed in no small degree to the success of the opera. This was Mademoiselle Taglioni, whose *tyrolienne* danced to the music of the charming unaccompanied chorus, was of course understood and applauded by every one from the very first.

After the first run of *Guillaume Tell*, the Opera returned to *La Muette de Portici*, and then for a time Auber's and Rossini's masterpieces were played alternate nights. On Wednesday, July 3rd, 1830, *La Muette de Portici* was performed, and with a certain political appropriateness;—for the " days of

---

* I was in Paris at the time, but, I forget the specific objections urged by the doctor against the *Freischütz* set before him at the " Académie Nationale," as the theatre was then called. Doubtless, however, he did not, among other changes, approve of added recitatives.

July" were now at hand, and the insurrectionary spirit had already manifested itself in the streets of Paris.   The fortunes of *La Muette de Portici* have been affected in various ways by the revolutionary character of the plot.   Even in London it was more than once made a pretext for a " demonstration " by the radicals of William the Fourth's time.   At most of the Italian theatres it has been either forbidden altogether or has had to be altered considerably before the authorities would allow it to be played.   Strange as it may appear, in absolute Russia it has been represented times out of number in its original shape, under the title of *Fenella*.

We have seen that *Masaniello* was represented in Paris four days before the commencement of the outbreak which ended in the elder branch of the Bourbons being driven from the throne.   On the 26th of July, *Guillaume Tell* was to have been represented, but the city was in such a state of agitation, in consequence of the issue of the *ordonnances,* signed at St. Cloud the day before, that the Opera was closed. On the 27th the fighting began and lasted until the 29th, when the Opera was re-opened. · On the 4th of August, *La Muette de Portici* was performed, and created the greatest enthusiasm,—the public finding in almost every scene some reminder, and now and then a tolerably exact representation, of what had just taken place within a stone's throw of the theatre. *La Muette*, apart from its music, became now the great piece of the day; and the representations at the Opera were rendered still more popular by Nourrit singing *"La Parisienne"* every evening. The melody of this temporary national song, like that of its predecessor (so infinitely superior to it), *"La Marseillaise"* (according to Castil Blaze), was borrowed from Germany. France, never wanting in national spirit, has yet no national air. It has four party songs, not one of which can be considered truly patriotic, and of which the only one that possesses any musical merit, disfigured as it has been by its French adapters, is of German origin.

Nourrit is said to have delivered *" La Parisienne "* with wonderful vigour and animation, and to this and to Casimir Delavigne's verses (or rather to Delavigne's name, for the verses in themselves are not very remarkable) may be attributed the reputation which the French national song, No. 4,* for some time enjoyed.

Guillaume Tell is Rossini's last opera. To surpass that admirable work would have been difficult for its own composer, impossible for any one else; and Rossini appears to have resolved to terminate his artistic career when it had reached its climax. In carrying out this resolution, he has displayed a strength of character, of which it is almost impossible to find another instance. Many other reasons

---

* No. 1.—*Vive Henri IV.* No. 2.—*La Marseillaise.* No. 3.—*Partant pour la Syrie.* No. 4.—*La Parisienne.* No. 5.—*Partant pour la Syrie* (encored). No. 6.—?

have been given for Rossini's abstaining from composition during so many years, such as the coldness
with which *Guillaume Tell* was received (when, as we
have seen, its *immediate* reception by those whose
opinion Rossini would chiefly have valued, was
marked by the greatest enthusiasm), and the success
of Meyerbeer's operas, though who would think of
placing the most successful of Meyerbeer's works on
a level with *Guillaume Tell?*

" *Je reviendrai quand les juifs auront fini leur
sabbat,*" is a speech (somewhat uncharacteristic of the
speaker, as it seems to me), attributed to Rossini by
M. Castil Blaze ; who, however, also mentions, that
when *Robert le Diable* was produced, every journal
in Paris said that it was the finest opera, *except
Guillaume Tell*, that had been produced at the Académie for years.   It appears certain, now, that Rossini simply made up his mind to abdicate at the height
of his power.   There were plenty of composers who
could write works inferior to *Guillaume Tell*, and to
them he left the kingdom of opera, to be divided as
they might arrange it among themselves.   He was
succeeded by Meyerbeer at the Académie ; by Donizetti and Bellini at the Italian opera-houses of all
Europe.

Rossini had already found a follower, and, so to
speak, an original imitator, in Auber, whose eminently
Rossinian overture to *La Muette*, was heard at the
Académie the year before *Guillaume Tell*.

I need scarcely remind the intelligent reader, that the composer of three master-pieces in such very different styles as *Il Barbiere*, *Semiramide*, and *Guillaume Tell*, might have a dozen followers, whose works, while all resembling in certain points those of their predecessor and master, should yet bear no great general resemblance to one another. All the composers who came immediately after Rossini, accepted, as a matter of course, those important changes which he had introduced in the treatment of the operatic drama, and to which he had now so accustomed the public, that a return to the style of the old Italian masters, would have been not merely injudicious, but intolerable. Thus, all the post-Rossinian composers adopted Rossini's manner of accompanying recitative with the full band; his substitution of dialogued pieces, written in measured music, with a prominent connecting part assigned to the orchestra, for the interminable dialogues in simple recitative, employed by the earlier Italian composers; his mode of constructing finales; and his new distribution of characters, by which basses and baritones become as eligible for first parts as tenors, while great importance is given to the chorus, which, in certain operas, according to the nature of the plot, becomes an important dramatic agent. I may repeat, by way of memorandum, what has before been observed, that nearly all these forms originated with Mozart, though it was reserved for Rossini to introduce and establish them on the Italian stage. In short, with the exception of the very greatest masters of Germany, all the composers of the last thirty or forty years, have been to some, and often to a very great extent, influenced by Rossini. The general truth of this remark is not lessened by the fact, that Hérold and Auber, and even Donizetti and Bellini (the last. especially, in the simplicity of his melodies), afterwards found distinctive styles; and that Meyerbeer, after *Il Crociato*, took Weber, rather than Rossini, for his model—the composer of *Robert* at the same time exhibiting a strongly marked individuality, which none of his adverse critics think of denying, and which is partly, no doubt, the cause of their adverse criticism.

What will make it appear to some persons still more astonishing, that Rossini should have retired after producing *Guillaume Tell* is, that he had signed an agreement with the Académie, by which he engaged to write three grand operas for it in six years. In addition to his " author's rights," he was to receive ten thousand francs annually until the expiration of the sixth year, and the completion of the third opera. No. 1 was *Guillaume Tell*. The librettos of Nos. 2 and 3 were *Gustave* and *Le Duc d'Albe*, both of which were returned by Rossini to M. Scribe, perhaps, with an explanation, but with none that has ever been made public. Rossini was at this time thirty-seven years of age, strong and vigorous enough to have outlived, not only his earliest, but his latest compositions, had

they not been the most remarkable dramatic works
of this century. If Rossini had been a composer who produced with difficulty, his retirement
would have been more easy to explain; but the difficulty with him must have been to avoid producing.
The story is probably known to many readers of his
writing a duet one morning, in bed, letting the music
paper fall, and, rather than leave his warm sheets to
pick it up, writing another duet, which was quite
different from the first. A hundred similar anecdotes are told of the facility with which Rossini
composed. Who knows but that he wished his
career to be measured against those of so many other
composers whose days were cut short, at about the
age he had reached when he produced *Guillaume
Tell?* A very improbable supposition, certainly,
when we consider how little mysticism there is in
the character of Rossini. However this may be, he
ceased to write operas at about the age when many
of his immediate predecessors and followers ceased to
live.*

And even Rossini had a narrow escape. About
the critical period, when the composer of *Guillaume
Tell* was a little more than half way between thirty
and forty, the Italian Theatre of Paris was burnt to
the ground. This, at first sight, appears to have
nothing to do with the question; but Rossini lived
in the theatre, and his apartments were near the roof.

* Mozart, Cimarosa, Weber, Hérold, Bellini, and Mendelssohn.

He had started for Italy two days previously; had he remained in Paris, he certainly would have shared the fate of the other inmates who perished in the flames.

Meyerbeer is a composer who defies classification, or who, at least, may be classified in three different ways. As the author of the *Crociato*, he belongs to Italy, and the school of Rossini; *Robert le Diable* exhibits him as a composer chiefly of the German school, with a tendency to follow in the steps of Weber; but *Robert, les Huguenots, le Prophète, l'Etoile du Nord*, and, above all *Dinorah*, are also characteristic of the composer himself. The committee of the London International Exhibition has justly decided that Meyerbeer is a German composer, and there is no doubt about his having been born in Germany, and educated for some time under the same professor as Karl Maria Von Weber; but it is equally certain that he wrote those works to which he owes his great celebrity for the Académie Royale of Paris, and as we are just now dealing with the history of the French Opera, this, I think, is the proper place in which to introduce the most illustrious of living and working composers.

"The composer of *Il Crociato in Egitto,* an amateur, is a native of Berlin, where his father, a Jew, who is since dead, was a banker of great riches. The father's name was Beer, Meyer being merely a Jewish prefix, which the son thought fit to incorporate with his surname. He was a companion of Weber, in his musical studies. He had produced other operas which had been well received, but none of them was followed by or merited the success that attended *Il Crociato*." So far Mr. Ebers, who, in a few words, tells us a great deal of Meyerbeer's early career. The said *Crociato*, written for Venice, in 1824, was afterwards produced at the Italian Opera of Paris in 1825, six years before *Robert le Diable* was brought out at the Académie. In the summer of 1825, a few months before its production in Paris, it was modified in London, and Mr. Ebers informs us that the getting up of the opera, to which nine months were devoted at the Théâtre Italien, occupied at the King's Theatre only one. Such rapid feats are familiar enough to our operatic managers and musical conductors. But it must be remembered that a first performance in England is very often less perfect than a dress rehearsal in France ; and, moreover, that between bringing out an original work (or an old work, in an original style), in Paris, and bringing out the same work afterwards, more or less conformably to the Parisian* model, in London, there is the same difference as between composing a picture and merely copying one. No singers and musicians read better than those of the French Académie, and it is a terrible mistake to suppose that so much time is required at that theatre for the production of a grand opera on account of any difficulty in making the *artistes* acquainted with

---

* In the case of *Il Crociato*, however. the model was an Italian one.

their parts.   *Guillaume Tell* was many months in rehearsal, but the orchestra played the overture at first
sight in a manner which astonished and delighted
Rossini.   The great, and I may add, the inevitable
fault of our system of management in England is that
it is impossible to procure for a new opera a sufficient
number of rehearsals before it is publicly produced.
It is surprising how few "repetitions" suffice, but
they would *not* suffice if the same perfection was
thought necessary on the first night which is obtained
at the Paris and Berlin Operas, and which, in London,
in the case of very difficult, elaborate works, is not
reached until after several representations.

However, *Il Crociato* was brought out in London
after a month's rehearsal.   The manager left the
musical direction almost entirely in the hands of
Velluti, who had already superintended its production at Venice, and Florence, and who was engaged, as a matter of course, for the principal part
written specially for him.   The opera (of which the
cast included, besides Velluti, Mademoiselle Garcia,
Madame Caradori and Crivelli the tenor) was very
successful, and was performed ten nights without in-
termission when the "run" was brought to a ter-
mination by the closing of the theatre.   The following
account of the music by Lord Mount Edgcumbe,
shows the sort of impression it made upon the old
amateurs of the period.

It was "quite of the new school, but not copied
from its founder, Rossini; original, odd, flighty, and

it might even be termed *fantastic,* but at times beautiful; here and there most delightful melodies and harmonies occurred, but it was unequal, solos were as rare as in all the modern operas, but the numerous concerted pieces much shorter and far less noisy than Rossini's, consisting chiefly of duets and terzettos, with but few choruses and no overwhelming accompaniments. Indeed, Meyerbeer has rather gone into the contrary extreme, the instrumental parts being frequently so slight as to be almost meagre, while he has sought to produce new and striking effects from the voices alone."

Before speaking of Meyerbeer's better known and more celebrated works, I must say a few words about Velluti, a singer of great powers, but of a peculiar kind (*"non vir sed Veluti"*) who, as I have said before, played the principal part in *Il Crociato.* He was the last of his tribe, and living at a time when too much license was allowed to singers in the execution of the music entrusted to them, so disgusted Rossini by his extravagant style of ornamentation, that the composer resolved to write his airs in future in such elaborate detail, that to embellish them would be beyond the power of any singer. Be this how it may, Rossini did not like Velluti's singing, nor Velluti Rossini's music—which sufficiently proves that the last of the sopranists was not a musician of taste.* Mr. Ebers tells us that " after making the

---

* Rossini's natural inability to sympathize with sopranists is one more great point in his favour.

tour of the principal Italian and German theatres, Velluti arrived in Paris, where the musical taste was not prepared for him," and that, " Rossini being at this time engaged at Paris under his agreement to direct there, Velluti did not enter into his plans, and having made no engagement there, came over to England without any invitation, but strongly recommended by Lord Burghersh." The re-appearance of a musico in London when the race was thought to be extinct, caused a great sensation, and not altogether of an agreeable kind. However, the Opera was crowded the night of his *début;* to the old amateurs it recalled the days of Pacchierotti, to the young ones, it was simply a strange and unexpected novelty. Some are said to have come to the theatre expressly to oppose him, while others were there for the avowed purpose of supporting him, from a feeling that public opinion had dealt harshly with the unfortunate man. Velluti had already sung at concerts, where his reception was by no means favourable. Indeed, Lord Mount Edgcumbe tells us " that the scurrilous abuse lavished upon him before he was heard, was cruel and illiberal," and that " it was not till after long deliberation, much persuasion, and assurances of support that the manager ventured to engage him for the remainder of the season."

Velluti's demeanour on entering the stage was highly prepossessing. Mr. Ebers says that " it was at once graceful and dignified," and that " he was in look and action the son of chivalry he represented."

He adds, that " his appearance was received with mingled applause and disapprobation ; but that " the scanty symptoms of the latter were instantly over- whelmed." The effect produced on the audience by the first notes Velluti uttered was most peculiar. According to Mr. Ebers, " there was a something of a preternatural harshness about them, which jarred even more strongly on the imagination than on the ear ;" though, as he proceeded, " the sweetness and flexibility of those of his tones which yet remained unimpaired by time, were fully perceived and felt." Lord Mount Edgcumbe informs us, that " the first note he uttered gave a shock of surprise, almost of disgust, to inexperienced ears ;" though, afterwards, " his performance was listened to with great atten- tion and applause throughout, with but few *audible* expressions of disapprobation speedily suppressed." The general effect of his performance is summed up in the following words :—" To the old he brought back some pleasing recollections ; others, to whom his voice was new, became reconciled to it, and sen- sible of his merits ; whilst many declared, to the last, his tones gave them more pain than pleasure." However, he drew crowded audiences, and no opera but Meyerbeer's *Crociato* was performed until the end of the season.

Some years after the production of *Il Crociato*, Meyerbeer had written an *opéra comique*, entitled *Robert le Diable*, which was to have been represented at the Ventadour Theatre, specially devoted to that kind of performance. The company, however, at the "Théâtre de l'Opera Comique," was not found competent to execute the difficult music of *Robert*, and the interesting libretto by M. M. Scribe and Delavigne, was altered and reduced, so as to suit the Académie. The celebrated "pruning knife" was brought out, and vigorously applied. What remained of the dialogue was adapted for recitative, and the character of "Raimbaud" was cut out in the fourth and fifth acts. With all these suppressions, the opera, as newly arranged, to be recited or sung from beginning to end, was still very long, and not particularly intelligible. However, the legend on which *Robert le Diable* is founded is well suited for musical illustration, and the plot, with a little attention and a careful study of the book, may be understood, in spite of the absence of "Raimbaud," who, in the original piece, is said to have served materially to aid and explain the progress of the drama.

If *Robert le Diable* had been produced at the Opéra Comique, in the form in which it was originally conceived, the many points of resemblance it presents to *Der Freischütz* would have struck every one. Meyerbeer seems to have determined to write a romantic semi-fantastic legendary opera, like *Der Freischütz*, and, in doing so, naturally followed in the footsteps of Weber. He certainly treats these legendary subjects with particular felicity, and I fancy there is more spontaneity in the music of

Robert le Diable, and *Dinorah,* than in any other that he has composed; but this does not alter the fact that such subjects were first treated in music, and in a thoroughly congenial manner, by Karl Maria von Weber. Without considering how far Meyerbeer, in *Robert le Diable,* has borrowed his instrumentation and harmonic combinations from Weber, there can be no doubt about its being a work of much the same class as *Der Freischütz;* and it would have been looked upon as quite of that class, had it been produced, like *Der Freischütz,* with spoken dialogue, and with the popular characters more in relief.

Robert le Diable, converted into a grand opera, was produced at the Académie, on the 21st of November, 1831. Dr. Véron, in his " Mémoires d'un Bourgeois de Paris," has given a most interesting account of all the circumstances which attended the rehearsals and first representation of this celebrated work. Dr. Véron had just undertaken the management of the Académie; and to have such an opera as *Robert le Diable,* with which to mark the commencement of his reign, was a piece of rare good fortune. The libretto, the music, the ballet, were all full of interest, and many of the airs had the advantage (in Paris) of being somewhat in the French style. The applause with which this, the best constructed of all M. Meyerbeer's works, was received, went on increasing from act to act; and, altogether, the success it obtained was immense, and, in some respects, unprecedented.

Nourrit played the part of "Robert," Madame Cinti Damoreau that of "Isabelle." Mademoiselle Dorus and Levasseur were the "Alice" and the "Bertram." In the *pas de cinq* of the second act, Noblet, Montessu, and Perrot appeared; and in the nuns' scene, the troop of resuscitated virgins was led by the graceful and seductive Taglioni. All the scenery was admirably painted, especially that of the moonlight *tableau* in the third act. The costumes were rich and brilliant, the *mise en scène*, generally, was remarkable for its completeness; in short, every one connected with the "getting up" of the opera from Habeneck, the musical conductor, to the property-men, gas-fitters and carpenters, whose names history has not preserved, did their utmost to ensure its success.

In 1832, *Robert le Diable* was brought out at the King's Theatre, with the principal parts sustained, as in Paris, by Nourrit, Levasseur, and Madame Damoreau. The part of "Alice" appears to have been given to Mademoiselle de Méric. This opera met with no success at the King's Theatre, and was scarcely better received at Covent Garden, where an English version was performed, with such alterations in Meyerbeer's music as will easily be conceived by those who remember how the works of Rossini, and, indeed, all foreign composers, were treated at this time, on the English stage.

In 1832, and, indeed, many years afterwards, when
Robert and *Les Huguenots* had been efficiently represented in London by German companies, Meyerbeer's
music was still most severely handled by some of our
best musical critics.   At present there is perhaps an
inclination to go to the other extreme; but, at all
events, full justice has now been rendered to M.
Meyerbeer's musical genius.   Let us hear what Lord
Mount Edgcumbe (whose opinion I do not regard as
one of authority, but only as an interesting index to
that of the connoisseurs of the old school), has to say
of the first, and, on the whole, the most celebrated
of Meyerbeer's operas.   He entertains the greatest
admiration for *Don Giovanni, Fidelio, Der Freischütz,* and *Euryanthe;* but neither the subject, nor
even the music of *Robert le Diable,* pleases him in
the least.   "Never," he says, "did I see a more
disagreeable or disgusting performance.   The sight
of the resurrection of a whole convent of nuns, who
rise from their graves, and begin dancing, like so
many bacchants, is revolting; and a sacred service in
a church, accompanied by an organ on the stage, not
very decorous.   Neither does the music of Meyerbeer compensate for a fable, which is a tissue of nonsense and improbability.   Of course, I was not
tempted to hear it again in its original form, and it
did credit to the taste of the English public, that it
was not endured at the Opera House, and was acted
only a very few nights."

Meyerbeer's second grand opera, *Les Huguenots,* was produced at the Académie Royale on the 26th of January, 1836, after twenty-eight full rehearsals, occasioning a delay which cost the composer a fine of thirty thousand francs. The expense of getting up the *Huguenots* (in scenery, dresses, properties, &c.), amounted to one hundred and sixty thousand francs.

In London, and I believe everywhere on the continent except in Paris, the most popular of M. Meyerbeer's three grand operas is *Les Huguenots.* At the Académie, *Robert le Diable* seems still to carry away the palm. Of late years, the admirable performance of Mario and Grisi, and of Titiens and Giuglini, in the duet of the fourth act, has had an immense effect in increasing the popularity of *Les Huguenots* with the English. This duet, the septett for male voices, the blessing of the daggers and the whole of the dramatic and animated scene of which it forms part, are certainly magnificent compositions; but the duet for "Raoul" and "Valentine" is the very soul of the work. At the theatres of Italy, the opera in question is generally "cut" with a free hand; and it is so long, that even after plentiful excisions an immense deal of music, and of fine music, still remains. But who would go to hear *Les Huguenots,* if the duet of the fourth act were omitted, or if the performance stopped at the end of act III.? On the other hand, the fourth act alone would always attract an audience; for, looked upon as a work by itself, it is by far the most dramatic, the most moving of all M. Meyerbeer's compositions. The construction of this act is most creditable to the librettist ; while the composer, in filling up, and giving musical life to the librettist's design, has shown the very highest genius. It ends with a scene for two personages, but the whole act is of one piece. While the daggers are being distributed, while the plans of the chief agents in the massacre are being developed in so striking and forcible a manner, the scene between the alarmed "Raoul" and the terrified "Valentine " is, throughout, anticipated ; and equally necessary for the success of the duet, from a musical as well as from a dramatic point of view, is the massive concerted piece by which this duet is preceded. To a composer, incapable or less capable than M. Meyerbeer, of turning to advantage the admirable but difficult situation here presented, there would, of course, have been the risk of an anti-climax ; there was the danger that, after a stageful of fanatical soldiers and monks, crying out at the top of their voices for blood, it would be impossible further to impress the audience by any known musical means. Meyerbeer, however, has had recourse to the expression of an entirely different kind of emotion, or rather a series of emotions, full of admirable variations and gradations; and everyone who has heard the great duet of *Les Huguenots* knows how wonderfully he has succeeded. It has been said that the idea of this scene originated with Nourrit. In any case, it was an idea which Scribe lost no time in profiting by, and the question does not in any way affect the transcendent merit of the composer.

Le Prophète, M. Meyerbeer's third grand opera, was produced at the Académie on the 16th of April, 1849, with Roger, Viardot-Garcia, and Castellan, in the principal characters. This opera, like *Les Huguenots,* has been performed with great success in London. The part of "Jean" has given the two great tenors of the Royal Italian Opera—Mario and Tamberlik—opportunities of displaying many of their highest qualities as dramatic singers. The magnificent Covent Garden orchestra achieves a triumph quite of its own, in the grand march of the coronation scene ; and the opera enables the management to display all its immense resources in the scenic department.

In passing from *Masaniello* to Rossini's *Guillaume Tell,* and from Rossini to Meyerbeer, we have lost sight too soon of the greatest composer France ever produced, and one who is ranked in all countries among the first composers of the century. I mean, of course, M. Auber, of whose works I should have more to say, if I had not determined, in this brief "History of the Opera" to pay but little attention to the French "Opéra Comique," which, with the exception of a very few examples (all by M. Auber)* is not a *genre* that has been accepted anywhere out of France. In sketching, however, the history

* For instance : *Fra Diavolo* and *Les Diamans de la Couronne.*

of the Grand Opera, it would be impossible to omit *Gustave III*. *Gustave ou le Bal Masqué*, composed on one of the two librettos returned to M. Scribe by Rossini,* was performed for the first time on the 27th of February, 1833. This admirable work is not nearly so well known in England, or even in France, as it deserves to be. The government of Louis Philippe seems to have thought it imprudent to familiarize the Parisians with regicide, by exhibiting it to them three or four times a week on the stage, as the main incident of a very interesting drama; and after a certain number of representations, *Gustave*, which, taken altogether, is certainly Auber's masterpiece, was cut down to the ball-scene. In England, no one objected to the theatrical assassination of *Gustavus*; but unfortunately, also, no scruple was made about mutilating and murdering Auber's music. In short, the *Gustavus* of Auber was far more cruelly ill-treated in London than the Gustavus of Sweden at his own masqued ball. Mr. Gye ought to produce *Gustavus* at the Royal Italian Opera, where, for the first time in England, it would be worthily represented. The frequenters of this theatre have long been expecting it, though I am not aware that it has ever been officially promised.

The original caste of *Gustave* included Nourrit, Levasseur, Massol, Dabadie, Dupont, Mademoiselle Falcon, Mademoiselle Dorus, and Madame Dabadie.

* The second, *Le Duc d'Albe*, was entrusted to Donizetti, who died without completing the score.

Nourrit, the original "Guillaume Tell," the original
"Robert," the original "Raoul," the original "Gustave," was then at the height of his fame; but he was
destined to be challenged four years afterwards by a
very formidable rival.   He was the first, and the only
first tenor at the Académie Royale de Musique, where
he had been singing with a zeal and ardour equal to
his genius for the last sixteen years, when the management engaged Duprez, to divide the principal parts
with the vocalist already in office.   After his long
series of triumphs, Nourrit had no idea of sharing
his laurels in this manner; nor was he at all sure
that he was not about to be deprived of them altogether.   "One of the two must succeed at the expense of the other," he declared; and knowing the
attraction of novelty for the public, he was not at all
sure that the unfortunate one would not be himself.

"Duprez knows me," he said, "and comes to sing
where I am.   I do not know him, and naturally fear
his approach."   After thinking over the matter for a
few days he resolved to leave the theatre.   He chose
for his last appearance the second act of *Armide*, in
which "Renaud," the character assigned to the tenor,
has to exclaim to the warrior, "Artemidore" —

> "Allez, allez remplir ma place,
>   Aux lieux d'où mon malheur me chasse," &c.

To which "Artemidore" replies—

> "Sans vous que peut on entreprendre?
>   Celui qui vous bannit ne pourra se défendre
>   De souhaiter votre retour."

The scene was very appropriate to the position of

the singer who was about to be succeeded by Duprez. The public felt this equally with Nourrit himself, and testified their sympathy for the departing Renaud, by the most enthusiastic applause.

Nourrit took his farewell of the French public on the 1st of April, 1837, and on the 17th of the same month Duprez made his *début* at the Académie, as "Arnold," in *William Tell*. The latter singer had already appeared at the Comédie Française, where, at the age of fifteen, he was entrusted with the soprano solos in the choruses of *Athalie*, and afterwards at the Odéon, where he played the parts of "Almaviva," in the *Barber of Seville*, and Ottavio," in *Don Juan*. He then visited Italy for a short time, returned to Paris, and was engaged at the Opéra Comique. Here his style was much admired, but his singing, on the whole, produced no great impression on the public. He once more crossed the Alps, studied assiduously, performed at various theatres in a great number of operas, and by incessant practice, and thanks also to the wonderful effect of the climate on his voice, attained the highest position on the Italian stage, and was the favourite tenor of Italy at a time when Rubini was singing every summer in London, and every winter in Paris. Before visiting Italy the second time, Duprez was a "light tenor," and was particularly remarkable for the "agility" of his execution. A long residence in a southern climate appears to have quite changed the nature of his voice; a transformation, however, which must have been considerably aided by the nature of his studies.   He returned to France a *tenore robusto*, an impressive, energetic singer, excelling in the declamatory style, and in many respects the greatest dramatic vocalist the French had ever heard.   As an actor, however, he was not equal to Nourrit, whose demeanour as an operatic hero is said to have been perfection.   *Guillaume Tell*, with Duprez, in the part of "Arnold," commenced a new career, and Rossini's great work now obtained from the general public that applause which, on its first production, it had, for the most part, received only from connoisseurs.

In the meanwhile, Nourrit, after performing with great success at Marseilles, Toulouse, Lyons, and elsewhere, went to Italy, and was engaged first at Milan, and afterwards at Florence and Naples.   At each city fresh triumphs awaited him, but an incident occurred at Naples which sorely troubled the equanimity of the failing singer, whose mind, as we have seen, had already been disturbed by painful presentiments.   Nourrit, to be sure, was only "failing" in this sense, that he was losing confidence in his own powers, which, however, by all accounts, remained undiminished to the last.   He was a well-educated and a highly accomplished man, and besides being an excellent musician, possessed considerable literary talent, and a thorough knowledge of dramatic effect.*   He had prepared two librettos, in which the

---

* Nourrit was the author of *la Sylphide*, one of the most interesting and best designed ballets ever produced; that is to say, he

part adapted for the tenor would serve to exhibit his double talent as an actor and as a singer. One of these musical dramas was founded on Corneille's *Polyeucte,* and, in the hands of Donizetti, became *I Martiri ;* but just when it was about to be produced, the Neapolitan censorship forbade its production on the ground of the unfitness of religious subjects for stage representation. Nourrit was much dejected at being thus prevented from appearing in a part composed specially for him at his own suggestion, and in which he felt sure he would be seen and heard to the greatest advantage. A deep melancholy, such as he had already suffered from at Marseilles, to an extent which alarmed all his friends, now settled upon him. He appeared, and was greatly applauded, in Mercadante's *Il Giuramento,* and in Bellini's *Norma,* but soon afterwards his despondency was increased, and assumed an irritated form, from a notion that the applause the Neapolitans bestowed upon him was ironical.

Nothing could alter his conviction on this point, which at last had the effect of completely unsettling his mind—unless it be more correct to say that mental derangement was itself the cause of the unhappy delusion. Finally, after a performance given for the benefit of another singer, in which Nourrit took part, his malady increased to such an extent that on his return home he became delirious, threw himself out of window, at five in the morning, and was picked up

composed the libretto for which Taglioni arranged the groups and dances.

in the street quite dead.   This deplorable event occurred on the 8th of March, 1839.

The late "Académie Royale de Musique," the
Théatre Italien of Paris, and all the chief opera
houses of Italy are connected inseparably with the
history of Opera in England.   All the great works
written by Rossini and Meyerbeer for the Académie
have since been represented in London; the same
singers for nearly half a century past have for the
most part sung alternately at the Italian operas of
Paris and of London; finally, from Italy we have
drawn the great majority of the works represented at
our best musical theatres, and nearly all our finest
singers.

German opera, in the meanwhile, stands in a
certain way apart.   Germany, compared with Italy,
has sent us very few great singers.   We have never
looked to Germany for a constant supply of operas,
and, indeed, Germany has not produced altogether
half a dozen thoroughly German operas (that is to
say, founded on German libretti, and written for
German singers and German audiences), which have
ever become naturalized in this country, or, indeed,
anywhere out of their native land.   Moreover, the
most celebrated of the said *thoroughly* German operas,
such as *Fidelio* and *Der Freischutz*, exercised no such
influence on contemporary dramatic music as to give
their composers a well-marked place in the operatic
history of the present century, such as clearly belongs

to Rossini. Beethoven, with his one great masterpiece, stands quite alone, and in the same way, Weber, with his strongly marked individuality has nothing in common with his contemporaries; and, living at the same time as Rossini, neither affected, nor was affected, by the style of a composer whose influence all the composers of the Italian school experienced. Accordingly, and that I may not entangle too much the threads of my narrative, I will now, having followed Rossini to Paris, and given some account of his successors at the French Opera, proceed to speak of Donizetti and Bellini, who were followers of Rossini in every sense. Of Weber and Beethoven, who are not in any way associated with the Rossini school, and only through the accident of birth with the Rossini period, I must speak in a later chapter.

CHAPTER XVIII.

DONIZETTI AND BELLINI.

SIGISMONDI, the librarian of the Neapolitan Conservatory, had a horror of Rossini's music, and took care that all his printed works in the library should be placed beyond the reach of the young and innocent pupils. He was determined to preserve them, as far as possible, from the corrupt but seductive influence of this composer's brilliant, extravagant, meretricious style. But Donizetti, who at this time was studying at Naples, had heard several of the proscribed operas, and was most anxious to examine, on the music paper, the causes of the effects which had so delighted his ear at the theatre. The desired scores were on the highest shelf of the library; and the careful, conscientious librarian had removed the ladder by means of which alone it seemed possible to get to them.

Donizetti stood watching the shelves which held the operas of Rossini like a cat before a bird cage; but the ladder was locked up, and the key in safe keeping in Sigismondi's pocket. Under a northern climate, the proper mode of action for Donizetti would have been to invite the jailor to a banquet, ply him with wine, and rob him of his keys as soon as he had reached a sufficiently advanced state of intoxication. Being in Italy, Donizetti should have made love to Sigismondi's daughter, and persuaded her to steal the keys from the old man during his mid-day *siesta*. Perhaps, however, Sigismondi was childless, or his family may have consisted only of sons; in any case, the young musician adopted neither of the schemes, by combining which the troubadour Blondel was enabled to release from captivity his adored Richard.* He resorted to a means which, if not wonderfully ingenious, was at least to the point, and which promised to be successful. He climbed, monkey-like, or cat-like, not to abandon our former simile, to the top shelf, and had his claws on the *Barber of Seville*, when who should enter the library but Sigismondi.

The old man was fairly shocked at this perversity on the part of Gaetan Donizetti, reputed the best behaved student of the Academy. His morals would be corrupted, his young blood poisoned!—but fortunately the librarian had arrived in time, and he might yet be saved.

Donizetti sprang to the ground with his prey—the full score of the *Barber of Seville*—in his clutches. He was about to devour it, when a hand touched him

* See Raynouard's veracious "Histoire des Troubadours."

on the shoulder: he turned round, and before him
stood the austere Sigismondi.

The old librarian spoke to Gaetan as to a son;
appealed to his sense of propriety, his honour, his
conscience; and asked him, almost with tears in his
eyes, how he could so far forget himself as to come
secretly into the library to read forbidden books—and
Rossini's above all? He pointed out the terrible
effects of the course upon which the youthful Donizetti had so nearly entered; reminded him that one
brass instrument led to another; and that when once
he had given himself up to violent orchestration,
there was no saying where he would stop.

Donizetti could not or would not argue with the
venerable and determined Sigismondi. At least, he
did not oppose him; but he inquired whether, as a
lesson in cacophony, it was not worth while just to
look at Rossini's notorious productions. He reminded
his stern adviser, that he had already studied good
models under Mayer, Pilotti, and Mattei, and that
it was natural he should now wish to complete his
musical education, by learning what to avoid. He
quoted the well known case of the Spartans and their
Helots; inquired, with some emotion, whether the
frightful example of Rossini was not sufficient to
deter any well meaning composer, with a little strength
of character, from following in his unholy path; and
finally declared, with undisguised indignation, that
Rossini ought to be made the object of a serious
study, so that once for all his musical iniquities might

be exposed and his name rendered a bye-word among the lovers and cultivators of pure, unsophisticated art !

" Come to my arms, Gaetano," cried Sigismondi, much moved. " I can refuse nothing to a young man like you, now that I know your excellent intentions. A musician, who is imbued with the true principles of his art, may look upon the picture of Rossini's depravity not only without danger, but with positive advantage. Some it might weaken and destroy ;—*you* it can only fortify and uphold. Let us open these monstrous scores ; their buffooneries may amuse us for an hour.

" *Il Barbiere di Siviglia !* I have not much to say about that," commenced Sigismondi. " It is a trifle; besides, full justice was done to it at Rome. The notion of re-setting one of the master-pieces of the great Paisiello,—what audacity ! No wonder it was hissed !"

" Under Paisiello's direction," suggested Donizetti.

"All a calumny, my young friend ; pure calumny, I can assure you. There are so many Don Basilios in the musical world ! Rossini's music was hissed because it was bad and because it recalled to the public Paisiello's, which was good." " But I have heard," rejoined Donizetti, " that at the second representation there was a great deal of applause, and that the enthusiasm of the audience at last reached such a point, that they honoured Rossini with a torch-light procession and conducted him home in triumph.

"An invention of the newspapers," replied Sigismondi; "I believe there was a certain clique present prepared to support the composer through everything, but the public had already expressed its opinion. Never mind this musical burlesque, and let us take a glance at one of Rossini's serious operas."

Donizetti wished for nothing better. This time he had no occasion to scale the shelf in his former feline style. The librarian produced the key of the mysterious closet in which the ladder was kept. The young musician ran up to the Rossini shelf like a lamplighter and brought down with him not one but half-a-dozen volumes.

"Too many, too many," said Sigismondi, "one would have been quite enough. Well, let us open *Otello*."

In the score which the old and young musician proposed to examine together, the three trombone parts, according to the Italian custom, were written on one and the same staff, thus 1o, 2o, 3o *tromboni*. Sigismondi began his lecture on the enormities of Rossini as displayed in *Otello* by reading the list of the instruments employed.

"*Flutes*, two flutes; well there is not much harm in that. No one will hear them; only, with diabolical perfidy, one of these modern flutists will be sure to take a *piccolo* and pierce all sensitive ears with his shrill whistling.

"*Hautboys*, two hautboys; also good. Here Rossini follows the old school. I say nothing against his two hautboys; indeed, I quite approve of them.

" *Clarionets !* a barbarous invention, which the *Tedeschi* might have kept them for themselves. They may be very good pipes for calling cows, but should be used for nothing else.

" *Bassoons ;* useless instruments, or nearly so. Our good masters employed them for strengthening the bass ; but now the bassoon has acquired such importance, that solos are written for it. This is also a German innovation. Mozart would have done well to have left the bassoon in its original obscurity.

" 1st and 2nd *Horns;* very good. Horns and hautboys combine admirably. I say nothing against Rossini's horns.

" 3rd and 4th *Horns !* How many horns does the man want? *Quattro Corni, Corpo di Bacco !* The greatest of our composers have always been contented with two. Shades of Pergolese, of Leo, of Jomelli ! How they must shudder at the bare mention of such a thing. Four horns ! Are we at a hunting party ? Four horns ! Enough to blow us to perdition."

.The indignation and rage of the old musician went on increasing as he followed the gradual development of a *crescendo* until he arrived at the explosion of the *fortissimo.* Then Sigismondi uttered a cry of despair, struck the score violently with his fist, upset the table which the imprudent Donizetti had loaded with the nefarious productions of Rossini, raised his hands to heaven and rushed from the room, exclaiming, "a hundred and twenty-three trombones ! A hundred and twenty-three trombones !"

Donizetti followed the performer and endeavoured to explain the mistake.

"Not 123 trombones, but 1st, 2nd, 3rd trombones," he gently observed. Sigismondi however, would not hear another word, and disappeared from the library crying "a hundred and twenty-three trombones," to the last.

Donizetti came back, lifted up the table, placed the scores upon it and examined them in peace. He then, in his turn, concealed them so that he might be able another time to find them whenever he pleased without clambering up walls or intriguing to get possession of ladders.

The inquiring student of the Conservatory of Naples was born, in 1798, at Bergamo, and when he was seventeen years of age was put to study under Mayer, who, before the appearance of Rossini, shared with Paer the honour of being the most popular composer of the day. His first opera *Enrico di Borgogna* was produced at Venice in 1818, and obtained so much success that the composer was entrusted with another commission for the same city in the following year. After writing an opera for Mantua in 1819 *Il Falegname di Livonia*, Donizetti visited Rome, where his *Zoraide di Granata* procured him an exemption from the conscription and the honour of being carried in triumph and crowned at the Capitol. Hitherto he may be said to have owed his success chiefly to his skilful imitation of Rossini's style, and it was not until 1830, when *Anna Bolena* was produced at

Milan (and when, curiously enough, Rossini had just written his last opera), that he exhibited any striking signs of original talent. This work, which is generally regarded as Donizetti's master-piece, or at least was some time ago (for of late years no one has had an opportunity of hearing it), was composed for Pasta and Rubini, and was first represented for Pasta's benefit in 1831. It was in this opera that Lablache gained his first great triumph in London.

Donizetti visited Paris in 1835, and there produced his *Marino Faliero*, which contains several spirited and characteristic pieces, such as the opening chorus of workmen in the Arsenal and the gondolier chorus at the commencement of the second act. The charming *Elisir d'Amore*, the most graceful, melodious, moreover the most characteristic, and in many respects the best of all Donizetti's works, was written for Milan in 1832. In this work Signor Mario made his re-appearance at the Italian Opera of Paris in 1839; he had previously sung for some time at the Académie Royale in *Robert* and other operas.

Lucia di Lammermoor, Donizetti's most popular opera, containing some of the most beautiful melodies in the sentimental style that he has composed, and altogether his best finale, was produced at Naples in 1835. The part of "Edgardo" was composed specially for Duprez, that of "Lucia" for Persiani.

The pretty little opera or operetta entitled *Il Campanello di Notte* was written under very interesting circumstances to save a little Neapolitan theatre from ruin. Donizetti heard that the establishment was in a failing condition, and that the performers were without money and in great distress. He sought them out, supplied their immediate wants, and one of the singers happening to say that if Donizetti would give them a new opera, their fortunes would be made : "As to that," replied the Maestro, "you shall have one within a week." To begin with, a libretto was necessary, but none was to be had. The composer, however, possessed considerable literary talent, and recollecting a vaudeville which he had seen some years before in Paris, called *La Sonnette de Nuit*, he took that for his subject, re-arranged it in an operatic form, and in nine days the libretto was written, the music composed, the parts learnt, the opera perfomed, and the theatre saved. It would have been difficult to have given a greater proof of generosity, and of fertility and versatility of talent. I may here mention that Donizetti designed, and wrote the words, as well as the music of the last act of the *Lucia ;* that the last act of *La Favorite* was also an afterthought of his; and that he himself translated into Italian the libretti of Betly and *La Fille du Regiment.*

When *Lucrezia Borgia* (written for Milan in 1834) was produced in Paris. in 1840, Victor Hugo, the author of the admirable tragedy on which it is founded, contested the right of the Italian librettists, to borrow their plots from French dramas ; maintaining that the representation of such libretti in France constituted an infringement of the French dramatists' "*droits d'auteur*." He gained his action, and *Lucrezia Borgia* became, at the Italian Opera of Paris, *La Rinegata*, the Italians at the court of Pope Alexander the Sixth being metamorphosed into Turks. A French version of *Lucrezia Borgia* was prepared for the provinces, and entitled *Nizza di Grenada*.

A year or two afterwards, Verdi's *Hernani* experienced the same fate at the Théâtre Italien as *Lucrezia Borgia*. Then the original authors of *La Pie Voleuse*, *La Grace de Dieu*, &c., followed Victor Hugo's example, and objected to the performance of *La Gazza Ladra* and *Linda di Chamouni*, &c. Finally, an arrangement was made, and at present exists, by which Italian operas founded on French dramas may be performed in Paris on condition of an indemnity being paid to the French dramatists. Marsolier, the author of the Opéra Comique, entitled *Nina, ou la Folle par Amour*, set to music by Dalayrac, had applied for an injunction twenty-three years before, to prevent the representation of Paisiello's *Nina*, in Paris; but the Italian disappeared before the question was tried. The principle, however, of an author's right of property in a work, or any portion of a work, had been established nearly two centuries before. In a "privilege" granted to St. Amant in 1653, for the publication of his *Moise Sauvé*, it is expressly forbidden to extract from that "epic poem" subjects for novels and plays. These cautions proved

unnecessary, as the work so strictly protected contained no available materials for plays, novels, or
any other species of literary composition, including
even "epic poems;" but *Moise Sauvé* has nevertheless been the salvation of several French authors
whose property might otherwise have been trespassed
upon to a considerable extent.   Nevertheless, the
principle of an author's sole, inalienable interest in
the incidents he may have invented or combined,
without reference to the new form in which they
may be presented, cannot, as a matter of course, be
entertained anywhere ; but the system of " author's
rights " so energetically fought for and conquered by
Beaumarchais has a very wide application in France,
and only the other day it was decided that the transla-
tors and arrangers of *Le Nozze di Figaro*, for the
Théâtre Lyrique must share their receipts with the
descendants and heirs of the author of *Le Mariage de
Figaro*.   It will appear monstrous to many persons
in England who cannot conceive of property otherwise
than of a material, palpable kind, that Beaumarchais's
representatives should enjoy any interest in a work
produced three-quarters of a century ago ; but as his
literary productions possess an actual, easily attainable value, it would be difficult to say who ought to
profit by it, if not those who, under any system of
laws, would benefit by whatever other possessions he
might have left.   It may be a slight advantage to
society, in an almost inappreciable degree, that
"author's rights" should cease after a certain period;

but, if so, the same principle ought to be applied to other forms of created value. The case was well put by M. de Vigny, in the "Revue des Deux Mondes," in advocating the claims of a grand-daughter, or great grand-daughter of Sedaine. He pointed out, that if the dramatist in question, who was originally an architect, had built a palace, and it had lasted until the present day, no one would have denied that it descended naturally to his heirs; and that as, instead of building in stone, he devoted himself to the construction of operas and plays, the results of his talent and industry ought equally to be regarded as the inalienable property of his descendants.

But to return to *Lucrezia Borgia*, which, with *Lucia* and *La Favorite*, may be ranked amongst the most successful of Donizetti's productions. The favour with which *Lucrezia* is received by audiences of all kinds may be explained, in addition to the merit of much of the music, by the manner in which the principal parts are distributed, so that the caste, to be efficient, must always include four leading singers, each of whom has been well-provided for by the composer. It contains less recitative than any of Rossini's operas—a great advantage, from a popular point of view, it having been shown by experience that the public of the present day do not care for recitative (especially when they do not understand a word of it), but like to pass as quickly as possible from one musical piece to another. From an artistic point of view the shortness of Donizetti's recitatives

is not at all to be regretted, for the simple reason that
he has never written any at all comparable to those
of Rossini, whose dramatic genius he was far from
possessing.   The most striking situation in the drama,
a thoroughly musical situation of which a great composer, or even an energetic, passionate, melo-dramatic
composer, like Verdi, would have made a great deal,
is quite lost in the hands of Dònizetti.   The *Brindisi*
is undeniably pretty, and was never considered vulgar
until it had been vulgarised.   But Donizetti has shown
no dramatic power in the general arrangement of the
principal scene, and the manner in which the drinking song is interrupted by the funeral chorus, has rather
a disagreeable, than a terrible or a solemn effect.   The
finale to the first act, or " prologue," is finely treated,
but " Gennaro's " dying scene and song, is the most
dramatic portion of the work, which it ought to terminate, but unfortunately does not.   I think it
might be shown that *Lucrezia* marks the distance
about half way between the style of Rossini and
that of Verdi.   Not that it is so much inferior to
the works of the former, or so much superior to
those of the latter ; but that among Donizetti's later
operas, portions of *Maria di Rohan* (Vienna, 1843),
might almost have been written by the composer of
Rigoletto ; whereas, the resemblance for good or for
bad, between these two musicians, of the decadence,
is not nearly so remarkable, if we compare *Lucrezia
Borgia* with one of Verdi's works.   Still, in *Lucrezia*
we already notice that but little space is accorded to

recitative, which in the *Trovatore* finds next to none; we meet with choruses written in the manner afterwards adopted by Verdi, and persisted in by him to the exclusion of all other modes; while as regards melody, we should certainly rather class the tenor's air in *I Lombardi* with that in *Lucrezia Borgia*, than the latter with any air ever composed by Rossini.

When Donizetti revisited Paris in 1840, he produced in succession *I Martiri* (the work written for Nourrit and objected to by the Neapolitan censorship), *La Fille du Regiment*, written for the Opéra Comique, and *La Favorite*, composed in the first instance for the Théâtre de la Renaissance, but re-arranged for the Académie, when the brief existence of the Théâtre de la Renaissance had come to an end. As long as it lasted, this establishment, opened for the representation of foreign operas in the French language, owed its passing prosperity entirely to a French version of the *Lucia*.

Jenny Lind, Sontag, Alboni, have all appeared in *La Figlia del Reggimento* with great success; but when this work was first produced in Paris, with Madame Thillon in the principal part, it was not received with any remarkable favour. It is full of smooth, melodious, and highly animated music, but is, perhaps, wanting in that piquancy of which the French are such great admirers, and which rendered the duet for the vivandières, in Meyerbeer's *Etoile du Nord*, so much to their taste. *L'Ange de Nisida*, converted into *La Favorite* (and founded in the first instance on a French drama, *Le Comte de Commingues*) was brought out at the Académie, without any expense in scenery and " getting up," and achieved a decided success. This was owing partly to the pretty choral airs at the commencement, partly to the baritone's cavatina (admirably sung by Barroilhet, who made his *début* in the part of " Alphonse") ; but, above all, to the fourth act, with its beautiful melody for the tenor, and its highly dramatic scene for the tenor and soprano, including a final duet, which, if not essentially dramatic in itself, occurs at least in a most dramatic situation.

The whole of the fourth act of *La Favorite*, except the cavatina, *Ange si pur*, which originally belonged to the Duc d'Albe, and the *andante* of the duet, which was added at the rehearsals, was written in three hours. Donizetti had been dining at the house of a friend, who was engaged in the evening to go to a party. On leaving the house, the host, after many apologies for absenting himself, intreated Donizetti to remain, and finish his coffee, which Donizetti, being inordinately fond of that stimulant, took care to do. He asked at the same time for some music paper, began his fourth act, and finding himself in the vein for composition, went on writing until he had completed it. He had just put the final stroke to the celebrated " *Viens dans une autre patrie*," when his friend returned, at one in the morning, and congratulated him on the excellent manner in which he had employed his time.

After visiting Rome, Milan, and Vienna, for which

last city he wrote *Linda di Chamouni*, Donizetti returned to Paris, and in 1843 composed *Don Pasquale* for the Théâtre Italien, and *Don Sebastien* for the Académie. The lugubrious drama to which the music of *Don Sebastien* is wedded, proved fatal to its success. On the other hand, the brilliant gaiety of *Don Pasquale*, rendered doubly attractive by the admirable execution of Grisi, Mario, Tamburini, and Lablache, delighted all who heard it. The pure musical beauty of the serenade, and of the quartett, one of the finest pieces of concerted music Donizetti ever wrote, were even more admired than the lively animated dialogue-scenes, which are in Donizetti's very best style; and the two pieces just specified, as well as the baritone's cavatina, *Bella siccome un angelo*, aided the general success of the work, not only by their own intrinsic merit, but also by the contrast they present to the comic conversational music, and the buffo airs of the bass. The music of *Don Pasquale* is probably the cleverest Donizetti ever wrote; but it wants the *charm* which belongs to that of his *Elisir d'Amore*, around which a certain sentiment, a certain atmosphere of rustic poetry seems to hang, especially when we are listening to the music of Nemorino" or "Norina." Even the comic portions in the *Elisir* are full of grace, as for instance, the admirable duet between " Norina " and " Dulcamara;" and the whole work possesses what is called " colour," that is to say, each character is well painted by the music, which, moreover, is always appropriate to the general scene. To look for "colour," or for any kind of poetry in a modern drawing-room piece of intrigue, like *Don Pasquale,* with the notaries of real life, and with lovers in black coats, would be absurd. I may mention that the libretto of *Don Pasquale* is a re-arrangement of Pavesi's *Ser Marcantonio* (was "*Ser*" *Marcantonio* an Englishman?) produced in 1813.

In the same year that Donizetti brought out *Don Pasquale* in Paris, he produced *Maria di Rohan* at Vienna. The latter work contains an admirable part for the baritone, which has given Ronconi the opportunity of showing that he is not only an excellent buffo, but is also one of the finest tragic actors on the stage. The music of *Maria di Rohan* is highly dramatic : that is to say, very appropriate to the various personages, and to the great "situations" of the piece. In pourtraying the rage of the jealous husband, the composer exhibits all that earnestness and vigour for which Verdi has since been praised—somewhat sparingly, it is true, but praised nevertheless by his admirers. The contralto part, on the other hand, is treated with remarkable elegance, and contains more graceful melodies than Verdi is in the habit of composing. I do not say that Donizetti is in all respects superior to Verdi; indeed, it seems to me that he has not produced any one opera so thoroughly dramatic as *Rigoletto ;* but as Donizetti and Verdi are sometimes contrasted, and as it was the fashion during Donizetti's lifetime, to speak of his music as light and frivolous, I wish to remark that in one of his latest operas he wrote several scenes, which, if written by Verdi, would be said to be in that composer's best style.

Donizetti's last opera, *Catarina Comaro*, was produced in Naples in the year 1844. This was his sixty-third dramatic work, counting those only which have been represented. There are still two operas of Donizetti's in existence, which the public have not heard. One, a piece in one act, composed for the Opéra Comique, and which is said every now and then to be on the point of being performed; the other, *Le Duc d'Albe*, which, as before-mentioned, was written for the Académie Royale, on one of the two libretti returned by Rossini to Scribe, after the composer of *William Tell* came to his mysterious resolution of retiring from operatic life.

Of Donizetti's sixty-three operas, about two-thirds are quite unknown to England, and of the nine or ten which may still be said to keep the stage, the earliest produced, *Anna Bolena*, is the composer's thirty-second work. *Anna Bolena, L'Elisir d'Amore, Lucrezia Borgia, Lucia di Lammermoor,* and *Roberto Devereux,* are included between the numbers 31 and 52, while between the numbers 53 and 62, *La Fille du Regiment, La Favorite, Linda di Chamouni, Don Pasquale,* and *Maria di Rohan,* are found. The first five of Donizetti's most popular operas, were produced between the years 1830 and 1840; the last five between the years 1840 and 1844.

Donizetti appears, then, to have produced his best serious operas during the middle period of his career—unless it be considered that *La Favorite, Linda di Chamouni*, and *Maria di Rohan*, are superior to *Anna Bolena, Lucrezia Borgia*, and *Lucia di Lammermoor;* and to the same epoch belongs *L'Elisir d'Amore*, which in my opinion is the freshest, most graceful, and most melodious of his comic operas, though some may prefer *La Fille du Regiment* or *Don Pasquale*, both full of spirit and animation.

It is also tolerably clear, from an examination of Donizetti's works in the order in which they were produced, that during the last four or five years of his artistic life he produced more than his average number of operas, possessing such merit that they have taken their place in the repertoires of the principal opera houses of Europe. Donizetti had lost nothing either in fertility or in power, while he appeared in some respects to be modifying and improving his style. Thus, in the Swiss opera of *Linda di Chamouni* (Vienna, 1842), we find, especially in the music of the contralto part, a considerable amount of local colour—an important dramatic element which Donizetti had previously overlooked, or, at least, had not turned to any account; while *Maria di Rohan* contains the best dramatic music of a passionate kind that Donizetti has ever written.

In composing, Donizetti made no use of the pianoforte, and wrote, as may be imagined, with great rapidity, never stopping to make a correction, though he is celebrated among the modern Italian composers for the accuracy of his style. Curiously enough, he never went to work without having a small ivory scraper by his side; and any one who has studied intellectual peculiarities will understand, that once wanting this instrument, he might have felt it necessary to scratch out notes and passages every minute. Mr. J. Wrey Mould, in his interesting " memoir," tells us that this ivory scraper was given to Donizetti by his father when he consented, after a long and strenuous opposition, to his becoming a musician. An unfilial son might have looked upon the present as not conveying the highest possible compliment that could be paid him. The old gentleman, however, was quite right in impressing upon the bearer of his name, that having once resolved to be a composer, he had better make up his mind to produce as little rubbish as possible.

The first signs of the dreadful malady to which Donizetti ultimately succumbed, manifested themselves during his last visit to Paris, in 1845. Fits of absence of mind, followed by hallucinations and all the symptoms of mental derangement followed one another rapidly, and with increasing intensity. In January, 1846, it was found necessary to place the unfortunate composer in an asylum at Ivry, and in the autumn of 1847, his medical advisers recommended as a final experiment, that he should be removed to Bergamo, in the hope that the air and scenes of his birth-place would have a favourable influence in dispelling, or, at least, diminishing the profound melancholy to which he was now subject. During his journey, however, he was attacked by paralysis, and his illness assumed a desperate and incurable character.

Donizetti was received at Bergamo by the Maestro Dolci, one of his dearest friends. Here paralysis again attacked him, and a few days afterwards, on the 8th of April, 1848, he expired, in his fifty-second year, having, during the twenty-seven years of his life, as a composer, written sixty-four operas; several masses and vesper services; and innumerable pieces of chamber music, including, besides arias, cavatinas, and vocal concerted pieces, a dozen quartetts for stringed instruments, a series of songs and duets, entitled *Les soirées du Pausilippe*, a cantata entitled *la Morte d'Ugolino*, &c., &c.

Antoine, Donizetti's attendant at Ivry, became much attached to him, and followed him to Bergamo, whence he forwarded to M. Adolphe Adam, a letter describing his illustrious patient's last moments, and the public honours paid to his memory at the funeral.

" More than four thousand persons," he relates, " were present at the ceremony. The procession was composed of the numerous clergy of Bergamo; the most illustrious members of the community and its environs, and of the civic guard of the town and suburbs. The discharges of musketry, mingled with the light of three or four hundred large torches, presented a fine effect—the whole was enhanced by the presence of three military bands, and the most propitious weather it was possible to behold. The service commenced at ten o'clock in the morning, and did not conclude until half-past two. The young gentlemen of Burgamo insisted on bearing the remains of their illustrious fellow-citizen, although the cemetery in which they finally rested lay at a distance of a league-and-a-half from the town. The road there was crowded along its whole length by people who came from the surrounding country to witness the procession—and, to give due praise to the inhabitants of Bergamo, never, hitherto, had such great honours been bestowed upon any member of that city."

Bellini, who was Donizetti's contemporary, but who was born nine years after him, and died thirteen years before, was a native of Sicily. His father was an organist at Catania, and under him the future composer of *Norma* and *La Sonnambula*, took his first lessons in music. A Sicilian nobleman, struck by the signs of genius which young Bellini evinced at an early age, persuaded his father to send him to Naples, supporting his arguments with an offer to pay his expenses at the celebrated Conservatorio. Here one of Bellini's fellow pupils was Mercadante, the future composer of *Il Giuramento*, an opera which, in spite of the frequent attempts of the Italian singers to familiarize the English

public with its numerous beauties, has never been
much liked in this country.   I do not say that it has
not been justly appreciated on the whole, but that
the grace of some of the melodies, the acknowledged
merit of the orchestration and the elegance and distinction which seem to me to characterize the composer's style generally, have not been accepted as
compensating for his want of passion and of that
spontaneity without which the expression of strong
emotion of any kind is naturally impossible.   Mercadante could never have written *Rigoletto,* but,
probably, a composer of inferior natural gifts to Verdi
might, with a taste for study and a determination to
bring his talent to perfection, have produced a work
of equal artistic merit to *Il Giuramento.*   And here
we must take leave of Mercadante, whose place in
the history of the opera is not a considerable one,
and who, to the majority of English amateurs, is
known only by his *Bella adorata,* a melody of which
Verdi has shown his estimation by borrowing it, di-
luting it, and re-arranging it with a new accompaniment for the tenor's song in *Luisa Miller.*

I should think Mercadante must have written
better exercises, and passed better examinations at
the Conservatorio than his young friend Bellini,
though the latter must have begun at an earlier age
to compose operas.   Bellini's first dramatic work was
written and performed while he was still a student.
Encouraged by its success, he next composed music
to a libretto already " set " by Generali, and entitled

Adelson e Salvino. Adelson was represented before the illustrious Barbaja, who was at that time manager of the two most celebrated theatres in Italy, the St. Carlo at Naples, and La Scala at Milan, — as well as of the Italian opera at Vienna, to say nothing of some smaller operatic establishments also under his rule. The great impresario, struck by Bellini's promise, commissioned him to write an opera for Naples, and, in 1826, his *Bianca e Fernando* was produced at the St. Carlo. This work was so far successful, that it obtained a considerable amount of applause from the public, while it inspired Barbaja with so much confidence that he entrusted the young composer, now twenty years of age, with the libretto of *il Pirata*, to be composed for La Scala. The tenor part was written specially for Rubini, who retired into the country with Bellini, and studied, as they were produced, the simple, touching airs which he afterwards delivered on the stage with such admirable expression.

Il Pirata was received with enthusiasm by the audiences of La Scala, and the composer was requested to write another work for the same theatre. *La Straniera* was brought out at Milan in 1828, the principal parts being entrusted to Donzelli, Tamburini, and Madame Tosi. This, Bellini's third work, appears, on the whole, to have maintained, but scarcely to have advanced, his reputation. Nevertheless, when it was represented in London soon after its

M 2

original production, it was by no means so favourably received as *Il Pirato* had been.

Bellini's *Zaira*, executed at Parma, in 1829, was a failure—soon, however, to be redeemed by his fifth work, *Il Capuletti ed i Montecchi*, which was written for Venice, and was received with all possible expressions of approbation. In London, the new operatic version of *Romeo and Juliet* was not particularly admired, and owed what success it obtained entirely to the acting and singing of Madame Pasta in the principal part. It may be mentioned that the libretto of Bellini's *I Montecchi* had already served his master, Zingarelli, for his opera of *Romeo e Julietta*.

The time had now arrived at which Bellini was to produce his master-pieces, *La Sonnambula* and *Norma;* the former of which was written for *La Scala*, in 1831, the latter, for the same theatre, in the year following. The success of *La Sonnambula* has been great everywhere, but nowhere so great as in England, where it has been performed in English and in Italian, oftener than any other two or perhaps three operas, while probably no songs, certainly no songs by a foreign composer, were ever sold in such large numbers as *All is lost* and *Do not mingle*. The libretto of *La Sonnambula*, by Romani, is one of the most interesting and touching, and one of the best suited for musical illustration in the whole *répertoire* of *libretti*. To the late M. Scribe, belongs the merit of having invented the charming story on which

Romani's and Bellini's opera is founded; and it is worthy of remark that he had already presented it in two different dramatic forms before any one was struck with its capabilities for musical treatment. A thoroughly, essentially, dramatic story can be presented on the stage in any and every form; with music, with dialogue, or with nothing but dumb action. Tried by this test, the plots of a great number of merely well written comedies would prove worthless; and so in substance they are. On the other hand, the vaudeville of *La Somnambula*, became, as re-arranged by M. Scribe, the ballet of *La Somnambule*, (one of the prettiest, by the way, from a choregraphic point of view ever produced) ; which, in the hands of Romani, became the libretto of an opera; which again, vulgarly treated, has been made into a burlesque; and, loftily treated, might be changed (I will not say elevated, for the operatic form is poetical enough), into a tragedy.

The beauties of *La Sonnambula*, so full of pure melody and of emotional music, of the most simple and touching kind, can be appreciated by every one ; by the most learned musician and the most untutored amateur, or rather let us say by any play-goer, who, not having been born deaf to the voice of music, hears an opera for the first time in his life. It was given, however, to an English critic, to listen to this opera, as natural and as unmistakably beautiful as a bed of wild flowers, through a special ear-trumpet of his own ; and in number 197 of the most widely-

circulated of our literary journals, the following remarks on *La Sonnambula* appeared.   With the exception of one or two pretty *motivi*, exquisitely given
by Pasta and Rubini, the music is sometimes scarcely
on a level with that of *Il Pirata*, and often sinks
below it; there is a general thinness and want of
effect in the instrumentation not calculated to make
us overlook the other defects of this composition,
which, in our humble judgment, are compensated
by no redeeming beauties.   Bellini has soared too
high; there is nothing of grandeur, no touch of true
pathos in the common place workings of his mind.
He cannot reach the *Opera semi-seria;* he should
confine his powers to the lowest walk of the musical
drama, the one act *Opera buffa.*"

Equally ill fared *Norma* at the hands of another
musical critic to whose " reminiscences" I have often
had to refer, but who tells us that he did not hear
the work in question himself.   He speaks of it simply
as a production of which the scene is laid *in Wales,*
and adds that " it was not liked."

Yet *Norma* has been a good deal liked since its
first production at Milan, now nearly thirty years
ago; and from Madame Pasta's first to Madame
Grisi's last appearance in the principal part, no great
singer with any pretension to tragic power has considered her claims fully recognised until she has succeeded in the part of the Druid priestess.

Beatrice di Tenda, Bellini's next opera after *Norma,*
cannot be reckoned among his best works.   It was

written for Venice, in 1833, and was performed in England for the first time, in 1836. It met with no very great success in Italy or elsewhere.

In 1834, Bellini went to Paris, having been requested to write an opera for the excellent Théâtre Italien of that capital. The company at the period in question, included Grisi, Rubini, Tamburini and Lablache, all of whom were provided with parts in the new work. *I Puritani*, was played for the first time in London, for Grisi's benefit, in 1835, and with precisely the same distribution of characters as in Paris. The "*Puritani* Season" is still remembered by old habitués, as one of the most brilliant of these latter days. Rubini's romance in the first act *A te o cara*, Grisi's *Polonaise, Son vergin vezzosa* and the grand duet for Tamburini and Lablache, produced the greatest enthusiasm in all our musical circles, and the last movement of the duet was treated by "arrangers" for the piano, in every possible form. This is the movement, (destined, too soon, to find favour in the eyes of omnibus conductors, and all the worst amateurs of the cornet), of which Rossini wrote from Paris to a friend at Milan; "I need not describe the duet for the two basses, you must have heard it where you are."

I Puritani was Bellini's last opera. The season after its production he retired to the house of a Mr. Lewis at Puteaux, and there, while studying his art with an ardour which never deserted him, was attacked by a fatal illness. "From his youth up," says

Mr. J. W. Mould, in his interesting " Memoir of Bellini ;" "Vincenzo's eagerness in his art was such as to keep him at the piano day and night, till he was obliged forcibly to leave it.   The ruling passion accompanied him through his short life, and by the assiduity with which he pursued it, brought on the dysentery, which closed his brilliant career, peopling his last hours with the figures of those to whom his works were so largely indebted for their success. During the moments of delirium which preceded his death, he was constantly speaking of Lablache, Tamburini and Grisi, and one of his last recognisable impressions was, that he was present at a brilliant representation of his last opera, at the Salle Favart. His earthly career closed on Wednesday, the 23rd of September, 1835."

Thus died Bellini, in the twenty-ninth year of his age.   Immediately after his death, and on the very eve of his interment, the Théâtre Italien re-opened with the *Puritani*.   "The work," says the writer from whom I have just quoted, " was listened to throughout with a sad attention, betraying evidently how the general thoughts of both audience and artists were pre-occupied with the mournful fate of him so recently amongst them, now extended senseless, soulless, and mute, upon his funeral bier.   The solemn and mournful chords which commence the opera, excited a sorrowful emotion in the breasts of both those who sang and those who heard.   The feeling in which the orchestra and chorus participated, extended itself to the principal artists concerned, and the foremost amongst them displayed neither that vigour nor that neatness of execution which Paris was so accustomed to accept at their hands ; Tamburini in particular, was so broken down by the death of the young friend, whose presence amongst them spurred the glorious quartett on the season before, to such unprecedented exertions, that his magnificent organ, superb vocalisation were often considerably at fault during the evening, and his interrupted accent, joined to the melancholy depicted on the countenances of Grisi, Rubini, and Lablache, sent those to their homes with an aching heart who had presented themselves to that evening's hearing of *I Puritani*, previously disposed, moreover, to attend the mournful ceremony of the morrow."

A committee of Bellini's friends, including Rossini, Cherubini, Paer, and Carafa, undertook the general direction of the funeral of which the musical department was entrusted to M. Habeneck the *chef d'orchestre* of the Académie Royale. The expenses of the ceremony were defrayed by M. Panseron, of the Théâtre Italien. The most remarkable piece for the programme of the funeral music, was a lacrymosa for four voices, without accompaniment, in which the text of the Latin hymn was united to the beautiful melody (and of a thoroughly religious character), sung by the tenor in the third act of the *Puritani*. This lacrymosa was executed by Rubini, Ivanoff, Tamburini, and Lablache. The service was performed in the church of the In-

valides, and Bellini's remains were interred in the
cemetery of Père la Chaise.

Rossini had always shown the greatest affection for
Bellini; and Rosario Bellini, a few weeks after his
son's death, wrote a letter to the great composer,
thanking him for the almost paternal kindness which
he had shown to young Vincenzo during his lifetime,
and for the honour he had paid to his memory when
he was no more. After speaking of the grief and
despair in which the loss of his beloved son had
plunged him, the old man expressed himself as follows :—

"You always encouraged the object of my eternal
regret in his labours; you took him under your pro-
tection; you neglected nothing that could increase
his glory and his welfare. After my son's death
what have you not done to honour his memory and
render it dear to posterity ! I learnt this from the
newspapers; and I am penetrated with gratitude for
your excessive kindness, as well as for that of a number of distinguished artistes, which also I shall never
forget. Pray, sir, be my interpreter, and tell these
artistes that the father and family of Bellini, as well
as our compatriots of Catana, will cherish an imperish-
able recollection of this generous conduct. I shall
never cease to remember how much you did for my
son; I shall make known everywhere, in the midst
of my tears, what an affectionate heart belongs to the
great Rossini; and how kind, hospitable, and full of
feeling are the artistes of France."

If we compare Bellini with Donizetti, we find that the latter was the more prolific of the two, judging simply by the number of works produced; inasmuch as Donizetti, at the age of twenty-eight, had already produced thirteen operas; whereas the number of Bellini's dramatic works, when he died in his twenty-ninth year, amounted only to nine. But of the baker's dozen thrown off by Donizetti at so early an age, not one made any impression on the public, or on musicians, such as was caused by *I Capuletti*, or *Il Pirata*, or *La Straniera*, to say nothing of *Il Puritani*, which, in the opinion of many good judges, holds forth greater promise of dramatic excellence than is contained in any other of Bellini's works, including those masterpieces in two such different styles, *La Sonnambula* and *Norma*. When Donizetti had been composing for a dozen years, and had produced thirty one operas (*Anna Bolena* was his thirty-second), he had still written nothing which could be ranked on an equality with Bellini's second-rate works, such as *Il Pirata* and *I Capuletti;* and during the second half of Donizetti's operatic career, not one work of his in three met with the success which (*Beatrice* alone excepted) attended all Bellini's operas, as soon as Bellini had once passed that merely experimental period when, to fail, is, for a composer of real ability, to learn how not to fail a second time. I do not say that the composer of *Lucrezia*, *Lucia*, and *Elisir d'Amore* is so vastly inferior to the composer of *La Sonnambula* and *Norma;* but, simply, that Donizetti, during the first dozen years of his artistic life, did not approach the excellence shown by the young Bellini during the nine years which made up the whole of his brief musical career. More than that, Donizetti never produced a musical tragedy equal to *Norma*, nor a musical pastoral equal to *La Sonnambula;* while, dramatic considerations apart, he cannot be compared to Bellini as an inventor of melody. Indeed, it would be difficult in the whole range of opera to name three works which contain so many simple, tender, touching airs, of a refined character, yet possessing all the elements of popularity (in short, airs whose beauty is universally appreciable) as *Norma*, *La Sonnambula*, and *I Puritani*. The simplicity of Bellini's melodies is one of their chief characteristics; and this was especially remarkable, at a time when Rossini's imitators were exaggerating the florid style of their model in every air they produced.

Most of the great singers of the modern school,—indeed, all who have appeared since and including Madame Pasta, have gained their reputation chiefly in Bellini's and Donizetti's operas. They formed their style, it is true, by singing Rossini's music; but as the public will not listen for ever even to such operas as *Il Barbiere* and *Semiramide*, it was necessary to provide the new vocalists from time to time with new parts; and thus "Amina" and "Anna Bolena" were written for Pasta; "Elvino," &c., for Rubini; "Edgardo," in the *Lucia*, for Duprez; a complete quartett of parts in *I Puritani,* for Grisi, Rubini, Tamburini, and Lablache. Since Donizetti's *Don Pasquale,* composed for Grisi, Mario (Rubini's successor), Tamburini, and Lablache, no work of any importance has been composed for the Italian Opera of Paris—nor of London either, I may add, in spite of Verdi's *I Masnadieri,* and Halévy's *La Tempesta,* both manufactured expressly for Her Majesty's Theatre.

I have already spoken of Pasta's and Malibran's successes in Rossini's operas. The first part written for Pasta by Bellini was that of "Amina" in the *Sonnambula;* the second, that of "Norma." But though Pasta "created" these characters, she was destined to be surpassed in both of them by the former Marietta Garcia, now returned from America, and known everywhere as Malibran. This vocalist, by all accounts the most poetic and impassioned of all the great singers of her period, arrived in Italy just when *I Capuletti, La Sonnambula,* and *Norma,* were at the height of their popularity—thanks, in a great measure, to the admirable manner in which the part of the heroine in each of these works was represented by Pasta. Malibran appeared as "Amina," as "Norma," and also as "Romeo," in *I Capuletti.* She "interpreted" the characters (to borrow an expression, which is admissible, in this case, from the jargon of French musical critics) in her own manner, and very ingeniously brought into relief just those portions of the music of each which were not rendered prominent in the Pasta versions.   The new singer was applauded enthusiastically.   The public were really grateful to her for bringing to light beauties which, but for her, would have remained in the shade.   But it was also thought that Malibran feared her illustrious rival and predecessor too much, to attempt *her* readings.   This was just the impression she wished to produce ; and when she saw that the public had made up its mind on the subject, she changed her tactics, followed Pasta's interpretation, and beat her on her own ground.   She excelled wherever Pasta had excelled, and proved herself on the whole superior to her. Finally, she played the parts of " Norma " and " Amina " in her first and second manner combined. This rendered her triumph decisive.

Now Malibran commenced a triumphal progress through Italy.   Wherever she sang, showers of bouquets and garlands fell at her feet ; the horses were taken from her carriage on her leaving the theatre, and she was dragged home amid the shouts of an admiring crowd.   These so-called " ovations " * were renewed at every operatic city in Italy ; and managers disputed, in a manner previously unexampled, the honour and profit of engaging the all-successful vocalist.

* When are we to hear the last of the " ovations " which singers are said to receive when they obtain, or even do not obtain, any very triumphant success ?   A great many singers in the present day would be quite hurt if a journal were simply to record their "triumph." An " ovation " seems to them much more important ; and it cannot be said that this misapprehension is entirely their fault.

The director of the Trieste opera gave Malibran four thousand francs a night, and at the end of her engagement pressed her to accept a set of diamonds. Malibran refused, observing, that what she had already received was amply sufficient for her services, and more than she would ever have thought of asking for them, had not the terms been proposed by the director himself.

"Accept my present all the same," replied the liberal *impresario* ; " I can afford to offer you this little souvenir. It will remind you that I made an excellent thing out of your engagement, and it may, perhaps, help to induce you to come here again."

" The actions of this fiery existence," says M. Castil Blaze, " would appear fabulous if we had not seen Marietta amongst us, fulfilling her engagements at the theatre, resisting all the fatigue of the rehearsals, of the representations, after galloping morning and evening in the Bois de Boulogne, so as to tire out two horses. She used to breakfast during the rehearsals on the stage. I said to her, one morning, at the theatre :—' *Marietta carissima, non morrai. Che farò, dunque ? Nemica sorte ! Creperai.*'

" Her travels, her excursions, her studies, her performances might have filled the lives of two artists, and two very complete lives, moreover. She starts for Sinigaglia, during the heat of July, in man's clothes, takes her seat on the box of the carriage, drives the horses ; scorched by the sun of Italy, covered with dust, she arrives, jumps into the sea,

swims like a dolphin, and then goes to her hotel to
dress.   At Brussels, she is applauded as a French
Rosìna, delivering the prose of Beaumarchais as
Mademoiselle Mars would have delivered it.   She
leaves Brussels for London, comes back to Paris,
travels about in Brie, and returns to London, not like a
courier, but like a dove on the wing.   We all know
what the life of a singer is in the capital of England,
the life of a dramatic singer of the highest talent.
After a rehearsal at the opera, she may have three or
four matinée's to attend ; and when the curtain falls,
and she can escape from the theatre, there are soirées
which last till day-break.   Malibran kept all these
engagements, and, moreover, gave Sunday to her
friends ; this day of absolute rest to all England, was
to Marietta only another day of excitement."

Malibran spoke Spanish, Italian, French, English,
and a little German, and acted and sang in the first
four of these languages.   In London, she appeared
in an English version of *La Sonnambula* (1833), when
her representation of the character of "Amina"
created a general enthusiam such as can scarcely
have been equalled during the "Jenny Lind mania,"
—perfect vocalist as was Jenny Lind.   Malibran appears, however, to have been a more impassioned
singer, and was certainly a finer actress than the
Swedish Nightingale.   "Never losing sight of the
simplicity of the character," says a writer in describing her performance in *La Sonnambula*, "she gave
irresistible grace and force to the pathetic passages

with which it abounds, and excited the feeling of the audience to as high pitch as can be perceived. Her sleep-walking scenes, in which the slightest amount of exaggeration or want of caution would have destroyed the whole effect, were played with exquisite discrimination ; she sang the airs with refined taste and great power ; her voice, which was remarkable, rather for its flexibility and sweetness than for its volume, was as pure as ever, and her style displayed that high cultivation and luxuriance which marked the school in which she was educated, and which is almost identified with the name she formerly bore."

Drury Lane was the last theatre at which Madame Malibran sang ; but the last notes she ever uttered were heard at Manchester, where she performed only in oratorios and at concerts. Before leaving London, Madame Malibran had a fall from her horse, and all the time she was singing at Manchester, she was suffering from its effects. She had struck her head, and the violence of the blow, together with the general shock to her nerves, without weakening any of her faculties, seemed to have produced that feverish excitement which gave such tragic poetry to her last performances. At first, she would take no precautions, though inflammation of the brain was to be feared, and, indeed, might be said to have already declared itself. She continued to sing, and never was her voice more pure and melodious, never was her execution more daring and dazzling, never before had she sung with such inspiration and with a passion

which communicated itself in so electric a manner to
her audience.   She was bled; not one of the doctors
appears to have had sufficient strength of mind to enforce that absolute rest which everyone must have
known was necessary for her existence, and she still
went on singing.   There were no signs of any loss of
physical power, while her nervous force appeared to
have increased.   The last time she ever sang, she
executed the duet from *Andronico,* with Madame
Caradori, who, by a very natural sympathy, appeared
herself to have received something of that almost
supernatural fire which was burning within the breast
of Malibran, and which was now fast consuming her.
The public applauded with ecstacy, and as the general
excitement increased, the marvellous vocalisation of the
dying singer became almost miraculous.   She improvised a final cadence, which was the climax of her
triumph and of her life.   The bravos of the audience
were not at an end when she had already sunk exhausted into the arms of Madame·Alessandri, who
carried her, fainting, into the artist's room.   She
was removed immediately to the hotel.   It was now
impossible to save her, and so convinced of this was
her husband, that almost before she had breathed her
last, he was on his way to Paris, the better to secure
every farthing of her property !

Rubini, though he first gained his immense reputation by his mode of singing the airs of *Il Pirata,*
Anna Bolena, and *La Sonnambula,* formed his style in

the first instance, on the operas of Rossini. This vocalist, however, sang and acted in a great many different capacities before he was recognised as the first of all first tenors. At the age of twelve Rubini made his début at the theatre of Romano, his native town, in a woman's part. This curious *prima donna* afterwards sat down at the door of the theatre, between two candles, and behind a plate, in which the admiring public deposited their offerings to the fair bénéficiare. She is said to have been perfectly satisfied with the receipts and with the praise accorded to her for her first performance. Rubini afterwards went to Bergamo, where he was engaged to play the violin in the orchestra between the acts of comedies, and to sing in the choruses during the operatic season. A drama was to be brought out in which a certain cavatina was introduced. The manager was in great trouble to find a singer to whom this air could be entrusted. Rubini was mentioned, the manager offered him a few shillings to sing it, the bargain was made, and the new vocalist was immensely applauded. This air was the production of Lamberti. Rubini kept it, and many years afterwards, when he was at the height of his reputation, was fond of singing it in memory of his first composer.

In 1835, twenty-three years after Rubini's first engagement at Bergamo, the tenor of the Théâtre Italien of Paris was asked to intercede for a chorus-singer, who expected to be dismissed from the establishment. He told the unhappy man to write a letter to the manager, and then gave it the irresistible weight of his recommendation by signing it " Rubini, *Ancien Choriste*."

After leaving Bergamo, Rubini was engaged as second tenor in an operatic company of no great importance. He next joined a wandering troop, and among other feats he is said to have danced in a ballet somewhere in Piedmont, where, for his pains, he was violently hissed.

In 1814, he was engaged at Pavia as tenor, where he received about thirty-six shillings a month. Sixteen years afterwards, Rubini and his wife were offered an engagement of six thousand pounds, and at last the services of Rubini alone were retained at the Italian Opera of St. Petersburgh, at the rate of twenty thousand pounds a year.

Rubini was such a great singer, and possessed such admirable powers of expression, especially in pathetic airs (it was well said of him, " *qu'il avait des larmes dans la voix*,") that he may be looked upon as, in some measure, the creator of the operatic style which succeeded that of the Rossinian period up to the production of *Semiramide*, the last of Rossini's works, written specially for Italy. The florid mode of vocalization had been carried to an excess when Rubini showed what effect he could produce by singing melodies of a simple emotional character, without depending at all on vocalization merely as such. It has already been mentioned that Bellini wrote *Il Pirato* with Rubini at his side, and it is very remarkable that Donizetti never achieved any great success, and was never thought to have exhibited any style of his own until he produced *Anna Bolena*, in which the tenor part was composed expressly for Rubini. Every one who is acquainted with *Anna Bolena*, will understand how much Rossini's mode of singing the airs, *Ogni terra ove, &c.*, and *Vivi tu*, must have contributed to the immense favour with which it was received.

Rubini will long be remembered as the tenor of the incomparable quartett for whom the *Púritani* was written, and who performed together in it for seven consecutive years in Paris and in London. Rubini disappeared from the West in 1841, and was replaced in the part of " Arturo," by Mario. Tamburini was the next to disappear, and then Lablache. Neither Riccardo nor Giorgio have since found thoroughly efficient representatives, and now we have lost with Grisi the original " Elvira," without knowing precisely where another is to come from.

Before taking leave of Rubini, I must mention a sort of duel he once had with a rebellious B flat, the history of which has been related at length by M. Castil Blaze, in the *Revue de Paris*. Pacini's *Talismano* had just been produced with great success at *la Scala*. Rubini made his entry in this opera with an accompanied recitative, which the public always applauded enthusiastically. One phrase in particular, which the singer commenced by attacking the high B flat without preparation, and, holding it for a considerable period, excited their admiration to the highest point. Since Farinelli's celebrated trumpet song, no one note had ever obtained such a success as their wonderful B flat of Rubini's. The public of Milan went in crowds to hear it, and having heard it, never failed to encore it. *Un 'altra volta !* resounded through the house almost before the magic note itself had ceased to ring. The great singer had already distributed fourteen B flats among his admiring audiences, when, eager for the fifteenth and sixteenth, the Milanese thronged to their magnificent theatre to be present at the eighth performance of *Il Talismano.* The orchestra executed the brief prelude which announced the entry of the tenor. Rubini appeared, raised his eyes to heaven, extended his arms, planted himself firmly on his calves, inflated his breast, opened his mouth, and sought, by the usual means, to pronounce the wished-for B flat. But no B flat would come. *Os habet, et non clamabit.* Rubini was dumb; the public did their best to encourage the disconsolate singer, applauded him, cheered him, and gave him courage to attack the unhappy B flat a second time. On this occasion, Rubini was victorious. Determined to catch the fugitive note, which for a moment had escaped him, the singer brought all the muscular force of his immense lungs into play, struck the B flat, and threw it out among the audience with a vigour which surprised and delighted them. In the meanwhile, the tenor was by no means equally pleased with the triumph he had just gained. He felt, that in exerting himself to the utmost, he had injured himself in a manner which might prove very serious. Something in the mechanism of his voice had given way. He had felt the fracture at the time. He had, indeed, conquered the B flat, but at what an expense; that of a broken clavicle!

However, he continued his scene. He was wounded, but triumphant, and in his artistic elation he forgot the positive physical injury he had sustained. On leaving the stage he sent for the surgeon of the theatre, who, by inspecting and feeling Rubini's clavicle, convinced himself that it was indeed fractured. The bone had been unable to resist the tension of the singer's lungs. Rubini may have been said to have swelled his voice until it burst one of its natural barriers.

" It seems to me," said the wounded tenor, " that a man can go on singing with a broken clavicle."

" Certainly," replied the doctor, " you have just proved it."

" How long would it take to mend it ?" he enquired.

" Two months, if you remained perfectly quiet during the whole time."

" Two months ! And I have only sung seven times. I should have to give up my engagement. Can a person live comfortably with a broken clavicle ? "

" Very comfortably indeed. If you take care not

to lift any weight you will experience no disagreeable effects."

"Ah! there is my cue," exclaimed Rubini; "I shall go on singing."

"Rubini went on singing," says M. Castil Blaze, "and I do not think any one who heard him in 1831 could tell that he was listening to a wounded singer— wounded gloriously on the field of battle. As a musical doctor I was allowed to touch his wound, and I remarked on the left side of the clavicle a solution of continuity, three or four lines * in extent between the two parts of the fractured bone. I related the adventure in the *Revue de Paris*, and three hundred persons went to Rubini's house to touch the wound, and verify my statement."

Two other vocalists are mentioned in the history of music, who not only injured themselves in singing, but actually died of their injuries. Fabris had shown himself an unsuccessful rival of the celebrated Guadagni, when his master, determined that he should gain a complete victory, composed expressly for him an air of the greatest difficulty, which the young singer was to execute at the San Carlo Theatre, at Naples. Fabris protested that he could not sing, or that if so, it would cost him his life; but he yielded to his master's iron will, attacked the impossible air, and died on the stage of hæmorrhage of the lungs. In the same manner, an air which the tenor Labitte

* That is to say, a quarter or a third part of an inch.

was endeavouring to execute at the Lion's theatre, in 1820, was the cause of his own execution.

I have spoken of the versatility of talent displayed by Rubini in his youth. Tamburini and Lablache were equally expert singers in every style. In the year 1822 Tamburini was engaged at Palermo, where, on the last day of the carnival, the public attend, or used to attend, the Opera, with drums, trumpets, saucepans, shovels, and all kinds of musical and unmusical instruments—especially noisy ones. On this tumultuous evening, Tamburini, already a great favourite with the Palermitans, had to sing in Mercadante's *Elisa e Claudio*. The public received him with a salvo of their carnavalesque artillery, when Tamburini, finding that it was impossible to make himself heard in the ordinary way, determined to execute his part in falsetto ; and, the better to amuse the public, commenced singing with the voice of a soprano sfogato. The astonished audience laid their instruments aside to listen to the novel and entirely unexpected accents of their *basso cantante*. Tamburini's falsetto was of wonderful purity, and in using it he displayed the same agility for which he was remarkable when employing his ordinary thoroughly masculine voice. The Palermitans were interested by this novel display of vocal power, and were, moreover, pleased at Tamburini's readiness and ingenuity in replying to their seemingly unanswerable charivari. But the poor *prima donna* was unable to enter into the joke at all. She even imagined that the turbulent

demonstrations with which she was received whenever
she made her appearance, were intended to insult her,
and long before the opera was at an end she refused to
continue her part.   The manager was in great alarm,
for he knew that the public would not stand upon
any ceremony that evening ; and that, if the performance were interrupted by anything but their own noise,
they would probably break everything in the theatre.
Tamburini rushed to the *prima donna's* room.   Madame Lipparini, the lady in question, had already
left the theatre, but she had also left the costume of
" Elisa " behind.   The ingenious baritone threw off
his coat, contrived, by stretching and splitting, to get
on " Elisa's " satin dress, clapped her bonnet over his
own wig, and thus equipped appeared on the stage,
ready to take the part of the unhappy and now fugitive
Lipparini.   The audience applauded with one accord
the entry of the strangest " Elisa " ever seen.   Her
dress came only half way down her legs, the sleeves
did not extend anywhere near her wrists.   The soprano,
who at a moment's notice had replaced Madame Lipparini, had the largest hands and feet a *prima donna*
was ever known to possess.

    The band had played the ritornello of " Elisa's "
cavatina a dozen times, and the most turbulent among
the assembly had actually got up from their seats,
and were ready to scale the orchestra, and jump
on the stage, when Tamburini rushed on in the
costume above described.   After curtseying to the
audience, pressing one hand to his heart, and with

the other wiping away the tears of gratitude he
was supposed to shed for the enthusiastic reception
accorded to him, he commenced the cavatina, and
went through it admirably; burlesquing it a little for
the sake of the costume, but singing it, nevertheless,
with marvellous expression, and displaying executive
power far superior to any that Madame Lipparini
herself could have shown. As long as there were only
airs to sing, Tamburini got on easily enough. He
devoted his soprano voice to " Elisa," while the
" Count " remained still a basso, the singer performing his ordinary part in his ordinary voice. But a
duet for " Elisa " and the "Count " was approaching;
and the excited amateurs, now oblivious of their
drums, kettles, and kettle-drums, were speculating
with anxious interest as to how Tamburini would
manage to be soprano and basso-cantante in the same
piece. The vocalist found no difficulty in executing
the duet. He performed both parts—the bass replying to the soprano, and the soprano to the bass—
with the most perfect precision. The double representative even made a point of passing from right to
left and from left to right, according as he was the
father-in-law or the daughter. This was the crowning
success. The opera was now listened to with pleasure
and delight to the very end; and it was not until the
fall of the curtain that the audience re-commenced
their charivari, by way of testifying their admiration
for Tamburini, who was called upwards of a dozen
times on to the stage. This was not all: they were

so grieved at the idea of losing him, that they en-
treated him to appear again in the ballet.   He did
so, and gained fresh applause by his performance in
a *pas de quatre* with the Taglionis and Mademoiselle
Rinaldini.

Lablache was scarcely seventeen years of age, and
had just finished his studies at the Conservatorio of
Naples when he was engaged as " Neapolitan buffo "
at the little San Carlino theatre.   Here two performances were given every day, one in the afternoon, the other in the evening, while the morning
was devoted to rehearsals.   Lablache supported the
fatigue caused by this system without his voice suffering the slightest injury, though all the other members of the company were obliged to throw up their
engagements before the year was out, and several of
them never recovered their voices.   He had been
five months at San Carlino when he married Teresa
Pinotti, daughter of an actor engaged at the theatre,
and one of the greatest comedians of Italy.   This
union appears to have had a great effect on Lablache's
fate.   His wife saw what genius he possessed, and
thought of all possible means to get him away from
San Carlino, an establishment which she justly regarded as unworthy of him.   Lablache, for his part,
would have remained there all his life, playing the
part of Neapolitan buffo, without thinking of the
brilliant position within his reach.   There was at
that time a celebrated Neapolitan buffo, named Mili-

lotti, who, Madame Lablache thought, might advantageously replace her husband. She not only procured an engagement for Lablache's rival at the San Carlino theatre, but is even said to have packed the house the first night of his appearance (or re-appearance, for he was already known to the Neapolitans) so as to ensure him a favourable reception. Her intelligent love would, doubtless, have caused her to hiss her husband, had not Mililotti's success been sufficiently great to convince Lablache that he might as well seek his fortune elsewhere, and in a higher sphere. He had some hesitation, however, about singing in the Tuscan language, accustomed as he was to the Neapolitan jargon, but his wife determined him to make the change, and procured an engagement for him in Sicily. Arrived at Messina, however, he continued for some time to appear as Neapolitan buffo, a line for which he had always had a great predilection, and in which, spite of the forced success of Mililotti, he had no equal.

Lablache will be generally remembered as a true basso; but, before appearing as "Bartolo" in the *Barber of Seville*, he for many years played the part of "Figaro." I have seen it stated that Lablache has played not only the bass and baritone, but also the tenor part in Rossini's great comic opera; but I do not believe that he ever appeared as "Count Almaviva." I have said that he performed bass parts (the Neapolitan buffo was always a bass), when he first made his *début*; and during

the last five-and-twenty years of his career, his voice—
marvellously even and sound from one end to the
other—had at the same time no extraordinary compass; but from G to E all his notes were full,
clear, and sonorous, as the tones of a bronze bell.
Indeed, this bell-like quality of the great basso's
voice, is said on one occasion to have been the cause
of considerable alarm to his wife, who, hearing its
deep boom in the middle of the night, imagined, as
she started from her slumbers, that the house was
on fire.   This was the period of the great popularity of *I Puritani*, when Grisi, accompanied by
Lablache, was in the habit of singing the polacca
three times a week at the opera, and about twice
a day at morning concerts.   Lablache, after executing his part of this charming and popular piece
three times in nine hours, was so haunted by it, that
he continued to ring out his sounding *staccato*
accompaniment in his sleep.   Fortunately, Madame
Lablache succeeded in stopping this somnambulistic
performance before the engines arrived.

Like all complete artists, like Malibran, like Ronconi, like Garrick, the great type of the class, Lablache was equally happy in serious and in comic
parts.   Though Malibran is chiefly remembered in
England by her almost tragic rendering of the part
of " Amina " in the *Sonnambula*, many persons who
have heard her in all her *répertoire*, assure me that
she exhibited the greatest talent in comic opera, or
in such lively "half character" parts as "Norina" in

the *Elixir of Love*, and "Zerlina" in *Don Giovanni*.
Lord Mount Edgcumbe declares, after speaking of her
performance of "Semiramide" ("Semiramide" has
also been mentioned as one of Malibran's best parts)
that "in characters of less energy she is much better,
and best of all in the comic opera. She even con-
descended," he adds, "to make herself a buffa cari-
cata, and take the third and least important part in
Cimarosa's *Matrimonio Segretto*, that of an old woman (the Mrs. Heidelberg of the *Clandestine Marriage*), generally acted by the lowest singer of the
company. From an insignificant character she raised
it to a prominent one, and very greatly added to the
effect of that excellent opera." So of Lablache,
Lord Mount Edgcumbe, after remarking that his
voice was "not only of deeper compass than almost
any ever heard, but, when he chose, absolutely sten-
torian," tells his readers that "he was a most excellent actor, especially in comic operas, in which he
was (as I am told) as highly diverting as any of the
most laughable comedians." Yet the character in
which Lablache himself, and not Lablache's reputation, produced so favourable an impression on this
writer—not very favourably impressed by any singers,
or any music towards the close of his life—was
"Assur" in *Semiramide!* Who that remembers
Lablache as "Bartolo"— that remembers the promi-
nence and the genuine humour which he gave to
that slight and colourless part — can deny that he
was one of the greatest of comic actors? And did he
not communicate the same importance to the minor

character of "Oroveso" in *Norma*, in which nothing
could be more tragic and impressive than his scene
with the repentant dying priestess in the last act?
What a picture, too, was his "Henry VIII." in *Anna
Bolena!* A picture which Lablache himself composed from a careful study of the costume worn by
the original, and for which nature had certainly supplied him in the first place with a most suitable
form. Think, again, of his superb grandeur as
"Maometto," of his touching dignity as "Desdemona's" father; then forget both these characters,
and recollect how perfect, how unique a "Leporello"
was this same Lablache. One of our best critics has
taken objection to Lablache's version of this last-
named part—though, of course, without objecting to
his actual performance, which he as well, or better
than any one else, knows to have been almost beyond
praise. But it has been said that Lablache (and if
Lablache, then all his predecessors in the same character) indulged in an unbecoming spirit of burlesque
during the last scene of *Don Giovanni*, in which the
statue seizes the hero with his strong hand, and
takes him down a practicable trap-door to eternal
torments. "Leporello," however, is a burlesque
character, and a buffoon throughout; cowardly, superstitious, greedy, with all possible low qualities
developed to a ludicrous extent, and thus presenting
a fine dramatic contrast to his master, who possesses
all the noble qualities, except faith—this one great
flaw rendering all the use he makes of valour, generosity, and love of woman, an abuse. "Leporello"

is always thinking of the bad end which he is sure awaits him unless he quits the service of a master whom he is afraid to leave; always thinking, too, of maccaroni, money, and the wages which "Don Juan" certainly will not pay him, if he is taken to the infernal regions before his next quarter is due. "*Mes gages, mes gages*," cries the "Sganarelle" of Molière's comedy, and "Sganarelle" and "Leporello" are one and the same person. We may be sure that Molière and Lablache are right, and that Herr Formes, with his new reading of a good old part is wrong. At the same time it is natural and allowable that a singer who cannot be comic should be serious.

In addition to his other great accomplishments, Lablache possessed that of being able to whistle in a style that many a piccolo player would have envied. He could whistle all Rode's variations as perfectly as Louisa Pyne sings them. As to the vibratory force of his full voice, it was such that to have allowed Lablache to sing in a green house might have been a dangerous experiment. Chéron, a celebrated French bass, is said to have been able to burst a tumbler into a thousand pieces, by sounding, within a fragile and doubtless sympathetic glass, some particular note. Equally interesting, in connexion with a glass, is a performance in which I have seen the veteran,* but still almost juvenile basso, Signor Badiali, indulge.

* "What a pity I did not think of this city fifty years ago!" exclaimed Signor Badiali, when he made his first appearance in London, in 1859.

The artist takes a glass of particularly good claret, drinks it, and, while in the act of swallowing, sings a scale. The first time his execution is not quite perfect. He repeats the performance with a full glass, a loud voice, and without missing a note or a drop. To convince his friends that there is no deception, he offers to go through this refreshing species of vocalization a third time ; after which, if the supply of wine on the table happens to be limited, and the servants gone to bed, the audience generally declares itself satisfied.

Giulia Grisi, the last of the celebrated Puritani quartett, first distinguished herself by her performance of the part of " Adalgisa, in *Norma*, when that opera was produced at Milan, in 1832. Giulia or Giulietta Grisi, is the younger sister of Giuditta Grisi, also a singer, but to whom Giulietta was superior in all respects; and she is the elder sister of Carlotta Grisi, who, from an ordinary vocalist, became, under the tuition of Perrot, the most charming dancer of her time. When Madame Grisi first appeared, lord Mount Edgcumbe having ceased himself to attend the opera, tells us that she possessed " a handsome person, sweet, yet powerful voice, considerable execution, and still more expression ;" that " she is an excellent singer, and excellent actress ;" in short, is described to be as nearly perfect as possible, and is almost a greater favorite than even Pasta or Malibran. In his *Pencillings by the Way*, Mr. N. P. Willis writes, after seeing Grisi, who had then first appeared at the King's Theatre,

in the year 1833; " she is young, very pretty, and an
admirable actress—three great advantages to a singer;
her voice is under absolute command, and she manages
it beautifully; but it wants the infusion of soul—the
gushing uncontrollable passionate feeling of Malibran.
You merely feel that Grisi is an accomplished artist,
while Malibran melts all your criticism into love and
admiration. I am easily moved by music, but I come
away without much enthusiasm for the present passion
of London." The impression conveyed by Mr. N. P.
Willis is not precisely that which I received from hearing Grisi fourteen or fifteen years afterwards, and up
to her last season. Of late years, at least, Madame
Grisi has shown herself above all " a passionate
singer," though as " accomplished artists" superior
to her, if not in force at least in delicacy of expression,
she has, from the time of Madame Sontag to that of
Madame Bosio, had plenty of superiors. It seems
to us, in the present day, that the " incontrollable
passionate feeling of Grisi," is just what we admire
her for in "Norma," beyond doubt her best character;
but it is none the less interesting, or perhaps the more
interesting for that very reason, to know what a man
of taste in poetry and the drama, and who had heard
all the best singers of his time, thought of Madame
Grisi at a period when her most striking qualifications
may have been different from what they are now. She
was at all events a great singer and actress then, in
1833, and is a great actress and singer now, in 1861—
the year of her final retirement from the stage.

CHAPTER XIX.

ROSSINI——SPOHR——BEETHOVEN——WEBER AND
HOFFMANN.

BELLINI and Donizetti were contemporaries of
Rossini; so were Paisiello and Cimarosa; so are
M. Verdi and M. Meyerbeer; but Rossini has outlived most of them, and will certainly outlive them
all. It is now forty-eight years since *Tancredi*, forty-
five since *Otello*, and forty-five since *Il Barbiere di
Siviglia* were written. With the exception of Cimarosa's *Matrimonio Segretto*, which at long intervals
may still occasionally be heard, the works of Rossini's
Italian predecessors have been thrown into utter obscurity by the light of his superior genius. Let us
make all due allowances for such change of taste as
must result in music, as in all things, from the natural
changeableness of the human disposition; still no
variation has taken place in the estimation in which
Rossini's works are held. It was to be expected that
a musician of equal genius, coming after Paisiello and
his compeers, young and vigorous, when they were
old and exhausted, would in time completely eclipse
them, even in respect to those works which they

had written in their best days; but the remarkable thing is, that Rossini so re-modelled Italian opera, and gave to the world so many admirable examples of his own new style, that to opera-goers of the last thirty years he may be said to be the most ancient of those Italian composers who are not absolutely forgotten. At the same time, after hearing *William Tell*, it is impossible to deny that Rossini is also the most modern of operatic composers. That is to say, that since *William Tell* was produced, upwards of thirty years ago, the art of writing dramatic music has not advanced a step. Other composers have written admirable operas during Rossini's time; but if no Italian *opera seria*, produced prior to *Otello*, can be compared to *Otello*; if no opera, subsequent to *William Tell*, can be ranked on a level with *William Tell*; if rivals have arisen, and Rossini's operas of five-and-forty years ago still continue to be admired and applauded; above all, if a singer,* the favourite heroine of a composer† who is so boastfully modern that he fancies he belongs to the next age, and who is nothing if not an innovator; if even this ultra modern heroine appears, when she wishes really to distinguish herself in a Rossinian opera of 1813; ‡ then it follows that of our actual operatic period, and dating from the early part of the present century, Rossini is simply the Alpha and the Omega. Undoubtedly his works are full of beauty, gaiety, life, and of much poetry of a positive, pas-

* Joanna Wagner.   † Richard Wagner.   ‡ Tancredi.

sionate kind, but they are wanting in spiritualism, or rather they do not possess spirituality, and exhibit none of the poetry of romance. It would be difficult to say precisely in what the "romantic" consists; —and I am here reminded that several French writers have spoken of Rossini as a composer of the "romantic school," simply (as I imagine) because his works attained great popularity in France at the same time as those of Victor Hugo and his followers, and because he gave the same extension to the opera which the cultivators and naturalisers in France of the Shakspearian drama gave, *after* Rossini, to their plays.* I may safely say, however, that with the "romantic," as an element of poetry, we always associate somewhat of melancholy and vagueness, and of dreaminess, if not of actual mystery. A bright passionate love-song of Rossini's is no more "romantic" than is a magnificent summer's day under an Italian sky; but Schubert's well known *Serenade* is essentially "romantic;" and Schubert, as well as Hoffmann, (a composer of whom I shall afterwards have a few words to say), is decidedly of the same school as Weber, who is again of the same school, or rather of the same class, as Schubert and Beethoven, in so far that not one of the three ever visited Italy, or was influenced, further than was absolutely inevitable, by Italian composers.

* Once more, I may mention that the "romantic opera" (in the sense in which the French say "romantic drama,") was founded by Da Ponte and Mozart, the former furnishing the plan, the latter constructing the work—"The Opera of Operas.".

As a romantic composer Weber may almost be said to stand alone. As a thoroughly German composer he belongs to the same class as Beethoven and Spohr. Spohr, greatly as his symphonies and chamber compositions are admired, has yet never established himself in public favour as an operatic composer—at least not in England, nor indeed anywhere out of Germany. I may add, that in Germany itself, the land above all others of scientific music, the works which keep possession of the stage are, for the most part, those which the public also love to applaud in other countries. The truth is, that the success of an opera is seldom in proportion to its abstract musical merit, just as the success of a drama does not depend, or depends but very little, on the manner in which it is written. We have seen plays by Browning, Taylor (I mean the author of Philip Von Artevelde), Leigh Hunt, and other most distinguished writers, prove failures; while dramas and comedies put together by actors and playwrights have met with great success. This success is not to be undervalued; all I mean to say is, that it is not necessarily gained by the best writers in the drama, or by the best composers in the opera; though the best composers and the best writers ought to take care to achieve it in every department in which they present themselves. In the meanwhile, Spohr's dramatic works, with all their beauties, have never taken root in this country; while even Beethoven's *Fidelio*, one of the greatest of operas, does not occupy any clearly marked space in

the history of opera; nor is it as an operatic composer
that Beethoven has gained his immense celebrity.

All London opera-goers remember Mademoiselle
Sophie Cruvelli's admirable performance in *Fidelio ;*
and like Mademoiselle Cruvelli (or Cruwel), all the
great German singers who have visited England—
with the single exception of Mademoiselle Titiens—
have some time or other played the part of the heroine in Beethoven's famous dramatic work : but
Fidelio has never been translated into English or
French,—has never been played by any thoroughly
Italian company, and admired, as it must always be by
musicians—nor has ever excited any great enthusiasm
among the English public, except when it has been
executed by an entire company of Germans,—the only
people who can do justice to its magnificent choruses.
It is a work apart in more than one sense, and it has
not had that perceptible influence on the works
which have succeeded it, either in Germany or in
other countries, that has been exercised by Weber's
operas in Germany, and by Rossini's everywhere.
For full particulars respecting Beethoven and his
three styles, and *Fidelio* and its three overtures, the
reader may be referred to the works published at
St. Petersburgh by M. Lenz in 1852 (*Beethoven et ses
trois styles*), at Coblentz, by Dr. Wegeler and Ferdi-
nand Ries in 1838, and at Munster, by Schindler (that
friend of Beethoven's, who, according to the mali-
cious Heine, wrote "*Ami de Beethoven*" on his card),
in 1845. Schindler's book is the courseof nearly

all the biographical particulars since published respecting Beethoven; that of M. Lenz is chiefly remarkable for the inflated nonsense it contains in the shape of criticism. Thus Beethoven's third style is said to be "*un jugement porté sur le cosmos humain, et non plus une participation à ses impressions*,"—words which, I confess, I do not know how to render into intelligible English. His symphonies in general are "events of universal history rather than musical productions of more or less merit." Those who have read M. Lenz's extravagant production, will remember that he attacks here and there M. Oulibicheff, author of the "Life of Mozart," published at Moscow in 1844. M. Oulibicheff replied in a work devoted specially to Beethoven (and to M. Lenz), published at St. Petersburgh in 1854;[*] in which he is said by our best critics not to have done full justice to Beethoven, though he well maintains his assertion; an assertion which appears to me quite unassailable, that the composer of *Don Juan* combined all the merits of all the schools which had preceded him. I have already endeavoured, in more

---

[*] The gist of M. Lenz's accusations against M. Oulibicheff amounts to this: that the latter, believing Mozart to have attained perfection in music, considered it impossible to go beyond him. "*Ou ce caractère d'universalité que Mozart imprime à quelques-un de ses plus grandes chefs-d'œuvre,*" says M. Oulibicheff. "*M'avait paru le progrès immense que la musique attendait pour se constituer définitivement,—pour se constituer, avais-je dit, et non pour ne plus avancer.*" According to M. Lenz, on the other hand, Mozart's master-pieces (after those which M. Lenz discovers among his latest compositions), are what preparatory studies are to a great work.

than one place, to impress this truth upon such of
my readers as might not be sufficiently sensible of it,
and moreover, that all the important operatic reforms
attributed to the successors of Mozart, and especially to Rossini, belong to Mozart himself, who
from his eminence dominates equally over the present
and the past.

Karl Maria von Weber has had a very different
influence on the opera from that exercised by Beethoven and Spohr; and so much of his method of
operatic composition as could easily be imitated has
found abundance of imitators. Thus Weber's plan
of taking the principal melodies for his overtures
from the operas which they are to precede, has been
very generally followed; so also has his system of
introducing national airs, more or less modified,
when his great object is to give to his work a national colour.* This process, which produces admirable results in the hands of a composer of intelligence and taste, becomes, when adopted by inferior
musicians, simply a convenient mode of plagiarism.
Without for one moment ranking Rossini, Bellini, or
Donizetti in the latter class, I may nevertheless observe, that the cavatina of *La Gazza Ladra* is founded
on an air sung by the peasants of Sicily; that the
melody of the trio in the *Barber of Seville* (*Zitti,
Zitti*), is Simon's air in the *Seasons*, note for note;

---

* New form of his overtures, national melodies, &c.—(*Straker*).
Love of traditions, melancholy, fanciful, spiritual; also popular.—
(*Der Freischütz*).

that *Di tanti palpiti* was originally a Roman Catholic hymn; that the music of *La Sonnambula* is full of reminiscences of the popular music of Sicily; and that Donizetti has also had recourse to national airs for the tunes of his choruses in *La Favorite*. In the above instances, which might easily be multiplied the composers seem to me rather to have suited their own personal convenience, than to have aimed at giving any particular "colour" to their works. However that may be, I feel obliged to them for my part for having brought to light beautiful melodies, which but for them might have remained in obscurity, as I also do to Haydn, Mozart, Beethoven, and Mendelssohn, for the admirable use they also have occasionally made of popular themes. It appears to me, however, (to speak now of operatic composers alone) that there is a great difference between borrowing an air from an oratorio, a collection of national music, or any other source, simply because it happens to be beautiful, and doing so because it is appropriate to a particular personage or scene. We may not blame, but we cannot praise Rossini for taking a melody of Haydn's for his *Zitti, Zitti*, instead of inventing one for himself; nor was there any particular merit, except that of civility, in giving "Berta," in the same opera, a Russian air to sing, which Rossini had heard at the house of a Russian lady residing at Rome, for whom he had a certain admiration. But the *Ranz des Vaches*, introduced with such admirable effect into *Guillaume Tell*, where it is marvellously embellished, and yet loses nothing of its original character; this *Ranz des Vaches* at once transports us amongst the Swiss mountains. So Luther's hymn is in its proper place in the *Huguenots ;** so is the Persian air, made the subject of a chorus of Persian beauties by the Russian composer Glinka, in his *Rouslan e Loudmila ;* so also is the Arabian march (first published by Niebuhr in his "Travels in Arabia"), played behind the scenes by the guards of the seraglio in *Oberon,* and the old Spanish romance employed as the foundation to the overture of *Preciosa.*

Weber had a fondness not only for certain instrumental combinations and harmonic effects, but also for particular instruments, such as the clarionet and the horn, and particular chords (which caused Beethoven to say that Weber's *Euryanthe* was a collection of diminished sevenths). There are certain rhythms too, which, if Weber did not absolutely invent, he has employed so happily, and has shown such a marked liking for them (not only in his operas, but also in his pianoforte compositions, and other instrumental works), that they may almost be said to belong to him. With regard to the orchestral portion of his operas generally, I may remark that Weber, though too high-souled a poet to fall into the error of direct imitation of external noises,

---

* I will not here enter into the question whether or not Meyerbeer desecrated this hymn by introducing it into an opera. Such was the opinion of Mendelssohn, who thought that but for Meyerbeer and the *Huguenots,* Luther's hymn might have been befittingly introduced in an oratorio which he intended to compose on the subject of the Reformation.

has yet been able to suggest most charmingly and poetically, such vague natural sounds as the rustling of the leaves of the forest, and the murmuring of the waves of the sea. Finally, to speak of what defies analysis, but to assert what every one who has listened to Weber's music will I think admit, his music is full of that ideality and spirituality which in literature is regarded in the present day, if not as the absolute essence of poetry, at least, as one of its most essential elements. Read Weber's life, study his letters, listen again and again to his music, and you will find that he was a conscientious, dutiful, religious man, with a thoroughly musical organization, great imaginative powers, inexhaustible tenderness, and a deep, intuitive appreciation of all that is most beautiful in popular legends. He was an artist of the highest order, and with him art was truly a religion. He believed in its ennobling effect, and that it was to be used only for ennobling purposes. Thus, to have departed from the poetic exigencies of a subject to gratify the caprice of a singer, or to attain the momentary applause of the public would, to Weber, with the faith he held, have been a heresy and a crime.

Weber has not precisely founded a school, but his influence is perceptible in some of the works of Mendelssohn, (as, for instance, in the overture to a *Midsummer Night's Dream*) and in many portions of Meyerbeer's operas, especially in the fantastic music of *Robert le Diable*, and in certain passages of *Dinorah*—a legend which Weber himself would have loved to treat. Meyerbeer is said to have borrowed many of his instrumental combinations from Weber ; but in speaking of the points of resemblance between the two composers, I was thinking not of details of style, but of the general influence of Weber's thought and manner.   If Auber is indebted to Weber it is simply for the idea of making the overture out of the airs of an opera, and of colouring the melodic portion by the introduction of national airs.   Only while Weber gives to his operas a becoming national or poetic colour throughout, the musical tints in M. Auber's dramatic works are often by no means in harmony.   The Italian airs in *La Muette* are appropriate enough, and the whole of that work is in good keeping ; but in the *Domino Noir*, charming opera as it is, no one can help noticing that Spanish songs, and songs essentially French, follow one another in the most abrupt manner.   As nothing can be more Spanish than the second movement of " Angèle's " scene (in the third act) so nothing can be more French, more Parisian, more vaudevillistic than the first.

But to return to Weber and his operas. *Der Freischütz*, decidedly the most important of all Weber's works, and which expresses in a more remarkable manner than any other of his dramatic productions the natural bent of his genius, was performed for the first time at Berlin in 1821. *Euryanthe* was produced at Vienna in 1823, and *Oberon* at London in 1826. *Der Freischütz* is certainly the most perfect German opera that exists ; not that it is a superior work to *Don Giovanni*, but that *Don Giovanni* is less a German than a universal opera ; whereas *Der Freis-*

chütz is essentially of Germany, by its subject, by the physiognomy of the personages introduced, and by the general character of the music. There is this resemblance, however, between *Don Giovanni* and *Der Freischütz :* that in each the composer had met with a libretto peculiarly suited to his genius— the librettist having first conceived the plan of the opera, and having long carried its germ in his mind. Lorenzo da Ponte, in his memoirs (of which an interesting account was published some years ago by M. Scudo, the accomplished critic of the *Revue des Deux Mondes*) states, that he had long thought of Don Juan as an admirable subject for an opera, of which he felt the poetic truthfulness only too well, from reflecting on his own career ; and that he suggested it to Mozart, not only because he appreciated that composer's high dramatic genius, but also because he had studied his mental and moral nature ; and saw, from his simplicity, his loftiness of character, and his reverential, religious disposition, that he would do full justice to the marvellous legend. Frederic Kind has also published a little volume ("Der Freischütz-Buch "), in which he explains how the circumstances of his life led him to meditate from an early age on such legends as that which Weber has treated in his master-piece. When Weber was introduced to Kind, he was known as the director of the Opera at Prague, and also, and above all, as the composer of numerous popular and patriotic choruses, which were sung by all Germany during the national war of 1813. He had not at this time produced any opera;

nor had Kind, a poet of some reputation, ever written
the libretto of one.   Kind was unwilling at first to
attempt a style in which he did not feel at all sure
of success.   One day, however, taking up a book, he
said to Weber: " There ought to be some thing here
that would suit us, and especially you, who have
already treated popular subjects."   He at the same
time handed to the musician a collection of legends,
directing his attention in particular to Apel's Freischütz.   Weber, who already knew the story, was
delighted with the suggestion.   " Divine ! divine ! "
he exclaimed with enthusiasm ; and the poet at once
commenced his libretto.

No great work ever obtained a more complete and
immediate triumph than *Der Freischütz ;* and within
a few years of its production at Berlin it was translated and re-produced in all the principal capitals
of Europe.   It was played at London in English, at
Paris in French, and at both cities in German.   In
London it became so popular, that at the height of
its first success a gentleman, in advertising for a servant, is said to have found it necessary to stipulate
that he should *not* be able to whistle the airs from
Der Freischütz.   In Paris, its fate was curious,
and in some respects almost inexplicable.   It was
brought out in 1824 at the Odéon, in its original
form, and was hissed.   Whether the intelligent
French audience objected to the undeniable improbability of the chief incidents in the drama, or whether
the originality of the music offended their unprepared
ears, or whatever may have been the cause, Weber's

master-piece was damned. Its translator, M. Castil Blaze, withdrew it, but determined to offer it to the critical public of the Odéon in another form. He did not hesitate to remodel *Der Freischütz*, changing the order of the pieces, cutting out such beauties as the French thought laughable, interpolating here and there such compositions of his own as he thought would please them, and finally presenting them this remarkable medley (which, however, still consisted mainly of airs and choruses by Weber) nine days after the failure of *Der Freischütz*, under the title of *Robin des Bois*. The opera, as decomposed and recomposed by M. Castil Blaze, was so successful, that it was represented three hundred and fifty-seven times at the Odéon. Moreover, it had already been played sixty times at the Opéra Comique, when the French Dramatic Authors' Society interfered to prevent its further representation at that theatre, on the ground that it had not been specially written for it. M. Castil Blaze, in the version he has himself published of this curious affair, tells us, that his first version of *Der Freischütz,* in which his "respect for the work and the author had prevented him from making the least change" was " *siffié, meurtri, bafoué, navré, moqué, conspué, turlupiné, hué, vilipendié, terrassé, déchiré, lacéré, cruellement enfoncé, jusqu'au troisième dessous.*" This, and the after success of his modified version, justified him, he thinks, in depriving Weber's work of all its poetry, and reducing it to the level of the comprehension of a French musical audience in the year 1824.

Strangely enough, when Berlioz's version of *Der*

Freischütz was produced at the Académie in 1841, it met with scarcely more success than had been obtained by *Der Freischütz* in its original musical form at the Odéon.   The recitatives added by M. Berlioz, if not objectionable in themselves, are at least to be condemned in so far that they are not Weber's, that they prolong the music beyond Weber's intentions, and, above all, that they change the entire character of the work.   I cannot think, after Meyerbeer's *Dinorah*, that recitative is an inappropriate language in the mouths of peasants.   Recitative of an heroic character, would be so, no doubt ; but not such as a composer of genius, or even of taste or talent, would write for them.   Nevertheless, Weber conceived his master-piece as a species of melodrama, in which the personages were now to sing, now to speak, " through the music," (to adopt an expressive theatrical phrase), now to speak without any musical accompaniment at all.   If, at a theatre devoted exclusively to the performance of grand opera, it is absolutely necessary to replace the spoken dialogue by recitative, then this dialogue should, at least, be so compressed as to reduce the amount of added recitative to a minimum quantity.   *Der Freischütz*, however, will always be heard to the greatest advantage in the form in which it was originally produced.   The pauses between the pieces of music have, it must be remembered, been all premeditated, and their effect taken into account by the composer.

But the transformations of *Der Freischütz* are not yet at an end. Six years ago M. Castil Blaze re-arranged his *Robin des Bois* once more, restored what he had previously cut out, cut out what he had himself added to Weber's music, and produced his version, No. 3 (which must have differed very little, if at all, from his unfortunate version, No. 1), at the Théâtre Lyrique.

Every season, too, it is rumoured that *Der Freischütz* is to be produced at one of the Italian theatres of London, with Mademoiselle Titiens or Madame Csillag in the principal part. When managers are tired of tiring the public with perpetual variations between Verdi and Meyerbeer, (to whose monstrously long operas my sole but sufficient objection is, that there is too much of them, and—with the exception of the charming *Dinorah*—that they are stuffed full of ballets, processions, and other pretexts for unnecessary scenic display), then we shall assuredly have an opportunity of hearing once more in England the masterpiece of the chief of all the composers of the romantic and legendary school. In such a case, who will supply the necessary recitatives ? Those of M. Berlioz have been tried, and found wanting. Mr. Costa's were not a whit more satisfactory. M. Alary, the mutilator of *Don Giovanni*, would surely not be encouraged to try his hand on Weber's masterpiece ? Meyerbeer, between whose genius and that of Weber, considerable affinity exists, is, perhaps, the only composer of the present day whom it would be worth while to ask to write recitatives for *Der Freischütz*. The additions would have to be made with great discretion, so as not to encumber the opera; but who

would venture to give a word of advice, if the work
were undertaken by M. Meyerbeer?

Weber's *Preciosa* was produced at Berlin in 1820,
a year before *Der Freischütz*, which latter opera appears to have occupied its composer four years—
undoubtedly the four years best spent of all his
artistic life. The libretto of *Preciosa* is founded on
Cervantes' *Gipsy of Madrid*, (of which M. Louis Vi-
ardot has published an excellent French translation);
and here Weber, faithful to his system has given
abundant "colour" to his work, in which the Spanish
romance introduced into the overture, and the Gipsies'
march are, with the waltz (which may be said to be
in Weber's personal style), the most striking and
characteristic pieces.

Euryanthe was written for Vienna, where it was
represented for the first time in 1823, the part of
" Euryanthe " being filled by Mademoiselle Sontag,
that of "Adolar," by Heitzinger. The libretto of
this opera, composed by a lady, Madame Wilhelmine
de Chézy is by no means interesting, and the dulness
of the poem, though certainly not communicated to the
music, has caused the latter to suffer from the mere
fact of being attached to it. *Euryanthe* was received
coldly by the public of Vienna, and was called by its
wits—professors of the " *calembourg d'à-peu-près* "—
Ennuyante. If such facetiousness as this was thought
enlivening, it is easy to understand how Weber's music
was considered the reverse. I have already mentioned
Beethoven's remark about *Euryanthe* being " a collection of diminished sevenths." Weber was natu-

rally not enchanted with this observation ; indeed it is said to have pained him exceedingly, and some days after the first production of *Euryanthe* he paid a visit to Beethoven, in order to submit the score to his judgment. Beethoven received him kindly, but said to him, with a certain roughness which was habitual to him : "You should have come to me before the representation, not afterwards . . . . . "Nevertheless," he added, " I advise you to treat *Euryanthe* as I did *Fidelio*; that is to say, cut out a third."

Euryanthe, however, soon met with the success it deserved, not only at Berlin, Dresden, and Leipzig, but at Vienna itself, where the part created by Mademoiselle Sontag was performed in 1825 by Madame Schrœder-Devrient, in a manner which excited general enthusiasm. The passionate duet between " Adolar " and " Euryanthe," in the second act, as sung by Heitzinger and Madame Schrœder, would alone have sufficed to attract the public of Vienna to Weber's opera, now that it was revived.

Oberon, Weber's last opera, was composed for Covent Garden Theatre, in 1826. Some ingenious depreciators of English taste have discovered that Weber died from grief, caused by the coldness with which this work was received by the London public. With regard to this subject, I cannot do better than quote the excellent remarks of M. Scudo. After mentioning that *Oberon* was received with enthusiasm on its first production at Covent Garden—that it was " appreciated by those who were worthy of comprehending it"—and that an English musical journal, the

Harmonicon, "published a remarkable article, in which all the beauties of the score were brought out with great taste," he observes that "it is impossible to quote an instance of a great man in literature, or in the arts, whose merit was entirely overlooked by his contemporaries;" while, " as for the death of Weber, it may be explained by fatigue, by grief, without doubt, but, above all, by an organic disease, from which he had suffered for years." At the same time " the enthusiasm exhibited by the public, at the first representation of *Oberon*, did not keep at the same height at the following representations. The master-piece of the German composer experienced much the same fate as *William Tell* in Paris."

Weber himself, in a letter written to his wife, on the very night of the first performance, says :—" My dear Lina ; thanks to God and to his all powerful will, I obtained this evening the greatest success in my life. The emotion produced in my breast by such a triumph, is more than I can describe. To God alone belongs the glory. When I entered the orchestra, the house, crammed to the roof, burst into a frenzy of applause. Hats and handkerchiefs were waved in the air. The overture had to be executed twice, as had also several of the pieces in the opera itself. The air which Braham sings in the first act was encored; so was Fatima's romance, and a quartett in the second act. The public even wished to hear the finale over again. In the third act, Fatima's ballad was re-demanded. At the end of the representation I was called on to the stage by the enthusiastic acclamations of the public, an honour which no composer had ever before obtained in England. All went excellently, and every one around me was happy."

In spite of the enthusiasm inspired by Weber's works in England, when they were first produced, and for some years afterwards, we have now but rarely an opportunity of hearing one of them. *Oberon,* it is true, was brought out at Her Majesty's Theatre at the end of last season, when, not being able to achieve miracles, it did not save the manager from bankruptcy; but the existence of Weber's other works seems to be forgotten by our directors, English as well as Italian, though from time to time a rumour goes about, which proves to be a rumour and nothing more, that *Der Freischütz* is to be performed by one of our Italian companies. In the meanwhile Weber has found an abundance of appreciation in France, where, at the ably and artistically-conducted Théâtre Lyrique, *Der Freischütz, Oberon, Euryanthe* and *Preciosa* have all been brought out, and performed with remarkable success during the last few years.

A composer, whose works present many points of analogy with those of Weber, and which therefore belong essentially to the German romantic school, is Hoffmann—far better known by his tales than by his *Miserere,* his *Requiem,* his airs and choruses for Werner's *Crusade of the Baltic,* or his operas of *Love and Jealousy,* the *Canon of Milan,* or *Undine.* This last production has always been regarded as his master-piece. Indeed, with *Undine,* Hoffmann obtained his one great musical success; and it is easy to account for the marked favour with which that work was received in Germany. In the first place the fantastic nature of the subject was eminently suited to the peculiar genius of the composer. Then he possessed the advantage of having an excellent *libretto*, written by Lamotte-Fouqué, the author of the original tale; and, finally, the opera was admirably executed at the Royal Theatre of Berlin. Probably not one of my readers has heard Hoffmann's *Undine*, which was brought out in 1817, and I believe was never revived, though much of the music, for a time, enjoyed considerable popularity, and the composition, as a whole, was warmly and publicly praised by no less a personage than Karl Maria von Weber himself. On the other hand, *Undine*, and Hoffmann's music generally, have been condemned by Sir Walter Scott, who is reported not to have been able to distinguish one melody from another, though he had, of course, a profound admiration for Scotch ballads of all kinds. M. Fétis, too, after informing us that Hoffmann "gave music lessons, painted enormous pictures, and wrote *licentious novels* (where are Hoffman's licentious novels?) without succeeding in making himself remarked in any style," goes on to assure us, without ever having heard *Undine*, that although there were "certain parts" in which genius was evinced, yet "want of connexion, of conformity, of conception, and of plan, might be observed throughout;" and that "the judgment of the best critics was, that such a work could not be classed among those compositions which mark an epoch in art."

Weber had studied criticism less perhaps than

M. Fétis ; but he knew more about creativeness, and in an article on the opera of *Undine*, so far from complaining of any "want of connexion, of conformity, of conception, and of plan," the author of *Der Freischütz* says : " This work seems really to have been composed at one inspiration, and I do not remember, after hearing it several times, that any passage ever recalled me for a single minute from the circle of magic images that the artist evoked in my soul. Yes, from the beginning to the end, the author sustains the interest so powerfully, by the musical development of his theme, that after but a single hearing one really seizes the *ensemble* of the work ; and detail disappears in the *naïveté* and modesty of his art. With rare renunciation, such as can be appreciated only by him who knows what it costs to sacrifice the triumph of a momentary success, M. Hoffmann has disdained to enrich some pieces at the expense of others, which it is so easy to do by giving them an importance, which does not belong to them as members of the entire work. The composer always advances, visibly guided by this one aspiration—to be always truthful, and keep up the dramatic action without ceasing, instead of checking or fettering it in its rapid progress. Diverse and strongly marked as are the characters of the different personages, there is, nevertheless, something which surrounds them all ; it is that fabulous life, full of phantoms, and those soft whisperings of terror, which belong so peculiarly to the fantastic. Kühleborn is the character most strikingly put in relief, both by the choice of the melodies, and by the instrumentation which, never leaving him, always announces his sinister approach.* This is quite right, Kühleborn appearing, if not as destiny itself, at least as its appointed instrument. After him comes *Undine*, the charming daughter of the waves, which, made sonorous, now murmur and break in harmonious roulades, now powerful and commanding, announce her power. The 'arietta' of the second act, treated with rare and subtle grace, seems to me a thorough success, and to render the character perfectly. 'Hildebrand,' so passionate, yet full of hesitation, and allowing himself to be carried away by each amorous desire, and the pious and simple priest, with his grave choral melody, are the next in importance. In the back-ground are Bertalda, the fisherman, and his wife, and the duke and duchess. The strains sung by the suite of the latter breathe a joyous, animated life, and are developed with admirable gaiety; thus forming a contrast with the sombre choruses of the spirits of the earth and water, which are full of harsh, strange progressions. The end of the opera, in which the composer displays, as if to crown his work, all his abundance of harmony in the double chorus in eight parts, appears to me grandly conceived and perfectly rendered. He has expressed the words—'good night to all the cares and to all the magnificence of the earth'—with true loftiness, and with a soft melancholy, which, in spite of the tragic conclusion of the piece, leaves behind a

* Another proof that this device is not new in the hands of Herr Wagner.

delicious impression of calm and consolation. The overture and the final chorus which enclose the work here give one another the hand. The former, which evokes and opens the world of wonders, commences softly, goes on increasing, then bursts forth with passion; the latter is introduced without brusqueness, but mixes up with the action, and calms and satisfies it completely. The entire work is one of the most *spiritual* that these latter times have given us. It is the result of the most perfect and intimate comprehension of the subject, completed by a series of ideas profoundly reflected upon, and by the intelligent use of all the material resources of art; the whole rendered into a magnificent work by beautiful and admirably developed melodies."

M. Berlioz has said of Hoffmann's music, adding, however, that he had not heard a note of it, that it was "*de la musique de littérateur.*" M. Fétis, having heard about as much of it, has said a great deal more; but, after what has been written concerning Hoffmann's principal opera by such a master and judge as Karl Maria von Weber, neither the opinion of M. Fétis, nor of M. Berlioz, can be of any value on the subject. The merit of Hoffmann's music has probably been denied, because the world is not inclined to believe that the same man can be a great writer and also a great musician. Perhaps it is this perversity of human nature that makes us disposed to hold M. Berlioz in so little esteem as an author; and I have no doubt that there are many who would be equally unwilling to allow M. Fétis any tolerable rank as a composer.

INDEX,

HISTORICAL AND BIOGRAPHICAL.

P 2